ULTIMATE
UNITED STATES
TRAVEL LIST

Introduction

Extraordinary national parks, world-class museums, and places that illuminate aspects of our history that can be difficult to comprehend... While the final pair of its 50 constituent states may have only joined in 1959, the United States comprises a powerhouse of natural wonders, culture, and intrigue, from the glacial wildernesses of Alaska to the volcanic tropics of Hawai'i, via many of the planet's greatest cities. But where to start? That's where this book will help. Here you'll find our pick of 500 of the most memorable, beautiful, surprising, and compelling experiences to be had in the 50 states. And what's more, we've ranked them in order of their brilliance.

How did we come up with our selection? We started by compiling every sight, attraction, and experience in the Lonely Planet guidebooks to the United States, which totaled an amazing 46,997 entries across every state from Alabama to Wyoming. Our writers rate each place they research and visit with between one and five stars. We focused on the highlights that earned four or five stars. Once we had a long list, we asked everybody in the Lonely Planet community, including writers, editors, bloggers, and staff members, to vote for their 20 favorite spots and experiences. Hundreds of votes were cast. We also took into account whether the places listed had a sustainable tourism policy and what efforts they made to protect the environment or support their communities, giving those places that did bonus points. After some mathematical alchemy, we ended up with a score for each of the 500 experiences – and a very close top three.

Each entry listed gives a taste of what to expect from the sight or experience, plus practical advice to start planning your own trip. Turn to our guidebooks, apps, and lonelyplanet.com for more detailed travel information.

This is Lonely Planet's Ultimate United States Travel List. We think this diverse nation is incredibly rewarding to explore and hope this book will inspire your travels within it.

01–99 Contents

100–199

200–299

300—399

400–500

01—
99

© Joseph Dube-Arsenault / Shutterstock
© Roman Khomlyak / Shutterstock

📷

Left: Grand Canyon rafting. Below: riding down the South Rim. Right: Toroweap Overlook, North Rim.

ESSENTIAL NATIONAL PARKS

↓

In the rain-soaked Northwest, breathe deeply in the cool and fresh air of Olympic National Park.

👉 page 75

↓

Discover fossils from bygone ages and even dinosaur tracks at Capitol Reef National Park.

👉 page 109

↓

Waterfalls, wooded hollows and wildflowers delight visitors to Shenandoah National Park.

👉 page 123

© Matteo Colombo / Getty Images

Be awed by nature's power at Grand Canyon National Park

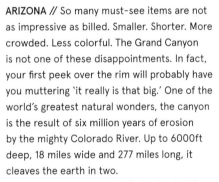

01

ARIZONA // So many must-see items are not as impressive as billed. Smaller. Shorter. More crowded. Less colorful. The Grand Canyon is not one of these disappointments. In fact, your first peek over the rim will probably have you muttering 'it really is that big.' One of the world's greatest natural wonders, the canyon is the result of six million years of erosion by the mighty Colorado River. Up to 6000ft deep, 18 miles wide and 277 miles long, it cleaves the earth in two.

Some visitors come simply to stand at the edge and gawk – and hey, that's experience enough. Others go further, descending down trails chiseled in sandstone cliffs and trekking through stands of pinyon and sagebrush. Mule trips to Phantom Ranch – stone cottages on the canyon floor accessible only to overnight guests – are a once-in-a-lifetime kind of thing, as are multi-day rafting excursions along the churning Colorado.

The vast majority of visitors come to the canyon's South Rim, which means more people but also more accommodations – book well ahead to stay in one of the majestic old National Park Service lodges, all local stone and dark timber beams. The North Rim is higher-altitude, colder and more difficult to access, so if you've got time and you're looking to get away from the crowds, this

is your spot. Other parts of the canyon are administered by Native American tribes, most notably the stomach-dropping see-through Skywalk of the Hualapai people and the milky blue waterfalls of the Havasupai.

For South Rim day-trippers, the flat 13-mile Rim Trail will get you to all the area's major sites. Gaze down on an infinite sea of mesas from Pipe Creek Vista, check out the panoramic views and topographic relief models of the canyon at Yavapai Geology Museum, then take in Mission-style Verkamp's Visitor Center and Hopi House, designed by pioneering female architect Mary Colter. Hopi Point is your spot for sunset viewing – don't expect solitude, but the crowds hardly detract from the symphony of golds, russets and purples playing on the canyon's crenelated walls. For more quad-burn, the seemingly endless staircase of the 8-mile Bright Angel Trail is a top South Rim choice. For overnight adventures, you can't do better than the 24-mile Rim to Rim, usually done north-to-south and requiring a backcountry camping permit. Do not try this in a single day: many have attempted it, with sometimes tragic results. The canyon is, above all, nature at its most awe-inspiring, a place where humans barely register in the ongoing march of geologic time.

☞ SEE IT ! *The entire canyon is in Arizona, with the nearest large airport in Phoenix, 230 miles south. The South Rim is 80 miles north of Flagstaff; the Grand Canyon Train runs from Williams to the South Rim. The North Rim entrance is 30 miles south of isolated Jacob Lake.*

© Nick Ocean Photography / Getty Images

02

Feel humbled by geological giants at unforgettable Yosemite National Park

CALIFORNIA // If there's one uniting quality in this monumental park, it's that Yosemite lifts your gaze. You'll crick your neck staring up at towering sequoias. You'll gape at lofty granite monoliths, and shield your eyes from sunshine bouncing off huge waterfalls. Everywhere you look, the only way is up: welcome to nature on its most mind-bending scale.

You could spend a decade exploring this 1187-sq-mile park but begin with the classics, like the giants of Mariposa Grove. Just south of Wawona, these 500 mighty trees with dramatically contorted trunks and monster roots are easily reached via boardwalks and fairly level trails.

Further north in the park, Tunnel View's lookout towards North Dome and Half Dome graces millions of Instagrams. According to Native American lore, these 87-million-year-old granite giants are quarrelling lovers frozen in time by the spirits of the land.

Ready for a walk? Ten minutes' drive away is Cook's Meadow Loop, glorious whether dappled with spring flowers or framed by golden leaves during fall. Close by, a short trail leads to Yosemite Falls; snowmelt brings the cascade to a thundering crescendo each spring.

A hair-raising drive leads you to Glacier Point (7214ft), where the air is thin and the panorama from Yosemite Falls to Half Dome draws gasps. Take time to survey the glacier-carved canyons and pine-furred valleys.

If these formidable views stir your appetite for wilderness, lace up your hiking boots. Trekking to the summit of Half Dome is a challenging 16-mile round-trip; pack supplies and start at sunrise. For skilled climbers, there's always the fearsome granite wall of El Capitan – though most prefer to watch daredevil ascents from a safe distance.

☛ SEE IT ! *Book well ahead for Yosemite campsites or accommodations in Wawona, or stay in gateway town Oakhurst and drive in.*

[camera icon]

Above: Yosemite's John Muir Trail traces the peak of Mount Whitney. Below: keep an eye out for black bears. Opposite: mighty Yosemite Falls.

© Mark Read / Lonely Planet

© Mark Read / Lonely Planet

Left: Black Pool in the West Thumb Geyser Basin used to have dark algae until the pool heated and turned a vivid blue.

03

Spy geysers, grizzlies, and grand canyons in Yellowstone National Park

WYOMING // The USA's oldest national park, Yellowstone is so incredible that, when the first Europeans to set eyes on its wonders related what they had seen, they were regarded as lunatics or liars. For over 50 years the reports of fire and brimstone, of boiling mud and spouting water were disregarded – until in 1872, when Yellowstone gained national park status and the recognition that its fantastical landscapes deserved. Here, alongside gushing geysers, hot springs and bubbling mud pots, is North America's largest super-volcano, all spread across a wonderland of mountains, canyons, forests, and lakes. And the second-largest park in the contiguous US wows with its wildlife as much as its topography, with just about the nation's best opportunities for spotting the many animals that call the area home. There are grizzly and black bears, elk, moose, the country's largest herd of bison and, following one of the most successful wildlife reintroduction stories in recent history, wolves. Where to begin? This geothermally animated place's geysers (60% of the planet's total) and hot springs are a good option.

Old Faithful, reliably spouting 100-200ft every hour or two, is the most visited. Grand Prismatic, the most impressive hot spring, vividly reflects the colors of the rainbow and resembles an immense, intense kaleidoscope. Giving Yellowstone yet greater bragging rights, this lauded wilderness contains the Rockies' biggest waterfall by volume, Lower Yellowstone Falls, which exuberantly leads the way into the park's own grand canyon, Grand Canyon of the Yellowstone. With imposingly sheer sides and surging waters, it's perhaps best left to the words of one of its earliest non-native visitors, Charles W. Cook, to describe: 'I sat there in amazement, while my companions came up, and after that, it seemed to me that it was five minutes before anyone spoke.' An apt summary of what any traveler stopping by this or any other Yellowstone sight today can still expect to feel.

☛ SEE IT ! *Coming from the north, Albright Visitor Center is the best park information point; from the south it's Grant Visitor Center, at Yellowstone Lake.*

04

Appreciate the entire span of human creativity at the Metropolitan Museum of Art

NEW YORK // To describe the Met, let's go ahead and lay out some stats. The largest art museum in the United States. The fourth-most-visited in the world. More than two million works across 17 acres of exhibit space. That might start to give you an idea of the enormity and importance of this 1870-built museum, with collections spanning prehistory through the present from every part of the globe. See ancient African textiles and Picasso abstractions. Stradivarius violins and Walker Evans photographs. Old Master oil paintings and medieval armor. Islamic calligraphy and Ming pottery and Indigenous Australian rock paintings and

Etruscan chariots and ceiling-hung Modernist sculptures and - oh yes - an entire first-century BCE Egyptian pyramid, the Temple of Dendur, relocated from the banks of the Nile to New York in the 1960s. If it's a big name, it's here: da Vinci, Botticelli, Rembrandt, Raphael, O'Keeffe, El Greco, Van Gogh - listing is rather pointless as there are so many. Enliven the experience further with a self-guided audio tour and, in warmer months, a visit to the rooftop sculpture garden, with its bird's-eye views of Central Park.

☛ SEE IT ! *The Met is at 1000 Fifth Ave; weekends are massively crowded.*

© poludziber / Shutterstock

05

Drive through dreamy landscapes in Bryce Canyon National Park

UTAH // It's always golden hour in Bryce Canyon National Park. Peachy rock arches and sandstone amphitheaters form a landscape that is ever-blushing. Battalions of copper-colored buttes stretch to the horizon, and turrets of rock glow bronze in the sun. Along Scenic Drive's numerous lookout points, it's hard to pick favorites – but the view of Bryce Amphitheater from Bryce Point truly brings home the staggering scale.

The park's collection of hoodoos, rippling columns of rock, is the largest found anywhere on the planet. These curvaceous fins of rock have been eroded over centuries by the relentless action of ice and thaw.

It's tempting to zip along Hwy 12, letting the serene beauty of this high-altitude park rush past in a blur. But allow time to hike through evergreen forests, along the walking trails that wind through crowds of rocky pinnacles. The 8-mile Fairyland Loop Trail provides an eye-popping introduction to the park's pinkish canyons and stately arches, and there's an easier 1.8 mile route at Queens Garden.

👉 SEE IT ! *Take Hwy 12 from Hwy 89 near Panguitch to reach the park visitor center. You can either self-drive, or park up and use shuttle buses between mid-April and mid-October.*

Opposite from top: Ellis Island's Registry Room; Kīlauea caldera, Hawai`i Volcanoes National Park.

06

Discover America's immigrant roots at Ellis Island

NEW YORK // Around 40% of Americans can trace their ancestry through this intimidating French Renaissance-style edifice in New York Harbor. Between 1892 and 1924, some 12 million people came through Ellis Island on their way to new lives. Today, it's a moving museum of the immigrant experience. Follow the steps of the induction process, which included intelligence tests and a medical – those suspected of disease or debility were marked with chalk. See abandoned possessions, listen to audio of immigrants' stories and search for your own roots at the American Family Immigration History Center. To stand here is to feel the hope – and the fear – of those who passed through. It's part of the Statue of Liberty National Monument; many combine a visit with a trip to Lady Liberty.

🖝 SEE IT ! *Ellis Island is accessible by Statue Cruises ferry; purchase tickets online.*

07

Thrill at the awesome might of lava at Hawai'i Volcanoes National Park

HAWAI`I // Two of the world's most active volcanoes, Kīlauea and Mauna Loa, rumble and churn beneath this ever-changing Big Island park, a micro-continent of rainforests, volcano-induced deserts, high-mountain meadows, and coastal plains. Kīlauea had been erupting continuously for 35 years when, in 2018, its summit collapsed, destroying 700 houses and totally altering the park's landscape. This area is sacred to native Hawai`ians, whose ancestors carved petroglyphs and buried the *piko* (umbilical cord) of their newborns in lava rocks. An essential activity is driving Crater Rim Drive or Chain of Craters Rd for views of craters, calderas, and lava plains. Stop for side-hikes and to explore the gigantic, eerie tubes left by molten lava like Nahuku (Thurston Lava Tube), nestled in the greenery just off Crater Rim Drive.

🖝 SEE IT ! *The park is on the southeast side of the Big Island, 30 miles south of Hilo airport or 90 miles southeast of bigger Kona airport.*

06

07

08

Learn important lessons at the NMAAHC

WASHINGTON, DC // The sensational National Museum of African American History and Culture explores the diverse experiences of African Americans and traces their part in shaping the nation. Start downstairs in the sobering 'Slavery and Freedom' exhibition (muted lighting and decor evoke being in a slave ship). Then work your way up to the community and culture galleries on the 3rd and 4th floors, where more recent African American achievements in sport, music, theater and visual arts are joyfully celebrated. Artifacts, state-of-the-art interactive exhibits and fascinating interpretative panels abound in the cleverly designed and dramatically lit exhibition spaces. Learn about the Civil Rights Movement and the death of Martin Luther King Jnr. Delight at Chuck Berry's Cadillac. Be inspired by Carl Lewis' track shoes. 'A Changing America: 1968 and Beyond' explores contemporary Black life through stories about African Americans' cultural experiences within the likes of the Black Arts Movement, hip hop, the Black Panthers and #BlackLivesMatter. And that's just the start of it.

☛ **SEE IT !** *In peak seasons, you must book a timed entry pass online. Alternatively, try for a weekday walk-up (when a smattering of tickets are released at 1pm Monday through Friday).*

MULTICULTURAL AMERICA

↓

The gravitas of the National Memorial for Peace and Justice in Alabama is inescapable.
☛ **page 168**

↓

Discover ancient Puebloan ruins at Chaco Culture National Historical Park.
☛ **page 179**

↓

The Museum of Contemporary Native Arts in Santa Fe displays Native American art.
☛ **page 183**

09

Admire big fauna and big peaks in Denali NP

ALASKA // Some head to the Serengeti and Kilimanjaro for their scenic safaris – but for Americans, the dynamic combo of big fauna and giant peaks is available on home turf. Grizzly bears, moose, caribou, wolves, and Dall's sheep all roam the flanks of Denali; known to native Athabascans as the 'Great One', it's the tallest mountain in North America, rising 20,310ft above the stark taiga of interior Alaska.

It's an impressive sight, and you don't have to be a hiker to view the wildlife. Special buses driven by expert naturalists ply the surrounding national park utilizing its only real road, the 92-mile unpaved Park Rd, closed to private vehicles after Mile 14.

For those with a bit more time and the desire to get further into the wild, there are vast expanses of untracked country to explore – more than 6 million acres of it, to be exact. Imagine a landmass the size of the US state of Massachusetts – without the people.

Most of the park is treeless and trail-less – welcome to a land of self-navigated off-trail hiking, a wonderfully liberating, if slightly intimidating, Alaskan wilderness experience.

☛ **SEE IT !** *The park is four hours north of Anchorage; you can drive in or catch a daily summer train called the Denali Star.*

Top: National Museum of African American History and Culture, Washington, DC. Bottom: spot caribou roaming in Denali National Park.

©ItzaVU / Shutterstock

© Martin Capek / Shutterstock

08

09

Top: hiking the
Kalalau Trail. Bottom:
Hanakāpīʻai Falls;
Opposite: Na Paliʻs
razor-rugged
coastline.

10

Trek the sinuous, slippery trail of Na Pali Coast State Wilderness Park

HAWAIʻI // No roads mean this 16-mile stretch of Kauaʻiʻs sublime Na Pali coast is one of the wildest, most pristine places in the Hawaiʻian islands. Visitors hike among the five rugged valleys, navigating silvery streams and waterfalls, or kayak the deep-green waters of the coastline, dipping in and out of sea caves and frolicking on bone-white beaches. The valley floors still contain the stone terraces where Hawaiʻians once grew taro and other crops – they used these trails for trading and travel. The word 'pali' means cliff, and these cliffs are like nowhere on earth – as ornately fluted as origami constructions, their peaks trailing shreds of cottony white clouds. Ambitious hikers tackle the narrow, winding track of the Kalalau Trail, 11 miles one-way. With dizzying basalt ledges, stands of screwpine, java plum and agave, slippery fern forests and open views of the snaking coastline and the crashing sea below, it's truly one of the world's most spectacular hikes. Spend the night at ultra-isolated Kalalau Beach, a crescent of silver sand at the base of the cliffs. On the way back, the side-hike to Hanakāpīʻai Falls is worth the sweat and the wet feet for the sight of water plunging 300ft down a lush volcanic slope into a milky jade pool. If you haven't snagged a precious overnight permit, the first part of the track, called the Hanakāpīʻai Trail, is 4 miles each way, taking in the falls. You can also see the coast with a commercial catamaran trip, no permit or hiking boots required.

☛ SEE IT ! *You need a permit to hike beyond Hanakāpīʻai Falls, and an overnight permit to camp at the Hanakoa and Kalalau sites.*

11

Explore Joshua Tree National Park's dramatic deserts

CALIFORNIA // Task a child to draw a desert, and they'll likely produce something resembling Joshua Tree – an expanse of stark silver sand punctuated by spiky cacti and rocky outcrops. The high, cool Mojave and the low, arid Colorado deserts come together here in a land of stark beauty that's inspired everyone from Mormon pioneers to U2, who named their fifth studio album after the park's namesake tree. Mormon settlers supposedly thought the tree branches were pointing towards heaven like the prophet Joshua guiding the Israelites – giving a new name to the *Yucca brevifolia* plant the Spanish called *izote de desierto*, desert dagger. Today, climbers scale the park's rough granite crags, hikers ascend for vistas across the Coachella Valley, bikers whizz down backcountry trails and stargazers take advantage of the ink-dark sky.

☛ SEE IT ! *Joshua Tree NP is about 130 miles east of Los Angeles. The access town is Twentynine Palms, with motels and restaurants.*

12

Witness the march of progress at the Civil Rights Museum

TENNESSEE // In the Lorraine Motel's otherwise uniform grid of balconies, a white wreath marks where Martin Luther King Jr was shot on April 4, 1968. The motel is now part of the National Civil Rights Museum, dedicated to recording centuries of civil rights struggles. Poring over the museum collections is a confronting education in the USA's racist history. Slavery, the Civil War and Reconstruction Era, and Jim Crow laws are explained in depth. Eyewitness accounts, photographs, and video footage detail tireless resistance to oppression – with spotlights on iconic activists like Rosa Parks. Life-size dioramas of segregated diners and buses encourage you to place yourself in the scene, prompting uncomfortable, but necessary, self-reflection: would you stand up for what's right?

☛ SEE IT ! *You'll see the sign at 450 Mulberry St in Memphis' South Main district.*

Opposite from top: fall colors in Central Park; sunrise over San Fran's iconic Golden Gate Bridge.

13

Wander Central Park, the lungs of New York

NEW YORK // New York might just boil over if it didn't have this cool green oasis in which to blow off steam. Urbanites come here to jog around the reservoir, play frisbee in Sheep Meadow, watch free concerts on the Great Lawn, birdwatch in the forested Ramble, rent rowboats at the Loeb Boathouse, and simply lie in the grass resting, reading, and people-watching. Designed by the venerable landscape architects Frederick Law Olmsted and Calvert Vaux, Central Park opened in 1858. Must-dos for visitors include snapping a photo on the pond's iconic Gapstow Bridge, watching the sea-lions lunch at the zoo, exploring the fanciful folly of Belvedere Castle, and joining the crowds paying their respects to John Lennon at Strawberry Fields. Get a deeper experience of the park's 843 acres with a tour from Central Park Conservancy.

🖝 SEE IT ! *The park runs from 59th to 110th streets, between Central Park West & Fifth Ave.*

14

Feel reverberations of history on the Golden Gate Bridge

CALIFORNIA // Traffic roars as you cross San Francisco's most famous bridge. It's too loud to think; all you can do is stare up at the Art Deco structure, whose graceful orange form clashes magnificently with a cobalt-blue sky. Completed in 1937, the Golden Gate Bridge is SF's emblem, a gift of architect Irving Morrow and engineer Joseph Strauss. Its mythic status endures through appearances in movies, from Hitchcock's *Vertigo* to *Interview with the Vampire*.

The pedestrian and bike-way is separate from the road, though you'll still feel heavy traffic vibrations. Stop to gaze at indigo San Francisco Bay and, at the northern end of the bridge, photograph the rugged Marin Headlands. Whichever end you start, you'll finish in part of the huge Golden Gate Bridge Recreation Area, where walking trails thread through florid gardens and across fog-draped cliffs.

🖝 SEE IT ! *Muni bus 28 trundles to the southern parking lot, from where you can cross the bridge.*

13

14

Opposite from top: hiking the dunes at White Sands National Park; Muir Woods' majestic redwoods.

© ferrantraite / Getty Images

15

Live out dystopian daydreams at White Sands National Park

NEW MEXICO // The Mad Max vibes are strong in this national park as you feel hot winds blowing sand around your ankles, undulating white gypsum dunes as far as you can see, sun glaring overhead. Even more dystopian: the park is completely surrounded by the White Sands Missile Range, where the first atomic bomb was tested in 1945. Entertain your post-apocalyptic fantasies with a 16-mile loop-drive through the world's largest gypsum dune field, hiking the 5-mile round-trip through the desiccated ancient lake of Alkali Flat. Or buy a plastic snow saucer at the visitor center and sled the dunes as if they were snowy hills. The hard-packed sand of Dunes Drive makes for excellent cycling.

👉 SEE IT ! *The entrance is 15 miles southwest of Alamogordo, and 52 miles northeast of Las Cruces.*

16

Forest-bathe amid ancient redwoods at Muir Woods

CALIFORNIA // The first thing you notice is the silence: here in Muir Woods National Monument, sound is muffled by some of the world's tallest trees. Many of these coastal redwoods are 1000 years old, so walking through them feels like exploring a primeval realm. Gigantic ferns overhang the path and rays of sunshine glance through the branches, spotlighting knotted roots and fire-blackened trunks.

Kept fresh by marine fog, this stand of old-growth redwoods has been protected since 1908. A mile-long loop delves into Cathedral Grove, where the tallest trees loom: watch for the blue flash of Steller's jay birds or occasional deer darting through the trees, and be inspired by the wild splendor that prompted John Muir's naturalist verse.

👉 SEE IT ! *Reserve a shuttle bus from the parking lot or hike from the Panoramic Hwy. Come early, or mid-week, to avoid the crowds.*

© Zack Frank / Shutterstock

15

16

© Alexander S. Kunz / Getty Images

Opposite: Take a summer boat trip to Crater Lake's Wizard Island.

17

Behold the spectacular volcanic remnants of Crater Lake

OREGON // The ancient remains of a cataclysmic volcanic explosion of some 7700 years ago, Crater Lake is testament to the recuperating power of nature and its ability to create something beautiful out of mass destruction.

The mountain whose remnants now form Crater Lake was Mt Mazama, a 12,000ft volcanic peak that was heavily glaciered and inactive for many thousands of years before it came apocalyptically back to life. The catastrophic explosion in around 5700 BCE scattered ash for hundreds of miles as flows of superheated pumice solidified into massive banks. These eruptions emptied the magma chambers at the heart of the volcano, and the summit cone collapsed to form a caldera.

Today, that spectacular caldera can be circumnavigated by car on the 33-mile-long Rim Drive, a formidable feat of 1930s engineering that undulates between 6500ft and 7900ft while blending subtly with the surrounding mountain-scape. In the hollow below lies a body of water unlike any other: Crater Lake. The deepest lake in the US (and the ninth deepest in the world) at 1949ft, it has no rivers feeding it – only snowfall and rain contribute to its frigid waters. This purity and the lake's great depth give it the glassy sapphire-blue sheen for which it is famous.

The fifth oldest national park in the nation, created in 1902, Crater Lake is a high-profile member of the national parks system and the only one in Oregon. Despite its location in the southern part of the state, it's known for its brutal snowfalls: up to 20ft can cover the Rim Drive in the winter. Summer is the best time to visit, when you can head to the historic Crater Lake Lodge, dating from 1915, and plan some energetic hiking.

☛ SEE IT ! *Most people visit Crater Lake by car. The nearest city is Klamath Falls, 60 miles to the south.*

At the intersection of Washington and State streets, the Freedom Trail passes the Old State House, Boston's oldest surviving public building.

18

Walk through revolutionary history on the Freedom Trail

MASSACHUSETTS // America's bloody fight to rid itself of British rule began among the cobblestone streets, red-brick churches, and humble tradesmen's homes of Boston. The 2.5-mile Freedom Trail commemorates that fight – follow the brick path from Boston Common, the USA's oldest public park, passing the golden dome of the Massachusetts State House and stopping at the graves of revolutionary heroes Paul Revere, John Hancock, and Samuel Adams at the Granary Burying Ground. Here too is the final resting place of Crispus Attucks, a freed enslaved man who was the first person to die in the Revolution. At Faneuil Hall, a public meeting place nicknamed the 'Cradle of Liberty,' stop at touristy-but-fun Quincy Market for a bread bowl of New England clam chowder. Paul Revere's battered clapboard house is another highlight: one of Boston's oldest remaining wooden homes, it was here that the silversmith began his legendary midnight ride. In the Charlestown Navy Yard, tour the USS *Constitution*, the world's oldest commissioned warship, launched in 1797. The trail ends at the 221ft Bunker Hill Monument.

🡢 TRY IT ! *There are 16 official sites on the trail. The NPS offices in Faneuil Hall has walking tours, audio guides and free maps.*

19

Experience the rawness of the Rockies in Glacier National Park

MONTANA // Few places in the US are as pure and pristine as Glacier. Protected since 1910, the park ranks with Yellowstone, Yosemite, and the Grand Canyon among the United States' most unsullied natural wonders. The glacially carved remnants of an ancient thrust fault have left a landscape of saw-toothed pinnacles laced with plunging waterfalls and turquoise lakes, endowed with a virtually intact pre-Columbian ecosystem. Smart park management keeps the unpolished backcountry accessible and authentically wild.

☞ SEE IT ! *Amtrak's* Empire Builder *train stops daily at West Glacier and East Glacier Park stations.*

20

Think of the victims at the September 11 Memorial and Museum

NEW YORK // The terrorist attacks on that bright September Tuesday in 2001 still scar America's heart and New York City's skyline. This moving museum uses video, photography, artifacts, and audio to honor the nearly 3000 people who lost their lives that day. Visitors stand below two 70ft steel tridents once supporting the base of the North Tower; contemplate the 'Survivors Staircase,' the ravaged stairs by which hundreds of workers fled to safety; and view the retaining wall that was still standing when the rubble was finally cleared.

☞ SEE IT ! *The memorial is free but the museum requires tickets; buy them online or at machines outside the building.*

Top: King's Canyon sequoias. Bottom: hiking Glen Pass in King's Canyon National Park.

© Larry Gerbrandt / Getty Images

21

Visit the world's biggest trees at Sequoia and Kings Canyon national parks

CALIFORNIA // You could come here just to see the superstar of these twin parks – that's General Sherman, the largest tree on Earth – and leave happy. But please, take a day – a week – to fully revel in the splendor of the granite-carved Sierra Nevada landscape. Hot in the summer, snowy in the winter, lashed by storms and occasionally ravaged by forest fires, these contiguous parks represent the wildest extremes of the California climate. Stroll through forests of giant sequoias reaching nearly 300ft into the sky. Watch out for rattlesnakes as you hike the arid foothills.

Mount the staircase at Moro Rock to see the Great Western Divide, the border between the two parks. The western slope of Mt Whitney, tallest mountain in the continental US, can be reached via Sequoia National Park; permits are required. In winter, the parks shimmer with snow and visitors snowshoe and cross-country ski through conifer forests.

☛ SEE IT ! *The parks are around 220 miles north of LA, 280 miles southeast of San Francisco. The nearest major airport is Fresno.*

22

Sunset-spot from the Empire State

© Benoît Daoust / Shutterstock

NEW YORK // Unless you're Ann Darrow (the unfortunate woman caught in King Kong's simian grip), heading to the top of the Empire State Building is an exhilarating experience. Two lofty observation decks (on the 86th and 102nd floors) offer mesmerizing views across the sweep of skyscraper-studded Manhattan, out to the islands of New York Harbor and far beyond – you can see for up to 80 miles on clear days. The Art Deco classic opened in 1931 after just 410 days of construction – using seven million hours of labor during the Great Depression.

☛ SEE IT ! *The Empire State Building is a short stroll from 34th St-Herald Sq subway station.*

© Robert Hoetink / Shutterstock

© Marianne Winther / Alamy

23

Explore Appalachian pioneer history at Cades Cove

TENNESSEE // This high mountain valley ('cove' to Appalachians) was settled by English, Welsh, and Scots-Irish pioneers in the early 1800s. They built homesteads, schools, and churches, raised a grist mill and buried their dead in hillside cemeteries. Today it's a ghost town, though it's hardly empty – Cades Cove is one of the top destinations in Great Smoky Mountains National Park. Tour the photogenic old buildings, ramble on wooded trails, picnic in wildflower-spangled meadows and bike the 11-mile loop road (closed to cars on summer Wednesdays). The large NPS campground is a popular and sociable spot.

 SEE IT ! *Cades Cove is 34 miles southwest of national park access town, Gatlinburg.*

24

Relish the mountain-themed amusements at Dollywood

TENNESSEE // Before you scoff at a Dolly Parton-brand Appalachian theme park, you must understand the goddess-like status Parton holds in East Tennessee. Born in a one-room cabin, the singer and actor has underwritten local schools and libraries, donated lavishly to wildfire victims, built a bald eagle preserve, and even helped fund one of the Covid-19 vaccines. Think about that when you're riding the *Dollywood Express* steam train, soaring on the Wild Eagle coaster or the Mystery Mine, watching country music performances, or visiting the replica of Dolly's childhood cabin. It's good, clean country fun.

 SEE IT ! *Dollywood is in Pigeon Forge, just outside Great Smoky Mountains National Park.*

Arrive early to catch morning-light vistas at Arches National Park's Double Arch.

25

Photograph breathtaking natural sculptures at Arches National Park

UTAH // Gazing at yet another elegant sandstone arch, you sense a kind of divine intervention. With more than 2000 natural rock bridges, Arches National Park looks as though a higher power tried their hand at sculpting, then left the results scattered around 119 sq miles of Utah desert. Some of these formations are small and squat, like bridges fit for gnomes; others, like Delicate Arch, look graceful; most impressive is Landscape Arch at 306ft wide – but whatever their size, the arches enhance already dream-like desertscapes. You'll find it impossible to resist using them as natural frames for photographs of the La Sal Mountains.

It took 65 million years to perfect this view. Buried sandstone was fractured under pressure, fissured by expanding ice and varnished by water flow. The result? Not only arches but myriad formations including castle-like ridges, fins of rock and boulders balanced improbably atop natural pillars.

☛ SEE IT ! *The park is 5 miles north of Moab. Visit in spring or fall for mild temperatures, or winter to see arches dusted in snow.*

© Peter Kunasz / Shutterstock

Left: The Virgin
River flows through
an autumnal Zion
National Park.

26

Adventure deep into the slot canyons of Zion National Park

UTAH // When it comes to national parks, Utah has an embarrassment of riches. Yet even among the state's 'mighty five' national parks, Zion stands just a little higher than the rest. Is it because of Angels Landing, a vertiginous hike involving chains bolted into the rocks, with sweeping views across the Colorado Plateau? Is it the Narrows, a wet walk along the Virgin River through slot canyons 1000ft high but only 20ft wide? Is it the crisp air and solitude among the juniper forests of the Kolob Canyons? Is it watching the sun set over 2000ft sandstone cliffs colored in the striated red and orange tones of the sun itself?

It's all this and more in this 229-sq-mile park, made of Navajo Sandstone carved by wind and water over millennia. The area was inhabited by Native Americans for some 8000 years, most recently by the Southern Paiute, before Mormon settlers arrived in the late 1850s. Established as a national park in 1919, it now sees nearly five million visitors a year.

This can mean crowds on popular trails in high season. Fortunately, many of the major attractions require permits, which cuts down congestion. Other activities are naturally self-selecting: only expert paddlers should attempt to kayak the whitewater of the Narrows, while casual climbers shouldn't tackle sheer sandstone walls with sparse protection.

Day-trippers can bike or ride the shuttle along Zion Canyon Scenic Drive; cycling is also allowed on the Pa'rus Trail, which follows the west bank of the Virgin River. The Canyon Trail Rides concession offers horseback treks along the river to the iconic sandstone formations known as the Court of the Patriarchs, or longer adventures up the dusty Sand Bench Trail for panoramic views of the park's southern end

☛ SEE IT ! *The park is just north of the Utah-Arizona line in Springdale. The nearest major airport is Las Vegas, 170 miles southwest.*

27

Go back to the 18th century in Colonial Williamsburg

VIRGINIA // It's the 21st century out there, but in here it's the 1700s, down to the very last button. Walk the streets of the former capital of colonial Virginia amidst costumed interpreters busy spinning wool, dipping beeswax candles and baking bread in wood-fired ovens, just as people would have done three centuries ago. The area encompasses some 300 acres of restored or recreated historic buildings, including the Governor's Palace, the Capitol, and the courthouse; walking around is free, though building tours have an entry fee. While some interpreters represent ordinary folks – including the many enslaved people who once worked here – others act as historical figures such as Thomas Jefferson and George Washington. Ask a question and they'll answer back with perfect colonial-era diction. Jealous of the costumes? Rent one for the day.

☛ SEE IT ! *Colonial Williamsburg is in the coastal city of Williamsburg. There's a free shuttle from the visitor center to the historic district.*

28

Enjoy the ups and downs of the Going-to-the-Sun Road

MONTANA // A strong contender for the most spectacular road in America, the 50-mile Going-to-the-Sun Rd was built for the express purpose of giving visitors to Glacier National Park a way to explore the mountainous interior without having to hike. This marvel of interwar engineering peaks at 6646ft Logan Pass on the continental divide, and is flanked by waterfalls, vertiginous drop-offs and broad Google Earth views. Constructed between 1921 and 1933 in the callow years of the motor car, the road is a National Historic Landmark.

The asphalt starts near iridescent Lake McDonald before angling sharply to the Garden Wall, a steep alpine escarpment known for its summer wildflowers. At Logan Pass you can stroll to Hidden Lake Overlook or hike the 7.6-mile Highline Trail, which contours across the Garden Wall to a backcountry chalet.

☛ SEE IT ! *In summer, Glacier National Park runs a free shuttle bus over Going-to-the-Sun Rd, from Apgar Transit Center to St Mary.*

Top: Haleakalā's Makahiku Falls. Bottom: a riot of colors along the park's Sliding Sands trail.

© Westend61 / Getty Images

© MNStudio / Shutterstock

29

Sleep in a volcano at Haleakalā National Park

HAWAI'I // Imagine camping on the crater floor of an ancient extinct volcano 10,000ft above the sea, the stars shining like silver fish in the black Hawai'ian sky. This is just one of the possible ways to spend your visit to Haleakalā National Park, one of the wildest landscapes in the United States. Native Hawai'ians tell the story of how the demigod Maui climbed to the summit of the Haleakalā volcano and lassoed the sun, forcing it to move more slowly across the sky so the people of Earth would have more warmth and light. Hike the cinder-cone volcano's slopes to see endangered wildlife like the

Haleakalā silversword plant, the kiwikiu (Maui parrotbill), and the nēnē (Hawai'ian goose). The most impressive cinder cones in the crater are nicknamed Pele's Paint Pot for their bronze and amber hues. Explore the ancient Hawai'ian village site at Kīpahulu, where the freshwater pools at 'Ohe'o Gulch cascade through a lush valley. And watch dawn break gold and purple over the crater – get up with plenty of time and make the short climb to Pa Ka'oao (White Hill) for the best spot.

👈 SEE IT ! *The park visitor center is 40 miles from Maui's main airport.*

Opposite from top: seeing stars through the Griffith Observatory's Zeiss Telescope; book ahead to view NYC from Lady Liberty's crown.

30

Feel starry-eyed at iconic Griffith Observatory

CALIFORNIA // From the outdoor terraces of Griffith Observatory, LA unfurls like a glittering carpet. Many visitors come to this 1935 landmark entirely for the views, arriving before sundown to admire the distant Hollywood sign and watch the fading light paint the City of Angels gold.

Even if it's your first time atop Mt Hollywood, the view is familiar – Griffith Observatory has had a starring role in movies like *Rebel Without a Cause*. But as well as inspiring Hollywood daydreams, the observatory reveals mysteries of the cosmic kind. Inside is the world's most advanced star projector, alongside interactive displays that map the solar system. Settle in at the Planetarium, where laser projections let you tour the heavens from your seat. Outside, obligatory selfie taken, you can peer into the Zeiss Telescope or wait until nightfall to stargaze.

☛ SEE IT ! *Organize a ride-share to beat peak-hour traffic, or take the DASH Observatory shuttle bus from Vermont/Sunset metro station.*

31

Get a view of freedom from the Statue of Liberty

NEW YORK // No other icon symbolizes the USA as much as Lady Liberty, soaring 151ft above Liberty Island. Representing opportunity and freedom, *Liberty Enlightening the World* (her full, if lesser-known name) was famously the first sight for millions of migrants who sailed into New York Harbor in the late 19th and early 20th centuries. These days, the massive statue remains one of the world's premier tourist attractions. It was conceived by French intellectual Édouard de Laboulaye around 1865 as a monument to the republican principles shared by France and the USA. French sculptor Frédéric-Auguste Bartholdi then spent more than 10 years in Paris designing it, before it was shipped to New York, erected on Bedloe's Island (the small harbor island later renamed Liberty Island) and unveiled in 1886.

☛ SEE IT ! *Liberty Island ferries run from Manhattan. Guided ranger tours and audio tours are available; book online to climb the crown.*

30

31

© karakurtis / Getty images

Left: hands-on at Kennedy Space Center. Below: Heroes & Legends. Right: the monumental engines of *Saturn V*

SCIENCE AND SPACE

↓

Marvel at America's first plane and its first space station at the Air and Space Museum.
page 52

↓

Get up to speed on space travel at NASA's Space Center Houston.
page 86

↓

Chicago's Museum of Science and Industry, America's largest, contains myriad wonders.
page 236

The Spirit of Space

Alan B. Shepard Jr.
First American in Space

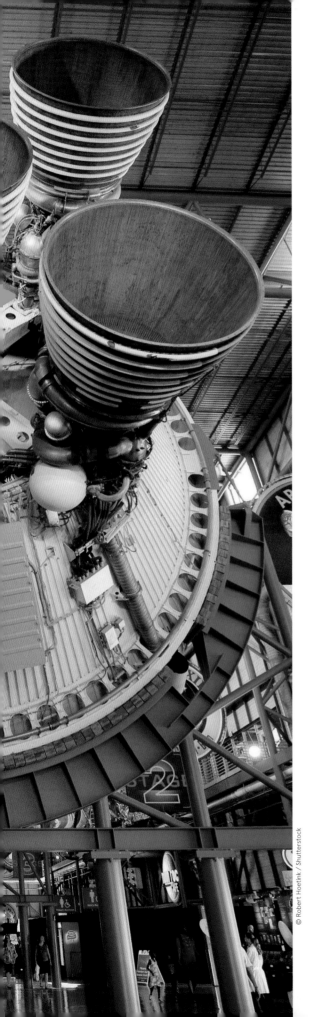

Blast off at Kennedy Space Center

FLORIDA // Some of humanity's most awe-inspiring feats have begun at this humid patch of Florida coast. Since 1968, NASA's Kennedy Space Center has been the main launch site for spaceflight. The Project Mercury flights that first took humans outside Earth's orbit took off from here, as did 1969's Apollo 11 mission to the moon. The 144-acre KSC complex now includes rocket-building facilities, astronaut crew quarters, and launch control. But for civilian space-lovers, it's all about the visitor complex. See artifacts like Gus Grissom's suborbital space suit and capsules from 1960s-era missions in the Heroes & Legends exhibit. Admire the famous rockets mounted upright, pointing at the sky, in the outdoor Rocket Garden. Ask your burning questions at the daily Q&A with a real veteran astronaut. Learn about space flight's future in displays about Mars. Pay respects at the Space Mirror Memorial, inscribed with the names of astronauts who have died in the quest to explore space.

There are also two IMAX theaters and a brand-new kids play area where aspiring astronauts can pilot pretend shuttles and scramble through tubes connecting glowing planets. But perhaps the most spine-tingling sight is the Space Shuttle *Atlantis*, retired since 2011 and now displayed inside a hangar. Suspended at an angle with the payload bay doors open, it's surrounded by interactive consoles giving visitors the chance to land the shuttle or dock it at the International Space Station. There's also a life-size Hubble Space Telescope replica. Go beyond the visitor center with a bus tour, which passes the launch facilities on the way to the Apollo/Saturn V Center, with a multimedia show in the Firing Room. Finish up with a foil packet of freeze-dried 'astronaut ice cream' at the gift shop.

☛ SEE IT ! *KSC is on Merritt Island (actually a peninsula); the nearest major airport is Orlando, 45 miles west.*

© Robert Hoetink / Shutterstock

33

Plunge into Great Smoky Mountains National Park

NORTH CAROLINA/TENNESSEE // With its foggy peaks, wildflower-spangled meadows, green glades, and tinkling waterfalls, it's no wonder this is the USA's most visited national park. The original Cherokee inhabitants called it 'Shaconage,' meaning 'place of the blue smoke' – wake up early on a misty morning and you'll understand why. As many visitors don't stray far from the main roads, it's easy to find solitude: hike along slopes abloom with trillium and columbine; wander across dramatic heaths; and go deep into mossy forests thick with ferns. Highlights include 6643ft Clingmans Dome, the Smokies' highest peak; the atmospheric valley of Cades Cove; and the stone peaks of Chimney Tops. Plan (way) ahead to stay at mountaintop LeConte Lodge, the park's only non-camping accommodation – only accessible by hiking in.

☛ SEE IT ! *The park spans the North Carolina-Tennessee border: the North Carolina access town is Cherokee; the Tennessee one is Gatlinburg.*

© Tony Barber / Getty Images

34

Goggle at the starchitect-designed Guggenheim Museum

NEW YORK // The Guggenheim's Frank Lloyd Wright-designed white nautilus spiral is one of New York's most recognizable buildings, sometimes overshadowing the works inside. Which is no small feat. The Guggenheim is home to one of the world's finest collections of modern and contemporary art. Picasso, Cézanne, Kandinsky, Monet, Van Gogh, Chagall, Modigliani, Klee, Pollock – they're all here, along with consistently amazing temporary exhibitions in the central rotunda. Completed in 1959, the gallery was the love child of mining scion Solomon R. Guggenheim and his art advisor, German baroness Hilla von Rebay, who had a falling out with the Guggenheim family and never saw the museum she helped create. Exhibits are installed from bottom to top along the rotunda ramp.

☛ SEE IT ! *The museum is on Fifth Ave at East 89th St; take the 4, 5 or 6 subway line to 86th St. Saturday 4-6pm is pay-what-you-wish – and crowded.*

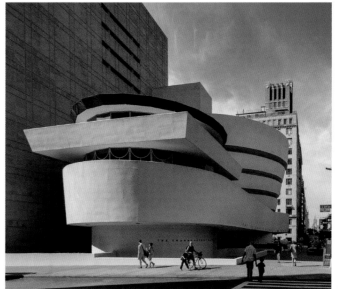

© Solomon R. Guggenheim Museum, New York. Photograph by David Heald. © SRGF

© Alex Pix / Shutterstock

© crbellette / Shutterstock

35

Marvel at the monumental sculpture of Mt Rushmore

SOUTH DAKOTA // One of America's most iconic sights, the four 60ft-high presidential heads of George Washington, Thomas Jefferson, Theodore Roosevelt, and Abraham Lincoln are really, truly awesome. Protruding from Mt Rushmore's craggy face in surely the nation's all-time greatest and most audacious rock-carving feat, these four heads of state were respectively selected for representing the USA's birth, growth, development, and preservation, and were carved between 1927 and 1941 by sculptor Gutzon Borglum, his son Lincoln and, presumably, some other helping hands.

☛ SEE IT ! *Mt Rushmore is off Hwy 244, 23 miles from Rapid City.*

36

Honor the millions at the United States Holocaust Memorial Museum

WASHINGTON, DC // Providing moving testament to the unimaginable horrors committed during WWII, this is one of America's most important remembrance sites. The staggering death toll is hard to fathom, though the museum does its best to humanize the suffering. Upon arrival you receive the identity card of a single Holocaust victim, whose story is revealed as you explore a hellish past marked by ghettos, rail cars, and death camps. It also shows the flip side of human nature, documenting the risks many citizens took to help the persecuted.

☛ SEE IT ! *The museum is south of the National Mall; a short walk from the Smithsonian metro station.*

37

Honor King's legacy at the Martin Luther King Jr National Historic Site

GEORGIA // Born in deeply segregated Atlanta in 1929, legendary freedom fighter Martin Luther King Jr grew up in a yellow Queen Anne-style house at 501 Auburn Avenue. Today, more than half a century after his assassination, the house is part of an historic site dedicated to his life and cause. The site includes King's Ebenezer Baptist church, exhibits on the Civil Rights Movement, and the graves of King and his wife, Coretta Scott King, next to a reflecting pool. In 2019 the National Park Service purchased King's last home, a brick split-level on Sunset Avenue on the other side of downtown; it's now a separate part of the Historic Site. The area is a moving, inspiring and often difficult place to visit, highlighting how far King took America, as well as how far the country still has to go.

☞ SEE IT ! *Most of the site is in Atlanta's Sweet Auburn neighborhood; King's last home is in Vine City.*

38

Look for the ghost of Abraham Lincoln inside the White House

WASHINGTON, DC // America's commander-in-chief works and resides in a decidedly grand abode. The White House has 132 rooms, 35 bathrooms, 28 fireplaces, eight staircases and three elevators, encompassing some 55,000 sq ft. Despite the size, Irish-born architect James Hoban envisioned a building that was simple and conservative, so as not to seem royal, in keeping with the new country's principles. He modeled the Neoclassical-style manor on Leinster House, a mid-18th-century duke's villa in Dublin that still stands and is now used by Ireland's parliament. If you can't score one of the free, self-guided inside tours (apply three months in advance), head to the White House Visitor Center for information-packed multimedia exhibits, including a presentation on the history and lives of the presidential families.

☞ SEE IT ! *For tours, US citizens apply via a home-state member of Congress, non-Americans via their country's embassy in DC.*

© Richard T. Nowitz / Getty Images

© Thomas Kreulen / Shutterstock

39

Learn about the past and the future at Jackson Square

LOUISIANA // One of the most photogenic corners of New Orleans, Jackson Square is a Paris-meets-the-Caribbean fantasy watched over by grand buildings and lush greenery. Originally known as the Place d'Armes, the block-sized square has played a pivotal civic role for more than 300 years: as a colonial meeting space, an open-air market, a military parade ground, and a public execution site. Today, it's a carnival-like hive of street musicians, sketch artists, and fortune tellers, all showing off their skills to the constant stream of visitors.

☛ SEE IT ! *Jackson Square lies in the French Quarter, one block from the riverfront.*

40

Pretend to be a robber baron at Biltmore Estate

NORTH CAROLINA // If there'd been reality TV in the Gilded Era, there certainly would have been a show called *Keeping Up With The Vanderbilts* set in this 250-room mansion. Built by George Washington Vanderbilt II, an heir to the family's shipping and railroad fortune, it remains America's largest privately owned home. You need to be fairly wealthy yourself just to visit – basic tickets start at $64. This buys you the chance to explore the French-style chateau, complete with its own bowling alley, and wander the exquisitely landscaped 8000-acre grounds.

☛ SEE IT ! *The estate is south of downtown Asheville. It has its own hotels, shopping, dining and winery.*

📷

Left: browse the haphazard City Lights shelves for some counter-culture inspo.

41

Summon your revolutionary spirit at City Lights Books

CALIFORNIA // Inspiration might strike while you saunter along Columbus Avenue. This strip of San Francisco's North Beach is lined with cafes, bookstores, and creaky-floored bars – favorite haunts of novelists, activists, and renegade poets during the 1960s.

The neighborhood's literary nucleus is City Lights Books. To understand its infamy, you have to turn back the clock to 1956. Authorities seized copies of Allen Ginsberg's *Howl*, an epic poem and rallying cry for creative and sexual freedom, while poet and City Lights owner Lawrence Ferlinghetti was arrested for distributing obscene material. The ensuing court case drew the nation's gaze to San Francisco's Beat generation writers.

Today, this independent publisher and bookstore still draws anti-establishment scribes and their admirers. Join them by leafing through counter-culture volumes and sitting in the 'poet's chair'. The store's sign says it best: this is 'A Kind of Library Where Books Are Sold.' The cellar is rumored to have been a former gathering place for shadowy cult rituals during the 1930s. Whether or not it's true, City Lights remains a portal to the written word at its most life-affirming.

🐾 SEE IT ! *City Lights (261 Columbus Ave) is between Chinatown and Coit Tower, a 10-minute walk from each.*

© Robert Mullan / Shutterstock

© Leonardo Pinheiro / Getty Images

© Sean Pavone / Shutterstock

Dip into democracy at the US Capitol

WASHINGTON, DC // No other US building better represents the nation's democratic traditions than the Capitol. Since 1800, this is where the legislative branch of American government – Congress – has met to debate and write the country's laws. The lower House of Representatives (435 members) and upper Senate (100 members) meet in the building's south and north wings respectively. To visit, you must take an hour-long tour which showcases the fascinating background of a building that fairly sweats history. You'll watch an introductory film first, then staff lead you into ornate halls and hushed chambers cluttered with the busts and statues of generations of Congress members. The highlight is the 180ft-high dome and its fresco, *The Apotheosis of Washington* (1865).

☛ SEE IT ! *For obligatory guided tours, enter via the underground visitor center below the East Front Plaza. To avoid lines, reserve online in advance.*

See world-changing inventions at the Air and Space Museum

WASHINGTON, DC // Forget the White House, the US Capitol and the Washington Monument – DC's biggest crowd pleaser is the staggering collection of all things aviation-related in the National Air and Space Museum. Anchored on the south side of the National Mall, the soaring halls are packed with historic aircraft, record-breaking rockets and otherworldly spacecraft. The Wright Brothers get their own gallery with its centerpiece the primitive biplane – the world's first airplane – they built and flew in 1903. You can also check out the natty red Lockheed Vega 5B that Amelia Earhart piloted solo across the Atlantic Ocean in 1932, the Apollo Lunar Module, and the cramped quarters (and exercise bicycle) of *Skylab*, America's first space station. For something less sedate, you can take the controls of a fighter jet in the Flight Simulator Zone, or get an awe-inspiring look at distant galaxies at the Albert Einstein Planetarium.

☛ SEE IT ! *The museum is close to L'Enfant Plaza metro station.*

44

Brave the lines to feel the magic at Walt Disney World

FLORIDA // It's called Walt Disney *World* for a reason: the country's most iconic resort park is a place apart. It's a world where adults wear mouse ears and squeal when Cinderella passes by; a world where employees are 'cast members' and the bus is a 'Magical Express'; a world where all children are seemingly dressed as either Elsa or Buzz Lightyear. Consisting of four 'Kingdoms' – the Magic Kingdom, Epcot, Hollywood Studios and Animal Kingdom – plus two waterparks and dozens of resorts, shopping and entertainment venues, it's truly a world unto itself.

☞ SEE IT ! *Fly into Orlando and take the bus (the Magical Express) 25 miles to the resort.*

45

Meet the ghosts of gangsters and escape from Alcatraz

CALIFORNIA // Disembarking the ferry at Alcatraz, a sense of isolation ensnares you instantly. There's nowhere to hide at this island prison, and swift currents made escape near-impossible. The dramatic setting is intentional, designed to send a strong message to criminal ringleaders. Touring the echoing cell blocks, you'll learn about daredevil escape attempts and walk in the footsteps of infamous criminals like Al 'Scarface' Capone. You'll also hear the sounds of San Francisco floating across the water – torturous reminders of freedom to inmates.

☞ SEE IT ! *Book online to reserve a DIY or guided tour, including return ferry from Pier 33.*

46

Seek inspiration on the Brooklyn Bridge

NEW YORK // Poets and painters (Hart Crane, Frank Stella), crooners and beatniks (Frank Sinatra, Jack Kerouac) have all found inspiration in the Brooklyn Bridge. And whether you sail beneath it, cycle past it, stroll over it, or simply admire its beauty from a distance, you can't help but feel the power of its presence, soaring high above the East River between Lower Manhattan and Brooklyn. Walking the clattering wooden boards above the traffic is the best way to experience this 1883 masterpiece; the mile-long journey offers staggering vistas along the way.

☞ SEE IT ! *The best views are Manhattan-bound so start in Brooklyn (take the A/C line to High St/Brooklyn Bridge station).*

Left: Make like a bison on an epic trek through Grand Teton National Park.

47

Hike until your legs are jelly at Grand Teton National Park

WYOMING // This national park in northwest Wyoming, craggy with icy peaks, rippling with sagebrush, dotted with high-altitude lakes, is a place for hikers. Sure, there are scenic views to be had from your car window, but the real magic happens halfway up a trail when you stop for a snack break and realize you're 1000ft above the valley floor, clouds blowing across the big western sky as fast as freight trains. Pass through conifer forest, alpine meadows and fields of scree, watching hawks circle overhead and chubby marmosets waddle between the rocks. The milky blue mountain lakes beckon invitingly; they're every bit as 'refreshing' as you'd expect.

Among the non-hiking adventures are cycling the path from Jackson, rafting the Snake River, riding the scenic passenger boat across Jenny Lake, and chowing down on cowboy cooking at Dornan's Chuckwagon.

Wildlife photography is big too: keep your camera ready for elk, grizzlies, bison, marmots, and cartoon-cute pikas. While Jackson has its luxe-Western hotels and restaurants, sleeping among the evergreens or staying at the 1920s NPS lodge is much more atmospheric.

☞ TRY IT ! *Grand Teton is just outside the town of Jackson. The airport is actually inside the park.*

© JacobH / Getty Images

© BrianScantlebury / Shutterstock

48

Visit America's oldest town, the extraordinary Taos Pueblo

NEW MEXICO // Tiwa-speaking Taos people have lived in this sun-baked northern New Mexico village for more than 1000 years, making it the oldest community in the US. About 150 people still inhabit the Pueblo itself, while some 1900 others live in the surrounding 99,000 acres of Taos lands. Their oral history and religious beliefs are closely guarded, though residents proudly share their village through guided tours. The Pueblo is centered on two five-story complexes, dating from 1450 and some of the finest examples of adobe architecture in existence. Artisans sell silver jewelry and unique mica-flecked pottery, as well as paintings and leatherwork like moccasins. Visitors can join the annual San Geronimo Feast Day in late September, as long as they abide by Pueblo rules, including no photography.

☛ SEE IT ! *Taos Pueblo is 3 miles northeast of Taos Plaza. Tours are optional and donation-based: take one and tip generously.*

49

Honor the dead at the Oklahoma City National Memorial and Museum

OKLAHOMA // The term 'domestic terrorism' was still unfamiliar to most Americans on April 19, 1995, when a truck bomb tore apart the Alfred P. Murrah Federal Building in downtown Oklahoma City. At least 168 people died – civil servants, grandparents collecting social security checks, babies in the daycare center. This respectful memorial includes a reflecting pool and a field of empty chairs representing the lives lost – the 19 tiny chairs meant for the children are especially moving. Hope springs from the Survivor Tree, an American elm that was damaged in the bombing but survived. Its seeds are planted each year and the saplings distributed around the country. The Children's Area has 5000 tiles hand-painted by children across America for whom the bombing was a generational trauma.

☛ SEE IT ! *The memorial is open daily at the site of the former federal building.*

Left: take a road trip through the epic scenery of Big Bend National Park.

© Denis Jr. Tangney / Getty Images

50

Embrace the enormity of Big Bend National Park

TEXAS // The phrase 'everything's bigger in Texas' gets bandied about a lot: the state's 'bigness' is in its DNA, from restaurant portions to ranches. But to really appreciate Texas' size, you need to park the car and head into enormous Big Bend National Park on foot. As well as being vast, these empty 1252 sq miles, brushing the US-Mexico border along the Rio Grande's distinctive kink, also show more sides to the state's topography than the cactus-dotted desert seen in movies. Within the park's borders are serious mountains reaching 7825ft at Emory Peak, plus verdant slopes of pinyon pine, quaking aspen, and bigtooth maple. At the other extreme, the Rio Grande cuts between canyon walls far, far below. In this huge, varied wilderness, where temperatures vary by up to 20°F from canyon bottom to mountaintop, adventurers must prepare for all eventualities – it can be punishingly hot on the 150 or so miles of hiking trails, but camping out can become mighty chilly.

In areas like the popular Chisos Mountains, Big Bend is well set up for visitors, with good infrastructure and an extensive network of trails. In other parts, the land is unpeopled and dauntingly inhospitable. Many big hikes depart from the Chisos Basin Visitor Center, including the 12.5-mile loop of the South Rim Trail which yields magical views of the Chihuahuan Desert and has the tantalizing out-and-back up to Emory Peak as an optional add-on. The park's chief pleasure? Feeling like a character in a Western, with a world to roam just a boot lace-up away. And as with most places of these proportions, you could keep coming back for a lifetime and never need to see the same spots twice.

☛ SEE IT ! *Get park information at Panther Junction Visitor Center, 30 miles east of Terlingua; Chisos Basin Visitor Center and Chisos Mountains trailhead are 9 miles further.*

© brians101 / Getty Images

© FiledIMAGE / Shutterstock

51

Listen to a bugle salute at Arlington National Cemetery

VIRGINIA // Simple white headstones cover the green hills at Arlington National Cemetery, the final resting place for soldiers from every war since the American Revolution. Apart from the 400,000 service members and their dependents, several US leaders and notable civilians are also buried here: an eternal flame flickers over the grave of John F. Kennedy; flowers pile up at the marker for the space shuttle *Challenger* crew; rifle-toting military guards maintain a 24-hour vigil at the Tomb of the Unknown Soldier. The elaborate changing of the guard (every hour on the hour October through March, every half-hour April through September) is one of Arlington's most moving sights. Still in active use, it's not uncommon here to see families gathered around flag-draped caskets or catch a lone bugle's heartrending lament.

 SEE IT ! *It's a five-minute walk from Arlington metro station to the entrance of the national cemetery.*

52

Cheer for the Chicago Cubs at Wrigley Field

ILLINOIS // The USA's second-oldest major league ballpark (after Fenway), Wrigley was built in 1914 and renamed for chewing-gum magnate William Wrigley Jr in 1927. Iconic for its ivy-covered outfield wall and hand-turned scoreboard, Wrigley has all the legends and superstitions you'd expect from a century-old stadium. The most famous, perhaps, is the 'Curse of the Billy Goat,' wherein a goat-owning local tavern owner cursed the Cubs with a losing streak in 1945. They didn't win another World Series until 2016. Learn this kind of quirky history on 90-minute park tours, or see the Cubs in action on a warm June night, bratwurst in one hand, beer in the other. Or come to the plaza at Gallagher Way for free concerts, outdoor fitness classes, and movie nights.

 SEE IT ! *The stadium's nearest station is Addison on the Red Line. The Cubs play April to October. Tours are available both on- and off-season.*

53

Goggle at skyscraper-sized trees in Redwood National and State Parks

CALIFORNIA // Nearly half the world's remaining old-growth coastal redwoods are protected within the foggy embrace of this park complex. Consisting of Redwood National Park plus Prairie Creek Redwoods, Del Norte Coast Redwoods, and Jedediah Smith Redwoods state parks, it's truly a land of giants. There's nothing to remind you of your tininess on this planet like walking through a grove of redwoods stretching nearly 300ft towards the California sky. Some of these trees were here when Julius Caesar ruled Rome. The Yurok people long lived in plank houses made from their wood – though only once it fell naturally – until they were displaced or killed by Gold Rush miners. After intense lobbying from environmentalists, Redwood National Park was finally created in 1968. Come here for the redwoods, of course, but also for the miles of undulating, often-foggy prairie, oak woodlands, and rugged coastline.

☛ SEE IT ! *The four parks are in far-north Humboldt and Del Norte counties. The nearest major airports are Sacramento and San Francisco.*

© photo.ua / Shutterstock / Hammering Man by Jonathan Borofsky

© Rush Jagoe / Lonely Planet

54

Escape the mainstream at Seattle Art Museum

WASHINGTON // It might not have the size or star power of New York and Chicago galleries, but Seattle Art Museum (SAM) feels uncommon, intimate and extraordinary. Aside from pulling in international-caliber temporary shows, SAM maintains a skilfully curated assemblage of permanent exhibits strongly biased toward contemporary and indigenous art, along with an avant-garde alfresco sculpture park overlooking Puget Sound. The slick modernity of the downtown HQ, with its grandiose entry staircase (the 'Art Ladder'), is echoed in the displays which include Andy Warhol, Jasper Johns, and some drippy (and trippy) Jackson Pollock. More local and relevant is the indigenous collection: large wooden masks and skilfully woven textiles from the Tlingit, Haida and Kwakwaka'wakw peoples of the Pacific Northwest.

☞ SEE IT ! *You can walk to the museum from anywhere in downtown Seattle. University St Station on Link light rail is close by.*

55

Salute the birthplace of rock & roll at Sun Studio

TENNESSEE // It's no exaggeration to say rock & roll was born in this Memphis storefront recording studio. Sam Phillips recorded blues legends Howlin' Wolf, BB King, and Ike Turner here, as well as rockabilly stars Jerry Lee Lewis, Johnny Cash, and Roy Orbison, before taking a chance on a local teen with hooded blue eyes and a pouty lower lip. Elvis was just what Phillips had been looking for: a white artist who could make Black music mainstream in deeply racist America. The rest, of course, is history. Studio tours are led by wisecracking guides, many of whom are musicians themselves. Hear tapes of historic recording sessions like the 'Million Dollar Quartet,' a 1956 jam session involving Elvis, Johnny Cash, Carl Perkins, and Jerry Lee Lewis, and pose for photos on the X where Elvis once sang.

☞ SEE IT ! *The studio is at 706 Union Ave; tours are hourly. A shuttle does a loop to Beale St and Graceland.*

56

See Atlantic swells on Cape Hatteras National Seashore

NORTH CAROLINA // This 70-mile ribbon of sand was once called the Graveyard of the Atlantic for all the ships that foundered in its treacherous waters. These barrier islands still feel wild today, with crashing gray waves, crab-filled marshes, flocks of migrating shorebirds, salt-splashed campgrounds, and family-run motels. Stop by the Cape Hatteras lighthouse, watching over the water since the early 19th century, and don't miss pirate lore, unique accents, wild ponies, and fig cake on Ocracoke Island, only accessible by car ferry.

☞ SEE IT ! *NC-12 runs down the Outer Banks; the National Seashore begins just south of Nags Head.*

57

Dig the acoustics at Red Rocks Park and Amphitheatre

COLORADO // The Beatles? Check. U2? Definitely. The Grateful Dead? Many times. Coldplay? Yup. Frankly, it would be easier to make a list of big-name bands that haven't played this legendary venue than the ones that have. In its natural setting with 9525 seats carved into dusky sandstone, Red Rocks has the kind of acoustics bands will cross oceans for. Snag tickets for whoever's playing and watch Denver light up on the horizon as night falls and the music starts. Or come for yoga, outdoor movies, and to hike miles of trails criss-crossing the 600-acre complex.

☞ SEE IT ! *Red Rocks is 15 miles southwest of Denver. You can visit in the daytime for free.*

58

Cross New York Harbor aboard the Staten Island Ferry

NEW YORK // One of NYC's finest free adventures can be had by boarding the hulking orange vessels that ply the waters between Lower Manhattan and Staten Island. From the outdoor decks, the 25-minute journey yields cinematic views of the city skyline, the Verrazzano-Narrows Bridge and the Statue of Liberty. And it provides a good excuse to explore New York's least-known borough, where you can catch a minor league baseball game at St George's waterfront stadium. Going strong since 1817, the ferry service runs 24 hours a day.

☞ SEE IT ! *Take the 1 line to South Ferry Station; avoid peak commuter times from 5-7pm.*

© EQRoy / Shutterstock

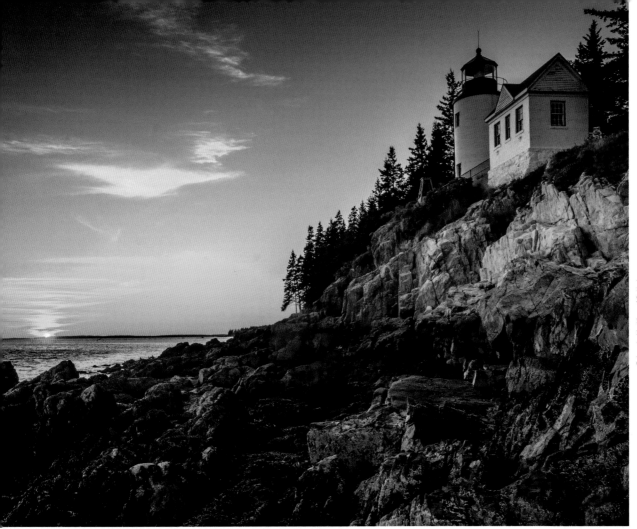

It's the first place in the US to see sunrise, but Acadia National Park is equally beautiful at sunset, here from Bass Harbor Lighthouse.

59

See the USA's first sunrise at Acadia National Park

MAINE // As well as being the first place in the country to see the sun's rays each morning, Acadia offers everything splendid about Maine in just 74 sq miles. There's the wild side: granite cliffs; crashing ocean; wheeling seabirds; thicketed mountains. And the genteel New England side: tea on the lawn at Jordan Pond; miles of hand-hewn stone roads for cycling and horseback-riding; quaint-but-refined inns and bistros in Bar Harbor.

Get your quads burning on the 7.5-mile hike up Cadillac Mountain, the North Atlantic's tallest peak; drive the Park Loop for views of Frenchman Bay; swim at Sand Beach – if you can handle the ever-chilly water – then press onwards to Thunder Hole, where waves hitting an underwater cave produce an unearthly roar. Longer trips mean time for paddling the secluded coves of Long Pond or taking a spin to the wind-whipped Schoodic Peninsula for a

craggy coastline, postcard-pretty lighthouse, and misty forests where daylight never quite seems to penetrate. Finish with butter-drenched lobster at park-adjacent mainstay, Trenton Bridge Lobster Pound.

☛ **SEE IT !** *Most of the park is on Mt Desert (pronounced 'dessert,' as in ice cream) Island, near the town of Bar Harbor. The nearest major airport is Bangor, 50 miles inland.*

60

Go gator-spotting in the vast Everglades National Park

FLORIDA // Endless vistas of swaying sawgrass have earned these extraordinary wetlands the nickname 'River of Grass.' America's largest tropical wilderness, with 2410 sq miles of sawgrass prairie, mangrove swamp, hardwood hammock, and pine forest covering Florida's southwestern tip, the Everglades is beautiful and foreboding, the muddy waters bubbling with gators and a-slither with snakes. Its long and complex history includes more than 10,000 years of Native American habitation and a role as a hiding place for people escaping slavery. Today it's a haven for birders, kayakers, and fishers, as well as day-trippers looking to take a tram tour or stroll one of the boardwalk trails. For paddlers, the Ten Thousand Islands area is a wonderland of mangrove islets and white beaches. If you're not afraid of dirt, try 'slogging' – donning special shoes to wade through the muck for close-ups with Everglades wildlife.

☛ SEE IT ! *The national park is around 40 miles southwest of Miami.*

61

Connect with natural wonders at the Garden of the Gods

COLORADO // Delicate red sandstone spires reach for the heavens as Pikes Peak looms in the background: the Garden of the Gods sure is a stunning park – and crowded, especially in summer. Formations like Kissing Camels and Steamboat Rock are chock-full with picture-takers, while trails are packed with e-bike and Segway riders. But with 21 miles of trails, it's easy to get away. Plus, colder weather thins the crowds and provides scenic snowy backdrops to boot. Rock Ledge Ranch is a fun stop, with costumed interpreters showcasing 19th-century Western life.

🐾 SEE IT ! *The park is in Colorado Springs, 70 miles south of Denver.*

62

Head into the clouds at One World Trade Center

NEW YORK // One World Trade Center soars with a touch of Manhattan's famous structural statistic-busting verve to the heights of highest building in the USA – *and* highest in the Western hemisphere, *and* sixth-highest in the world. A defiant and dramatic response to the terrorist attacks that razed the Twin Towers to the ground in 2001, this 1776ft giant was completed in 2013. On Levels 100-102, some 1268ft up, the observation deck is, even in a city filled with gargantuan skyscrapers, still New York's loftiest publicly accessible lookout.

🐾 SEE IT ! *You can't miss this sky-scraping building at 285 Fulton St, Lower Manhattan.*

63

Look for ghosts of the past in Lafayette Cemetery No. 1

LOUISIANA // Of all the New Orleans cemeteries, Lafayette exudes the strongest sense of subtropical Southern Gothic – the contrast of moldering crypts and gentle decay with fertile greenery is jarring. It's a place filled with stories – of German and Irish immigrants, deaths from yellow fever, societies doing right by their dead – that pulls the living into the city's long, troubled past. *Interview with the Vampire* author Anne Rice even staged her own mock funeral here, complete with horse-drawn hearse, brass band, and an antique wedding dress.

🐾 SEE IT ! *It's a two-block walk to the St Charles Avenue Streetcar.*

© bjul / Shutterstock

Opposite: find superlative solitude amid the highlands of Rocky Mountain National Park.

64

Gain altitude in Rocky Mountain National Park

COLORADO // There's one direction in Rocky Mountain National Park: up. Up Trail Ridge Rd, the highest all-paved road in the US, crossing alpine meadows and aspen forests to rise above the tree line at 12,183ft. Up Longs Peak, the park's only '14er' (mountain higher than 14,000ft), a bucket-list item for many a would-be mountaineer. Up to rustic campgrounds so high above sea level you may wake up dizzy.

The area was inhabited by Ute and Arapaho people before homesteaders began setting up ranches in the mid-1800s; Woodrow Wilson signed the park into existence in 1915. It's now 415 sq miles of mountains, valleys, lakes and rivers, with more than 350 miles of hiking trails ranging from kid-friendly strolls to epic multi-day treks. The fir, spruce, and aspen forests are as peaceful as cathedrals; the mountain meadows fit for filming your very own *The Sound of Music* Intro. Wildlife abounds:

moose, elk, and bighorn sheep graze; bobcats and mountain lions prowl; pikas and marmots scurry. In the summer people abound too, though with so much wilderness it's easy to find your own slice of mountain. Winter brings tranquillity and thick, glittering snow. Go for a guided snowshoe trip, whizz through the valleys on cross-country skis or lug your snow tube up to the old ski resort at Hidden Valley for a spot of sledding.

While Longs Peak is the only 14er, there are 72 mountains higher than 12,000ft in the park – meaning you get your pick of leg-testing hikes. We like Twin Sisters Peak, whose 11,433ft summit, reached via a scramble across landslide fields and loose scree, has views clear across the Continental Divide.

☛ SEE IT ! *The park's access towns are Estes Park to the east and Grand Lake to the west. Denver Airport is around 80 miles southeast.*

65

Wander a geological wonderland at Valley of Fire State Park

NEVADA // This masterpiece of Southwest desert scenery contains 40,000 acres of red Aztec sandstone, petrified trees and, at Atlatl Rock, ancient Native American petroglyphs depicting people, animals, and other symbols. Valley of Fire was Nevada's first designated state park when dedicated in 1935, but its psychedelic landscapes have been carved by wind and water for thousands of years.

Must-see spots include White Domes, Rainbow Vista, Fire Canyon, and Silica Dome: each as magnificent as it sounds. For more information on the park's unique geological features, the visitor center sells books and maps and takes reservations for guided hikes and ranger-led stargazing expeditions. You can also try your luck for one of the 72 extremely popular, first-come, first-served primitive campsites.

🐟 SEE IT ! *Valley of Fire Hwy cuts across the park, connecting with I-15 34 miles northeast of Las Vegas.*

66

Join the studious at the New York Public Library

NEW YORK // Loyally guarded by *Patience* and *Fortitude* (sculpted marble lions overlooking Fifth Ave), this Beaux Arts show-off is one of NYC's best free attractions. When dedicated in 1911, the city's flagship library ranked as the largest marble structure ever built in the US, and the lavish coffered ceiling of the remarkable Rose Main Reading Room still takes the breath away. But the reading room is not just for show: anybody can use what might well be the most glamorous co-working space in the world. This extraordinary library also houses precious manuscripts by just about every author of note in the English language, as well as an original copy of the Declaration of Independence and a Gutenberg Bible. Then there's the 431,000 maps, 16,000 atlases, and books on cartography, dating from the 16th century to the present.

🐟 SEE IT ! *Join a free guided tour or grab a free audioguide from the information desk. And ask about the seminar and workshop program.*

67

View big-name contemporary art at The Broad

CALIFORNIA // The Broad (rhymes with 'road', not 'board') has made a bold architectural and artistic impression in downtown Los Angeles since it first opened its doors in 2015. Billionaire philanthropist Eli Broad and his wife have amassed a heavy-hitting body of works in this outstanding collection, including pieces by Andy Warhol, Roy Lichtenstein, Cindy Sherman, and Jeff Koons. The building itself is a sight to behold too, a weird and wonderful white lattice shell that lifts at the corners.

☞ SEE IT ! *The Broad is an easy walk from Civic Center/Grand Park Metro station.*

68

Leap into literary utopia at Harry Ransom Center

TEXAS // Harry Ransom indisputably numbers among the University of Texas' most enterprising faculty members ever. He drove the expansion of its rare books collection from 1957 onwards, leading to the legacy of rare volumes and artifacts the facility protects today. Just being in this huge literature repository holding one of the few surviving Gutenberg Bibles, early Shakespeare folios, and fragments of a 10th-century Quran, not to mention the first nature photograph ever taken, will send shivers down any book-buff's spine. Many texts are available to members for viewing.

☞ SEE IT ! *The center is on Austin's University of Texas campus.*

69

Catch exquisite canyon views at Angels Landing

UTAH // Toughness on a trek means many things, and Zion National Park's Angels Landing is proof it doesn't always mean distance. Just 2.5 miles separate trailhead from top on this out-and-back slog, where physical hardship first tests your calves during 1488ft of ascent – and then tests your head for heights. The point at which many turn back is the chain-assist section near the summit, where you balance along a rocky 5ft-wide ridge with precipitous 1000ft drop-offs either side. Spying Zion Canyon's most magical views is your incentive to persevere.

☞ SEE IT ! *The hike starts at Grotto drop-off point on Floor of the Valley Rd.*

© Frank Bach / Shutterstock

Mesa Verde's astonishing Cliff Palace complex was mysteriously abandoned 80 years after it was built.

70

Adventure through archaeology at Mesa Verde National Park

COLORADO // Even by the benchmark of other ancient civilizations, the culture of the Ancestral Puebloans, who erected the edifices in the cliffs that make Mesa Verde National Park so mesmeric, remains mystery-shrouded. No one knows why, having lived atop the mesa for six centuries, these people moved beneath the cliffs around 1190 to build elaborate villages. Or why, having gone to such efforts, they permanently migrated south just 80-odd years later (a cooling climate is one theory). Those guys could teach today's construction industry plenty about building to last, though. A spectacular 600 cliff dwellings survive, besides an estimated 5000 sites of archaeological importance dating back over at least eight to 10 millennia – making this easily the nation's most significant archaeological preserve. Uniquely for the USA, the national park focuses on protecting these early cultural relics above its natural treasures, but the surrounding lonely cuesta country (a cuesta is a plateau, like a mesa, but plunges to sheer drops on one side only) impresses too, dotted with prickly pear cactus and fir. The best collection of dwellings is Cliff Palace, a one-time 150-room complex.

👉 SEE IT ! *The park entrance is halfway between Cortez and Mancos off Hwy 160.*

© Zack Frank / Shutterstock

© SBWorldphotography / Shutterstock / Mark di Suvero, Mother Peace, 1969–70

71

Take flight at the Wright Brothers National Memorial

NORTH CAROLINA // Ohio proclaims itself 'the birthplace of aviation' because self-taught engineers Wilbur and Orville Wright hailed from Dayton. But as any North Carolinian will tell you, flight itself was born on a wind-whipped December day in the Outer Banks town of Kitty Hawk, when Orville took to the air for 12 seconds in their homemade flying machine. This national memorial celebrates that historic 1903 moment with a boulder marking the take-off spot; a visitor center with interactive exhibits and a full-size replica of the 1903 aircraft; and a climbable bronze sculpture of the plane popular with the junior aviator set. There's also a reconstruction of the wooden camp where the brothers lived while pursuing their dream. Remarkably, both died of natural causes; Orville lived long enough to see the dawn of the Jet Age.

 SEE IT ! *Kitty Hawk, in the central Outer Banks, is accessible via both Manteo and Elizabeth City.*

72

Ponder massive sculptures at Storm King Art Center

NEW YORK // Rolling hills, shadow-filled forests, and wind-whipped meadows make a serene backdrop to one of America's finest open-air museums. Spread across 500 acres, the Storm King Art Center contains a treasure trove of artwork, with numerous large-scale site-specific pieces. Andy Goldsworthy's evocative *Storm King Wall* snakes around trees, down to a pond then emerges from the other side and up a hill, some 2278ft in all. There's Mark di Suvero's towering *Pyramidian*, a 65ft-high structure of powerful forms that anchors the grassy meadows; and Magdalena Abakanowicz' *Sarcophagi in Glass Houses*, whose industrial coffin-shaped sculptures reference human-made traumas inflicted on the natural world. Over 100 works by the great sculptors of the past century are on display, including pieces by Maya Lin, Alexander Calder, Richard Serra, Sol LeWitt, Isamu Noguchi, and Louise Bourgeois.

SEE IT ! *Storm King is 70 miles north of NYC; nearest train station (via Metro-North) is Beacon, a 30-minute taxi/ride-share away.*

© Xinhua News Agency / Getty Images

© Modoc Stories / Getty Images

73

Take off to the National Museum of the US Air Force

OHIO // Dayton, sixth-largest city in Ohio, might have stayed pretty pedestrian as a tourist destination were it not for its exceptional contribution to aviation – locals Orville and Wilbur Wright, creators of the first heavier-than-air powered aircraft, trialled their second and third planes in the skies above what is now Dayton Aviation Heritage National Historical Park. And then there is this, the world's oldest, largest military aviation museum. The collection, begun in 1923, displays over 360 flying vehicles and missiles, many rare or unique. Standout specimens include a Wright Brothers military plane from 1909, the original Air Force One (the plane fitted out for carrying the president), and one of the 'Little Boy' type atomic bombs dropped on Hiroshima (decommissioned and declared safe, you will be pleased to know).

☛ SEE IT ! *The museum is on Wright-Patterson Air Force Base, 6 miles northeast of downtown Dayton.*

74

Hike paths less trodden in North Cascades NP

WASHINGTON // Inaugurated in 1968, North Cascades National Park feels like Alaska transplanted into the lower 48: 1000 sq miles of dramatic, daunting wild country strafed with mountains, lakes, glaciers (over 300 of them) and wildlife, but with almost no trace of civilization and only one road. Erratic weather, massive precipitation, thick rainforest and vertiginous cliffs have long ensured the isolation of the park's mountains: steep, alpine behemoths furnished with names like Mt Terror, Mt Fury, Mt Despair, and Forbidden Peak. Aspiring bushwhackers and free-climbers love the unique challenges offered by this eerie wilderness (most of the peaks weren't climbed until the 1930s). The less adrenaline-hungry stick close to arterial Hwy 20 and prepare for the drive of a lifetime.

☛ SEE IT ! *You'll need your own wheels to explore the area. Note: Hwy 20 closes due to snow blockage in the winter.*

Come prepared for off-grid hiking in rain-drenched Olympic National Park.

75

Get rained on in Olympic National Park

WASHINGTON // Shimmering with a hundred shades of green, from teal lakes to emerald forests, Olympic National Park is a huge 1442-sq-mile protected zone that shelters a unique temperate rainforest, copious glaciated mountain peaks, and a separate 57-mile strip of unpopulated Pacific coastline. Despite its proximity to Seattle, it remains one of North America's last great wilderness areas. Most of it has been spared the scars of human habitation, with 1000-year-old cedar trees, a largely roadless interior, and a palpable end-of-the-continent feel.

Opportunities for independent exploration in the backcountry abound, spearheaded by hiking, fishing and kayaking. The main caveat? Inclement weather. It rains a lot here, some 100-170in per year. For a more civilized experience, bed down in one of three historic lodges, recline in natural hot springs at Sol Duc, or ski at Hurricane Ridge, one of only two ski areas inside a US national park.

The park's distinct and highly biodiverse ecosystem is rich in plant and animal life, much of it – such as the majestic Roosevelt elk – indigenous to the region.

☞ SEE IT ! *The nearest big airport is Seattle; best access towns are Port Angeles and Aberdeen. You'll need a car to explore.*

© Robert Szymanski / Shutterstock

© Oliver Foerstner / Shutterstock

76

Crisscross the vast expanses of Tongass National Forest

ALASKA // Dedicated in 1907 by President Teddy Roosevelt, the Tongass National Forest in Southeast Alaska covers a tract of land as big as South Carolina, incorporating over 1100 islands and 450 miles of fjord-punctuated coastline. Most people visit without realizing it. The 'forest' has a population of 75,000 which includes the settlements of Juneau, Haines, and Skagway; and in a good year, Tongass gets one million annual visitors (mostly cruise-shippers); nearly 14 times its actual population.

Despite being the world's largest temperate rainforest, packed with Sitka spruce, western hemlock and red cedar, 40% of the Tongass is treeless, comprised instead of muskeg (wetlands), ice and high-mountain terrain. Off-grid adventures abound, particularly in the forest's two national monuments, Misty Fjords and Admiralty Island.

☛ SEE IT ! *The Alaskan towns of Juneau and Skagway are both served by regular ferries and airplanes.*

77

Stroll above city streets atop New York's High Line

NEW YORK // It's hard to believe that the 1.5-mile-long High Line was once a gritty elevated freight line that anchored an unsavory district of slaughterhouses. This radically transformed green space now draws visitors who come to stroll, sit, and picnic 30ft above the city – while enjoying fabulous views of Manhattan's ever-changing urban landscape.

The attractions are numerous: stunning vistas of the Hudson River, specially commissioned public art installations, wide lounge chairs for sunbathing, willowy stretches of native-inspired landscaping (including a mini sumac forest), food and drink vendors, and a thoroughly unique perspective on the neighborhood streets below – particularly at various overlooks, where bleacher-like seating faces huge panes of glass that frame the traffic, buildings, and pedestrians below as living works of art.

☛ SEE IT ! *Handy subway stations include 14th St (A/C/E line) and 34th St-Hudson Yards, 7 line. Grab lunch from nearby Chelsea Market.*

Trip through celebrity history on Sunset Strip

CALIFORNIA // Domain of giant billboards and legendary music clubs where the planet's best bands once performed, this stretch of Sunset Blvd has had almost every A-lister from the 1920s to 2000s stop by (and get up to no end of antics). Marilyn Monroe's first date with Joe DiMaggio was at the Rainbow Bar & Grill; Led Zeppelin raced motorcycles at what's now the Andaz Hotel. From the 1980s on, the Strip's wild days were waning as other districts eclipsed it for nightlife, but it's still a must-visit for a taste of Hollywood celebrity.

☛ SEE IT ! *Sunset Strip runs between Laurel Canyon Blvd and Doheny Rd.*

Get sensory overload in Times Square

NEW YORK // The days when Times Square was best known for peep shows and muggings are long past: today, the intersection of Broadway and 7th Avenue is New York at its most manic. With glaring screens on every side, panhandlers dressed as superheroes, supersized chain restaurants, and skyscrapers blocking out the sky, it's a fever dream of urbanism. Snap a few selfies then let the crowds carry you along to the adjoining Theater District for a matinee musical.

☛ SEE IT ! *Numerous subway lines run through the Times Square-42nd St station; the S train runs to Grand Central.*

Pay tribute to Pearl Harbor at the USS Arizona Memorial

HAWAI'I // The USA's most important WWII site, the *Arizona* is one of four battleships sunk at Pearl Harbor following Japanese bombings on December 7, 1941. All other damaged battleships were later raised, but, rushing to recover from the attack, authorities decided to leave 900 servicemen interred inside this ship, where they remain still. Fallen crewmen's names are engraved inside the white shrine that floats over the wreck; you can peer down through the central section to see the battleship's remains.

☛ SEE IT ! *The memorial is part of Pearl Harbor National Memorial and accessible by boat from there.*

See whether the truth is out there in Roswell

NEW MEXICO // The comprehensive International UFO Museum and Research Center already assumes familiarity with Roswell's extraterrestrial past, so know that it was here that the world's most highly-publicized, widely-investigated, conspiracy-theory-generating incident of a UFO-landing did, or did not, take place in 1947. Displays share witness statements, newspaper cuttings and the like, while alien-themed models and mock-ups provide unearthly visuals. Alongside UFO incidents worldwide, Roswell's flying saucer escapades get the most vigorous treatment: great cover-up, hoax or hearsay? You decide.

☛ SEE IT ! *The museum is at 114 North Main St, Roswell.*

Contemplate the contemporary at Palm Springs Art Museum.

82

View compelling contemporary art in the desert at Palm Springs Art Museum

CALIFORNIA // With a permanent collection running the gamut of greats from Henry Moore to William Morris via pop artist Edward Ruscha and sculptor Mark di Suvero, this museum has contemporary painting, photography, sculpture, and glass art as its strongest suits amongst a catalogue of 12,000 objects. There's a fine assemblage of art from the American West, featuring exponents like Frederic Remington and William Robinson Leigh with their epic landscapes; and a substantial body of Native American art, including Cahuilla basketry and Navajo rugs. The glass art by Morris and Dale Chihuly is superb too. You can also visit architect Albert Frey's masterpiece, Frey House II, nestling on the hillside above. Nor should you miss the run 12 miles southeast to the museum's other site at Palm Desert, where many of the collection's best sculptures stand within a garden styled as a desert oasis. Fancy burning some energy either side of a visit? The Cactus to Clouds Trail, one of the most grueling day-hikes in the US, begins behind the main museum building.

SEE IT ! *The main museum is at 101 Museum Dr, Palm Springs.*

© Guillaume Goureau / Palm Springs Art Museum

78

83

Gasp at Graceland, the flamboyant home of rock royalty

TENNESSEE // Though he died in 1977, Elvis – and his white Memphis mansion – continues to occupy an outsized spot in the American imagination. In 1957, aged 22, Elvis bought this colonial-style house and turned it into a refuge where he and his buddies would shoot guns and ride go-karts. It was later redecorated in lurid 1970s-style, complete with an indoor faux waterfall and green shag carpet on the ceiling. Take an audio tour of the house and its adjacent memorabilia museums, paying respects to the King at his grave by the backyard pool.

 **SEE IT !** *Graceland is 9 miles south of downtown Memphis on US-51.*

84

Wander the wilds of Badlands National Park

SOUTH DAKOTA // Looking at this stark spectacle of perpendicular pinnacles stabbing into the arid air, you soon understand why Native Americans named it *mako sica* or badland. It might resemble a stormy sea someone boiled dry, but there is much color and life here too. The banded rocky buttes show off hues from burnished red-brown to olive; the nation's largest virgin tract of mixed-grass prairie offers green splashes; and prairie dogs, bighorn sheep, and bison can be spotted. Hiking is first-class, and the otherworldliness profound.

SEE IT ! *Ben Reifel Visitor Center, off Hwy 44 northeast of Interior, is an info hub for adventurers. Note that off-trail hiking is permitted here.*

85

Watch the fog roll in at Quoddy Head State Park

MAINE // Nowhere captures the beauty of Maine's northern coast quite like Quoddy Head State Park. You'll be far from the din of modern life as you hike the seaside trail past wave-crashed cliffs backed by thick forests or detour inland to coastal-plateau bogs full of rare plant species. In summer, keep an eye on the sea for migrating whales (finback, minke, humpback, and right whales) swimming along the coast. And pay a visit to the much-photographed, red-and-white-striped West Quoddy Head Lighthouse, the easternmost point in the US.

SEE IT ! *Quoddy Head is a 6-mile drive south of Lubec, a stone's throw from the Canadian border.*

A river definitely runs through it: take a watery walk through Zion's spectacular Narrows slot canyon.

86

Walk and wade through Zion Canyon's chilling Narrows

UTAH // The Narrows refer to the narrowest reaches of Zion Canyon, where the Virgin River forges glassily between sheer copper-colored rock faces and the spectacular hike traversing them. Whether you trek this geological wonderland bottom-up or top-bottom, know that you will be wading as much as walking – the majority of the trail is along the slippery boulder-strewn riverbed itself, in ankle- to chest-deep water. Most elect the bottom-up approach

as you get to the best bits more quickly, and no permit is required. Bottom-up begins straightforwardly on Riverside Walk, where the pretty path runs beside the river rather than through it. Then, though, it's time to get wet. Donning the waterproof gear and trekking poles that are essential for continuing, enter the river for the next 4 miles up to the turnaround point, Big Springs: a distance seeming easily doable on firm ground but much tougher when

walking upriver through chilly, fast-running water. The climax is at Wall St, where canyon sides come together to their neck-craning narrowest and the water is wall-to-wall. However far you venture, this is not only the defining Zion Canyon hike but up there with the USA's very finest canyon treks.

👉 TRY IT ! *The trail starts from Temple of Sinawava shuttle stop, at the end of Zion Canyon Rd, 9 miles northeast of Springdale.*

Appreciate artistic excellence at the Art Institute of Chicago

ILLINOIS // The USA's second-largest art museum has one of the world's ultimate collections of Impressionist and Post-Impressionist works, the kinds of paintings instantly recognizable from a million postcards and posters: Van Gogh's *The Bedroom*; Monet's *Water Lilies*; Seurat's *A Sunday Afternoon on the Island of La Grande Jatte*. Other highlights include Grant Wood's *American Gothic*; Edward Hopper's *Nighthawks*; and Georgia O'Keeffe's *Cow's Skull with Calico Roses*. But big-name works are only a taste of the pleasures that the Art Institute offers – temporary exhibits range from video installations to fiber art. Our favorite stop is the basement, home to the 68 Thorne Miniature Rooms – meticulous 1:12 scale recreations of upscale historic home interiors, complete with authentic miniature paintings on the walls.

SEE IT ! *The Art Institute is in central Chicago, next to Millennium Park. The free museum app is a must for navigating the collection.*

88

See a super-hot rainbow at Grand Prismatic

WYOMING // If you've seen one image of Yellowstone National Park it's probably of this: the psychedelic eye winking from the valley floor in shades of teal, marine, rust and mustard. At 370ft wide and 121ft deep, Grand Prismatic is the park's largest hot spring. Its rainbow rings are caused by microbes that thrive in hot water. Stroll through the steam on the boardwalk circling the pool, or climb up the hill from the Fairy Falls trailhead for a bird's-eye view. The spring drains into Excelsior Geyser Crater, a gusher mostly dormant since the 1900s, which drains some 4000 gallons of near-boiling water a minute into the Firehole River. Standing in the sulphur-scented steam, or admiring the yellow-and-orange runoff as you approach the basin over the bridge, it's easy to see why early explorers called Yellowstone 'the place where Hell bubbled up.'

 SEE IT ! *The spring is in the Midway Geyser Basin area; parking in summer is tough.*

NATURAL HISTORY

↓

Discover dinosaurs at the capital's National Museum of Natural History.
 page 125

↓

Watch breaching whales from Lime Kiln Point State Park in Washington state.
page 155

↓

View an artist's appreciation of the New Mexico landscape at the Georgia O'Keeffe Museum.
page 219

89

View natural history at the Field Museum

ILLINOIS // This grand colonnaded building sitting in verdant parkland alongside Chicago's lakeshore is no mere pretty face: its mind-boggling 40 million artifacts comprise one of the world's foremost natural history collections. The variety of what's on show is partly due to the institution inheriting myriad wonders from the 1893 cultural extravaganza, the World's Columbian Exposition. But there is so very much, encompassing so many walks of life and corners of the globe, that you need a long look at the museum map to formulate a plan of attack. Star of the show is Sue, the largest Tyrannosaurus rex yet discovered. Then there is the Northwest Coast and Arctic Peoples' wondrous totem poles, the 23 human mummies in the Inside Ancient Egypt exhibition and – oh, just visit. Making it even more interesting is how exhibits are brought alive by a slew of on-hand scientists – this remains an active research facility.

SEE IT ! *Museum Campus/11th St is the nearest station.*

Opposite from top: all the colors at Yellowstone's Grand Prismatic; say hello to T. Rex Sue at the Field Museum of Natural History.

88

89

Opposite:
Fallingwater is the
apogee of Frank
Lloyd Wright's organic
design style.

90

Marvel at the visionary design of Fallingwater

PENNSYLVANIA // Frank Lloyd Wright was a world-renowned architect, talented enough to have several celebrated works across the US, but Fallingwater, a staggering vacation home that straddles the rushing Bear Run stream in a pocket of Pennsylvanian forest, is his most aesthetically pleasing. Ironically, Wright had seemed to be past his prime, career-wise, when department store-owning bigwig Edgar J. Kauffman asked him to design his new getaway. The architect's response was, purportedly, to sketch the plan for what would be widely regarded as his masterwork in just two hours.

Fallingwater blends seamlessly into its serene setting, as many of Wright's buildings do, but this one's finest achievement is to actually let the landscape in to physically feature inside too. A highlight is the open stairway that descends to the stream, allowing the sound and smell of the water to become part of the interior experience,

and acting as natural ventilation. A rocky outcrop, meanwhile, protrudes into the living room, and each bedroom has its own terrace, bringing the majestic surrounding trees that much closer. Completed in 1938, the construction ran majorly over budget, costing a sweet $155,000 (to put that in context, a master mason working on the home at the time would have earned about $0.85 an hour). The Kauffmans were happy to pay up, though. They had long loved the Bear Run area but had expected a house within view of the stream's cascades, not, as Wright designed, somewhere that sat directly over the tumbling waters, and approved of Wright's bold creation. The architectural gem can be visited by guided tour only; afterwards you can roam the surrounding forest trails.

☛ SEE IT ! *Fallingwater is about 67 miles southeast of downtown Pittsburgh, between the villages of Mill Run and Ohiopyle.*

© seaOtter12 / Budget Travel

© John Silver / Shutterstock

91

Immerse yourself in marine life at Monterey Bay

CALIFORNIA // Behind the glass, an enormous sun fish floats mere inches from your face. A hammerhead shark races through the water, while silvery sardines shimmy en masse. You could stare at the Open Sea display in Monterey Bay Aquarium for hours: the tank is as large and glowing as a cinema screen, and just as engrossing.

This impressive aquarium showcases the majesty of California's native marine life, as well as underwater ecosystems from further afield. The exhibits indoors are familiar: gliding rays, pulsating jellyfish, and drifting kelp forests that send your brain into a state of utter relaxation. But Monterey Bay Aquarium blends its exhibits seamlessly with its oceanside setting – the outdoor Great Tide Pool looks right onto the power and beauty of the Pacific.

☛ SEE IT ! *Skip the line by booking ahead, and arrive early. Note the feeding times as you enter, or book a behind-the-scenes tour.*

92

Reach for the stars at Space Center Houston

TEXAS // 'Houston, we have a problem:' one of the best known space-age-related phrases and certainly the most famous mentioning a location back on Earth. Houston is forever linked to America's space program: despite manned US space flights all launching elsewhere, the planning, control, and most training happened here at NASA's Johnson Space Center. Alongside, Space Center Houston museum deals with the past, present, and future of space flight, including planned missions to Mars. Budding Buzz Aldrins will be over the moon here: tours whiz round Mission Control and the astronaut training facility. Oh, and that aforementioned phrase? In actuality it was 'Houston, we've had a problem'. Not quite so edge-of-the-seat. This attraction, though, full of fantastic hand-on exhibits that keep kids riveted, absolutely is.

☛ SEE IT ! *Get beamed up at 1601 East NASA Parkway, in Houston's southeast.*

TRADITIONAL Request 2.00
— OTHERS $5.00
The SAINTS $10.00

Pres Hall offers
a beautiful blast
of NoLA's French
Quarter aural history.

93

Feel the fiery brass rhythms of traditional jazz at Preservation Hall

LOUISIANA // If jazz is the lifeblood of New Orleans, its beating heart is Preservation Hall. The live-music venue opened in the French Quarter in 1961 and has been hosting intimate acoustic concerts ever since. Famous it may be, but Pres Hall has little in common with Carnegie, the Royal Albert or those other illustrious halls. It dates from the early 1800s and the rustic interior, with its creaky wooden floorboards and weathered walls strung with old portraits, evokes a bygone era. The humble space is more living room than concert chamber and accommodates 100 audience members at most. The last ones in might have to stand in the back, while those up front sometimes have to dodge a trombone extension from their perch on the floor just inches from the stage. Despite the informal vibe, the rousing power of the music is undeniable. The resident performers, some of whom are fourth-generation jazz musicians, are ludicrously talented and regularly tour the world. Preservation Hall also has its own record label as well as a non-profit foundation that gives lessons to young players – ensuring New Orleans jazz will live on for the next generation.

☛ SEE IT ! *All ages are welcome here, just arrive early for a good seat.*

© cdrin / Shutterstock

© Pung / Shutterstock

94

Tuck into Seattle's smorgasbord at Pike Place Market

WASHINGTON // In this labyrinth of fishmongers and sausage sellers, jewelry boutiques and vintage wares, you'll feel like a true Seattleite. You'll bump elbows with office workers on walk-and-talk lunches, squeeze past tourists photographing the lucky piggy-bank bronze named Rachel, and gape at monster lobsters presented in beds of sparkling ice. Since 1907, fish vendors at Pike Place Market have beckoned shoppers to their freshly-caught swordfish, crab, and oysters. There are ready-made delights, too: clam chowder is ladled into bread bowls; fruit compote swirled into thick Greek yogurt; and doughnuts rolled in sugar. Seize an armful of goodies and head to the water-facing outdoor seating for an eyeful of Elliott Bay. There are weather-protected areas, too, if you've had enough of Seattle's rain.

🖝 EAT IT ! *The market is walkable from downtown Seattle and Belltown; head to the waterfront, then follow the 'Public Market' sign.*

95

Snorkel at Hanauma Bay Nature Preserve

HAWAI'I // Consider a moment. What does your fantasy bay look like? Sheltered, horseshoe-shaped, and lapped by the Pacific Ocean? Check. Arc of white sand? Check. Phenomenal 7000-year-old coral reef a short paddle out in the turquoise waters, harboring an astonishing array of marine life? Check – and welcome to Hanauma Bay. It's true that a lot of other Hawai'i-bound vacationers think exactly the same thing, which means this bay, although a protected nature preserve, is in danger of being loved to death. But popularity does not diminish its appeal. And above all else, you're here for the sublime snorkelling – the underwater world's color spectrum spans the azure flashes of parrotfish to the olive hue of sea turtles seemingly unfazed by humans sporting fake flippers.

🖝 SEE IT ! *The bay is 12 miles east of Honolulu via Hwy H1 and Hwy 72, aka Kalaniana'ole Highway.*

96

Appreciate the astounding architectural excess of Hearst Castle

CALIFORNIA // This fabulously over-the-top homage to material excess was home to William Randolph Hearst, the newspaper magnate who once owned the planet's biggest media conglomerate. Hearst did not call his opulent residence a castle. He preferred referring to the 165-room estate, with its main building modestly designed on a Spanish cathedral, flanked by statues from ancient Greece and Moorish Spain and enveloped by 123 acres of landscaped grounds, as 'La Cuesta Encantada' (the Enchanted Hill) or simply 'The Ranch'. Getting invited here from the 1920s through to 1947, when Hearst had to leave because of deteriorating health, was as good as it got in high society, and numerous A-listers of the period visited. California's first licensed female architect, Julia Morgan, masterminded the design.

☞ SEE IT ! *The castle is about halfway between LA and San Francisco, approximately four hours' drive from either.*

97

Hug ancient trees in the Hoh Rain Forest

WASHINGTON // On the wet western side of Olympic National Park, the Hoh River basin is paradise for lovers of tall trees, springy moss, and incessant rain. With its deep green canopy of ferns, lichens, and foliage, the Hoh is probably the best example of a surviving temperate rainforest in the US. Most of it has never been logged and, as a result, many of the trees – Sitka spruce and western hemlock dominate – are very tall (300ft plus) and very old (500 years plus).

The bulk of the action takes place at the end of the paved Upper Hoh Rd, where a visitor center acts as a launch-pad for several short hikes. With luck and a sharp eye, you may spot a Roosevelt elk, the ungulate for which the surrounding Olympic National Park was created to protect.

☛ SEE IT ! *You'll need a car to get to the end of the Hoh River Rd, branching east off of Hwy 101 just south of Forks.*

© LizCoughlan / Shutterstock

© rusty426 / Shutterstock

98

99

Witness the power of faith at El Santuario de Chimayo

NEW MEXICO // Pilgrims journey by foot from as far as Albuquerque to this humble 1816 adobe chapel to pry a chunk of dirt from a hole in the sanctuary floor. Why? The faithful believe the dirt has healing powers. Some rub it on their skin, some save it in a special tin, some even eat it (though this is discouraged). Inside the cool dim church is a hand-painted altar and a room filled with tin *milagros* (charms) and testimonials of answered prayers. Outside, El Potrero Trading Post has been selling crucifixes, carved saints, and *milagros* since 1921.

☞ SEE IT ! *The chapel is 90 miles northeast of Albuquerque near the Sangre de Cristo Mountains.*

Pay tribute at Gettysburg National Military Park

PENNSYLVANIA // The air thunders with cannon shots. Gunpowder wafts on the breeze. Well, not quite. But so evocative is the Gettysburg National Military Park, the actual site of one of the bloodiest battles of the Civil War, that you almost think you're on the battlefield. These days, its 8 sq miles of land are marked with monuments and trails. Get your bearings in the park's visitor center, where the awe-inspiring cyclorama, a life-size, 360-degree painting of Pickett's Charge, puts you right in the action of the battle's last day.

☞ SEE IT ! *You can explore on your own, on a bus tour or – best option – on a two-hour guide-led tour in your own car or on a bike.*

100—
199

The Chilkoot Trail promises epic adventure through wild and varied landscapes.

100

Succumb to gold fever on the Chilkoot Trail

ALASKA // Undertaken by over 30,000 gold-rush stampeders on their way to the Klondike in 1897-8, this epic trek is sometimes known as the 'Last Great Adventure' or the 'Meanest 33 Miles in America.' Its appeal is legendary and, consequently, more than 3000 people spend 3-5 days hiking the historic route between Dyea in Alaska and Bennett in Canada every summer.

The trail crosses the US-Canadian border, takes in numerous climate zones, and traverses terrain etched with the discarded remnants of one of the 19th century's most incredible journeys. For contemporary hikers, it's a chance to connect with the past, emulate erstwhile struggles, and relive an adventure that played out in an age before cars and the internet made everything so easy. The trail ends at Lake Bennett in British

Columbia, where a special 'hikers train' uses the historic White Pass & Yukon Route Railroad to take you back to Skagway. Hiking the Chilkoot and returning by train is the ultimate Alaska excursion, combining superb scenery and incredible historical adventure.

☛ TRY IT ! *Get backpacking permits from the Trail Center in Skagway before heading to the trailhead at Dyea, 9 miles northwest.*

© Chamomile Alya / Shutterstock

© deimagine / Getty Images

101

Find your inner rock god at the Museum of Pop Culture

WASHINGTON // Between rocking out like Kurt Cobain and taking selfies by a fish tank filled with zombie heads, time passes quickly at Seattle's Museum of Pop Culture. The brainchild of Microsoft co-founder Paul Allen, MoPOP is a high-tech temple to movies, music, video games, and art. The modern exterior was designed by celebrated architect Frank Gehry; within, it's arranged into enclaves of pop culture. Very quickly, your inner super-fan reveals itself: you'll stalk through horror-movie history; frantically shoot arcade-game aliens; and admire the guitars of rock royalty. There's a big emphasis on Seattle's home-grown '90s grunge icons and metalheads; try replicating their signature songs at the interactive Sound Lab – and don't miss the dazzling temporary exhibs. When you finally leave, sporting a souvenir Foo Fighters T-shirt, your brain buzzing with movie trivia, you'll wonder 'where'd the hours go?'

☛ SEE IT ! *The museum is at the Seattle Center; travel from downtown via the Seattle Center Monorail.*

102

Catch virtuoso boarding at a vintage Venice Skate Park

CALIFORNIA // Even if skateboarding normally leaves you, ahem, bored, this beachside skate park might entice you for the spectacle: seriously talented skaters descend on this old-school run to tackle the 16,000-plus sq ft of molded concrete vert, tranny and street terrain. Somehow, none of them seems to get distracted by the palm-fringed vistas of pretty Venice Beach surrounding them – though you might. The two bowls and the snake run are where most high-flyers want to do their thing, usually to crowds of onlookers. The park hit the headlines in 2020 during the Covid-19 pandemic, when authorities went to what many saw as extreme lengths to fill it with sand to deter large groups from congregating – only for never-say-die skaters to dig it all out again. Bigger skate parks there may be, but Venice, LA, is considered the birthplace of modern skating, so to skate here wins you street cred.

☛ SEE IT ! *Find the skate park at 1500 Ocean Front Walk, Venice.*

103

Enjoy an excursion to the eccentric City Museum

MISSOURI // When artists win dominion over abandoned factories, consequences can be wild, as this highly original museum shows. Bob and Gail Cassilly acquired this St Louis former shoe factory in 1993, but no one saw what was happening for years: a concrete serpent erected in the parking lot was the only clue. The public were allowed inside in 1996 and, fortunately, the wait was worthwhile. Wacky acquisitions and creations include the world's largest pencil, the 1870s vault from the First National Bank of St Louis, a Ferris wheel – the zany list continues.

☛ SEE IT ! *The museum is at 750 North 16th St, St Louis.*

104

Graze gourmet treats at LA's Original Farmers Market

CALIFORNIA // Los Angeles is flooded with them today, but before those other farmers markets were so much as an apple in anyone's eye there was this one, the original. This 1934 food emporium was one of the world's first modern farmers markets, with over 100 gourmet grocers vending everything from cheese to chicken, roasted nuts to red snapper and coffee beans to spices to ice cream. The mouth-watering eating options include a Brazilian *churrascaria* (meat grill) and a Singaporean joint which serves its dishes on banana leaves.

☛ EAT IT ! *The daily market has made its address, West 3rd St & South Fairfax Ave, one of the city's most famous intersections.*

105

Light a candle in St Patrick's Cathedral

NEW YORK // You'd be forgiven for thinking that Midtown Manhattan is a godless domain devoted solely to materialistic pursuits. Yet in the middle of bank-branded high-rises and luxury retailers looms one of America's grandest cathedrals. Stepping into this hallowed space, which opened in 1878, is like peering back in time – you can feel the kinship of Europe's great spiritual monuments in St Patrick's soaring Neo-Gothic spires, its vast marble-clad interior (that holds up to 3000 people) and a magnificent rose window made of over 10,000 pieces of stained glass.

☛ SEE IT ! *For an expansive overview of the cathedral, head across to the Rockefeller Center's observation deck.*

© David Tonelson / Shutterstock

106

Gawp at the crazed geology of Devils Tower National Monument

WYOMING // This igneous rock monolith is so strikingly at odds with its surroundings that it will come as little surprise to know it holds a sacred place in legend for 20-plus Native American peoples, while even geologists continue to debate how such a structure could have formed. The huge strata-scored butte seems like an object just-landed from another world, shooting near-vertically 867ft out of the trees above the Belle Fourche River from comparatively low-lying, completely contrasting terrain. It was declared the USA's first National Monument in 1906.

🐾 SEE IT ! *Head 12 miles north of Carlile Junction on I-24 and then Hwy 110, from where the road to Devils Tower branches off.*

© Mark Read / Lonely Planet

© Courtesy Russ & Daughters

© Sean Pavone / Shutterstock

107

Find the meaning of 'appetizing' at Russ & Daughters

NEW YORK // You probably think of the word 'appetizing' as an adjective, but when it comes to New York Jewish food, it's a noun meaning 'food that goes with bagels.' Nowhere is the appetizing more, well, appetizing than at Russ & Daughters, a century-old deli on Manhattan's Lower East Side. Polish immigrant Joel Russ got his start peddling pickled herring from a barrel before opening up his Houston St store and bringing his daughters in as partners. Join the lines of locals to order bagels, bialys, lox, smoked whitefish, caviar, babka (a sweet braided bread), chopped liver, potato knishes, and way more from the brusque counter staff (Russ & Daughters is now run by the fourth generation of the Russ family). Then go find a bench in nearby Sara D. Roosevelt Park and eat yourself into a fish-and-carb coma.

☛ SEE IT ! *Russ & Daughters is at 179 East Houston St between Orchard & Allen streets.*

108

Explore the lives of the elite at the Flagler Museum

FLORIDA // If there's one place to immerse yourself in America's Gilded Age, this is it: the magnificent Flagler Museum, housed in the 1902 Whitehall Mansion, built by railway magnate and hotelier Henry Flagler as a gift for his bride, Mary Lily Kenan. Designed by John Carrère and Thomas Hastings (students of the École des Beaux-Arts in Paris and collaborators on other Gilded Age landmarks such as the New York Public Library), the house was one of the most modern of its era and quickly became the focus of the winter season for the wealthy. Wander its rooms and be wowed by the craftsmanship and opulence of the pink aluminum-leaf wallpaper, the very grand Grand Hall, and the silk- and wood-lined Drawing Room. Upstairs, intimate bedrooms give a insight into family life.

☛ SEE IT ! *Take a free one-hour tour or pick up an audioguide, then lunch 'Gilded Age Style' at the Café des Beaux-Arts in the glass pavilion.*

Wrap up warm to
kayak LeConte's chilly
tidewaters – and
watch out for the
'shooters'!

109

Paddle the tidewaters to LeConte Glacier

ALASKA // The southernmost tidewater glacier in the Northern Hemisphere, and an extremely active one at that, the LeConte crashes into a wide fjord 25 miles east of the quiet (read: no cruise ships) Norwegian-flavored fishing port of Petersburg.

While not as big or brawny as icy behemoths further north, the LeConte is easy to visit, popular with kayakers and frequented by herds of well-insulated seals who lounge

on its abundant ice floes. The Scottish-American naturalist John Muir claimed it was his favorite Alaskan glacier.

Adventurous kayakers pitch out from Petersburg, taking one to two days to reach the frozen monument by crossing Frederick Sound north of Coney Island. For a simpler approach, hire a local tour company to cruise you over to the glacier for careful paddling among the bobbing bergs. Easier still are the

kayak-free jet-boat tours available out of both Petersburg and Wrangell. Whichever you choose, beware: the LeConte is known for its 'shooters', bergs that calve underwater before springing unexpectedly to the surface.

SEE IT ! *Petersburg and Wrangell are island towns and off the main road network. You can either fly in from Seattle or cruise in on Alaska's public ferry.*

110

Sip tea in the Golden Gate Park's historic Japanese Tea Garden

CALIFORNIA // Five fecund acres within the wider green embrace of San Francisco's Golden Gate Park constitute the USA's oldest Japanese gardens – there's a sense of history to these gorgeous grounds, first planted in 1894, besides their beauty and tranquillity.

Spring, for blossom, and fall, for gorgeous maple tree colors, are prime times to visit, but you can enjoy the bonsai grove, koi ponds, Zen garden, and pagodas year-round. If strolling fuels a desire for refreshment, head for the garden tea house to take tea and

fortune cookies, the latter introduced to the US through garden creator Makoto Hagiwara.

 SEE IT ! *Light rail line N Judah runs along the south of Golden Gate Park: Irving St & 9th Ave is your closest stop.*

111

Dig your toes in the sand at Siesta Key

FLORIDA // A fat 3-mile arc of crushed quartz sand as fine as confectioners' sugar announces Siesta Key, a gangly isle just off the Sarasota coast that is bliss for beachgoers. You can indulge in a raft of beach sports from parasailing to jet-skiing or, for the more leisurely inclined, just slide between towel time and floating supine in the blue-green shallows. If you covet some Siesta Key without so many other beachgoers, try Turtle Beach, several miles south of the main action, where sea turtles nest May through October.

 TRY IT ! *SCAT bus 11 serves Siesta Key from downtown Sarasota.*

112

Stroll a section of Rhode Island's Cliff Walk

RHODE ISLAND // This 3.5-mile meander walks you through some of the finest scenery in the USA's dinkiest state. Beginning in affluent Newport by Easton Beach's tawny sands, you are soon skirting the grassy shore-abutting grounds of the area's famously lavish historic mansions on one of the country's most genteel little ambles. Beyond the architectural masterpieces, this coastline has huge natural variety too: sandy bays, cliffs, and relatively wild sections, where waves bombarding jagged seaboard is the sole sound.

SEE IT ! *Walk north to south, Easton Beach to Bailey's Beach: buses run between Bailey's Beach and Memorial Blvd near the start point.*

113

Explore Roosevelt's seaside getaway at Campobello Island

MAINE // President Franklin Delano Roosevelt and his wife Eleanor had a lot of great ideas – not least of which was where to spend wonderful summer vacations. Their favorite family retreat was Campobello Island, a 15-sq-mile expanse of forests and rocky coastline offering fabulous views over the Bay of Fundy. You can tour their summer cottage (more of a mansion), learn about the first lady's many civic contributions over 'Tea with Eleanor', and walk the serene paths around the island.

SEE IT ! *Though technically part of New Brunswick, Campobello Island is jointly run by the US and Canada, and is a five-minute drive from Lubec, Maine. Don't forget your passport!*

© Strattons.US / Shutterstock

Cross open water to isolated Dry Tortugas NP

FLORIDA // Hop on a ferry or a seaplane to this far-flung archipelago, one of the US' most remote national parks. Consisting of seven islands across 100 miles of sea, the Tortugas lie in the clear and balmy water off the Florida Keys. You'll disembark to a rather surprising sight – an enormous brick bastion. This is Fort Jefferson, built in the mid-1800s to protect this stretch of the Gulf of Mexico. Now it's a top snorkeling spot – look for goliath groupers, octopuses and sharks. Sleep under the twinkling stars at the ultra-basic campground.

☞ SEE IT ! *The* Yankee Freedom III *high-speed catamaran takes two hours to travel to the park from Key West.*

© Caselle11 / Shutterstock

Join the eccentric parade on the Venice Boardwalk

CALIFORNIA // Fortune-tellers, bongo drummers, elderly rollerbladers, barechested bodybuilders, street magicians, graffiti artists, surfers, and tourists all mingle along Venice's anything-goes beachfront promenade. Grab a sprout-filled sandwich at an old-school veggie cafe, pick up a cheesy T-shirt from a souvenir stall, and rent a bike to ride the 2-mile paved stretch, pedalling along the Pacific with the smell of salt air (and pot smoke) in your nose. Ride all the way to Santa Monica, or go inland to tour the iconic canals that give Venice its name.

☞ TRY IT ! *Venice is a 25-minute drive from downtown LA in perfect (so don't hold your breath) traffic conditions.*

Discover magnificent minimalist art at Chinati Foundation

TEXAS // Sequestered away in the west Texas desert is the anomaly of Marfa, which looks from the map like it would be a one-horse town, but is actually a thriving artistic hub. Things changed for Marfa in 1987 when Donald Judd transformed this former army post into an astonishing museum, inspiring the area's artsy renaissance. Huge windows installed throughout the one-time barracks usher in sweeping desert views, while inside perhaps the planet's largest, most preeminent collection of minimalist art beckons.

☞ SEE IT ! *The museum is just south of Marfa's center, accessed down South Hill St.*

117

Uncover centuries of Louisiana history at the Cabildo

LOUISIANA // As far as the French were concerned, New Orleans was born and died in or around the Cabildo. The 18th-century building lies near the spot where Bienville founded the settlement of La Nouvelle-Orléans in 1718. Less than a century later the French sold the city – along with 530 million acres of land – to the US, with the 1803 Louisiana Purchase being completed in the Cabildo. In between, the building served as the seat of government for both the French and Spanish administrations, and was destroyed by fire and rebuilt. Today, this fascinating link to the past houses New Orleans' best history museum with exhibitions covering Native American culture, colonial days, the horrific slavery era, and the Civil War. Don't miss Bellin's 1744 map of New Orleans (all four blocks of it) or Napoleon Bonaparte's death mask.

 SEE IT ! *The Cabildo overlooks Jackson Square in the heart of the French Quarter.*

118

Savor Frank Lloyd Wright's domicile of design

ILLINOIS // The home of a famous person is always great for learning about their life and legacy in a more tangible way than in a library, and still more so when that person numbers among the most influential architects of the 20th century. Frank Lloyd Wright both lived and worked here between 1899 and 1909, and it's the first home he designed, full of the touches that made his architectural style so distinctive. Highlights are the Children's Playroom with its arcing sky-lit ceiling, Arabian Nights mural, and oriel windows, and the beautiful studio where, as with many of his later works, the doorway is concealed, in this case behind striking columns with capitals representing fertility, nature, and knowledge. Incorporating hidden entrances compelled visitors to appreciate his buildings from outside before going in.

SEE IT ! *Frank Lloyd Wright's Home and Studio is in Oak Park, 10 miles west of downtown Chicago.*

Indiana Dunes offer a welcome pocket of peace on the shores of Lake Michigan.

119

Scale sandy peaks above a Midwestern ocean at Indiana Dunes

INDIANA // Wedged into an industrial corridor in northern Indiana, a 15,000-acre reserve on the edge of Lake Michigan seems an unlikely setting for a national park at first glance. But once you make peace with the surrounding area, you can appreciate this protected landmark for all its surprising allure. Shifting dunes, meandering rivers, oak savannas, windswept prairies, verdant wetlands, and 15 miles of ocean-like shoreline all form the backdrop to one of America's most biologically diverse national parks. Indiana Dunes has many unusual highlights including Mount Baldy, the largest 'living' dune here which moves about 4ft inland each year, consuming any grasses, shrubs and even trees in its path. There are rare plants – like the endangered fringed polygala which grows only on the north slope of one particular dune and is found nowhere else in Indiana – and more orchids than in all of Hawai'i. In fact, it was here in 1900 that botanist Henry Cowles and other scientists made groundbreaking studies in the newly emerging field of ecology,

☞ SEE IT ! *In a northwest patch of Indiana, the national park is 50 miles southeast of Chicago, and easy to reach by train (South Shore Line).*

Harry S. Truman on the lawn of his Independence home in 1944.

120

Gain insights into the 33rd US president's life at the Truman Home

MISSOURI // 'I hope to be remembered as the people's president' – so said the 33rd man to take on America's top job, Harry S. Truman. He certainly never forgot his roots: the aptly named city of Independence was where he grew up, married local girl Bess Wallace, and lived with her in this touchingly down-to-earth wooden house from 1919 to 1972 (excepting his eight years in office between 1945 and 1953). Here, the couple lived the simple life, especially for those accustomed to White House splendor. The home is furnished with their original belongings, and you fully expect one of the two to wander out at any moment and greet you. In his later years, Truman received dignitaries in the modest front room (and is said to have hoped no visitor would stay longer than 30 minutes). Few sites so powerfully convey the pre- and post-office life and character of a president, and this half-mile stretch of Truman Rd also features the Noland home, the Wallace home, and the Harry S. Truman National Historic Site, all of which shed further light on the man, his times, and his circle of acquaintances.

☛ SEE IT ! *Independence is 10 miles east of Kansas City, Missouri.*

© Jack Vartoogian/Getty Images

© Courtesy of New Orleans Museum of Art / Richard Sexto Left: Bernar Venet. *11 Acute Unequal Angles, 2016*
Middle: Larry Bell. *Pacific Red VI, 2016-17*

121

Let the world's finest musicians entertain you at Carnegie Hall

NEW YORK // 'Excuse me, sir, can you tell me how to get to Carnegie Hall?' says the lost ticket holder. 'Practice!' goes the famous reply. Indeed, budding musicians everywhere dream of playing in the fabled concert hall that has hosted the world's best entertainers since its opening in 1891: jazz legends Duke Ellington, Ella Fitzgerald, and Nina Simone, opera diva Maria Callas, and even The Beatles and Led Zeppelin. Learn about the venue's storied history on a guided tour, but don't miss a concert inside the auditorium with its astonishing acoustics.

 SEE IT ! *Just outside the hall is the 57th St-Seventh Avenue subway station (N/Q/R/W lines).*

122

Take in cutting-edge art and sculpture at the New Orleans Museum of Art

LOUISIANA // Set amid the sprawling greenery of City Park, the New Orleans Museum of Art houses one of the most important collections in the South. Opened in 1911, the Beaux-Arts-style building stages wide-ranging exhibitions that cover everything from Jain art in India to exquisite handmade quilts from Gee's Bend, Alabama. The permanent collection contains over 40,000 items dating from 3000 BCE to the present. Also part of NOMA is the nearby sculpture garden displaying masterpieces by Louise Bourgeois, René Magritte, and Frank Gehry, set amid tree-lined paths, verdant lawns, and a sparkling lake.

 SEE IT ! *Take the streetcar up Canal St (City Park/Museum line).*

Chimney Rock is one of the weird and wonderful geological delights of Capitol Reef.

123

Get into geology at Capitol Reef National Park

UTAH // Weird geology (ever heard of a monocline?), delightful wildlife (look for a rarely-spotted ringtail, an adorable arboreal mammal), and fascinating fossils (including three-billion-year-old stromatolites) set this southern Utah park apart. But just how did something hundreds of miles from any sea get the name 'reef'? The park's Waterpocket Fold monocline, an 87-mile-long buckle in the earth's crust, reminded early prospectors of the impassable reefs they'd encountered in their seafaring days. The 'Capitol' bit comes from the park's white Navajo Sandstone domes which made settlers think of the US Capitol building. Mormon homesteaders who arrived here in the late 1800s turned the banks of the Fremont River into a cool green oasis of apple, apricot, peach, pear, and cherry trees, now the park's Fruita Rural Historic District. You're welcome to pick all the ripe fruit you want, free, from June to October. Visit Fruita's old Gifford Homestead to learn about pioneer life and purchase their famous fruit pie. Off Hwy 24 you can see petroglyphs carved in the stone about 1000 years ago by people of the Fremont Culture.

☛ SEE IT ! *The park's access town is Torrey, 11 miles west. The nearest big airport is 200 miles east in Grand Junction, Colorado.*

124

Honor the activists at the Civil Rights Memorial Center

ALABAMA // A haunting memorial in Montgomery honors Civil Rights activists who paid the ultimate price. The names of 40 martyrs, and the history of the Civil Rights Movement, spread out like the hands of a clock across a circle of black granite created by celebrated architect and sculptor Maya Lin: water flows evenly over its surface, a nod to Martin Luther King Jr's well-known paraphrase from the Book of Amos ('until justice rolls down like waters'). After surveying the monument, tour the museum; it forms part of the Southern Poverty Law Center, which continues the fight for equal access to justice.

☛ SEE IT ! *The memorial at 400 Washington Ave is two blocks west of the Capitol. Nearby see a church where Dr King served as pastor.*

125

Enjoy easy riding along the bucolic Virginia Capital Trail

VIRGINIA // Woodlands and meadows drift past as you pedal along the Virginia Capital Trail, offering 52 scenic miles of family-friendly cycling between Richmond and Jamestown. There are plenty of picnic areas and bathrooms en route, and it's never far between historic sights: perhaps the Charles City Courthouse; the Richmond Battlefield Visitor Center (above) and cemetery; or Sherwood Forest, a plantation owned by two different US presidents. This is cycling at its most easy-going: you'll trundle over iron bridges, pause to ponder Virginia history, then pull up at barbecue joints for melt-in-the-mouth pork.

☛ SEE IT ! *Book a return shuttle service if you're tackling the trail one way.*

Ponder the past inhabitants of Gila Cliff as you wander their ancient rockside homes.

126

Travel back 700 years at Gila Cliff Dwellings National Monument

NEW MEXICO // People of the Mogollon culture built these imposing cliff dwellings sometime in the late 1200s, using local stone to turn five natural caves into more than 40 rooms. Yet they only stayed for one generation, abandoning their home about 20 years later. No one knows why, or where, they went.

More than seven centuries later the area is still remote. Getting here means a winding two-hour desert drive from Silver City, followed by a mile-long hike and a climb up bumpy stone stairs to the dwellings. Unlike many similar sites, the caves are open for exploration. Stand in the dusty, cool interiors, imagining what life was like for the families that raised children, cooked, and made unique brown and black pottery within these walls before disappearing forever. Explore the monument area, soaking in backcountry hot springs (keep water out of your nose, lest you acquire a dangerous amoeba), or hiking through a shady canyon and amid pine and fir forest. The 12-mile West Fork Loop takes you along the ridge tops for panoramic views of the silver-and-red desert.

☛ SEE IT ! *The drive from Silver City is 44 miles but can take up to 2 hours. There are no trash cans in the park: pack it out.*

You can forest-bathe amid a thousand shades of emerald at verdant 'Iao Valley.

127

Trek through the 'Iao Valley's teeming forests

HAWAI'I // Shield your eyes against the drizzle, and look up: you're in the emerald forests of west Maui, where fog hangs thick above the mountains and the 'Iao Needle (2250ft) looms high. This is the second-wettest place in Hawai'i: mists of rain make the entire forest feel alive, and guava and mountain apples drop from teeming trees.

'Iao Valley State Monument is where geological and spiritual histories collide.

The head of the valley is Kahālāwai Crater, the remains of a 1.7-million-year-old shield volcano. An epic battle raged here in 1790, when the Big Island's King Kamehameha the Great challenged the armies of Maui's Kalanikūpule. Burial sites are secreted deep in the forests, and keen-eyed hikers can spot ancient petroglyphs etched into the rocks.

The photogenic 'Iao Needle is your focal point: legend says it's an ill-fated daughter of Maui, turned to stone after her love affair with a merman. Climb up 133 steps to see a verdant panorama from the top of the needle. Other walking trails offer tantalizing glimpses of Maui's highest point, Pu'u Kukui (5788ft) and many are lined with panels telling stories of ancient gods and tribal warfare.

☛ SEE IT ! *The park is a 10-minute drive west of central Wailuku.*

© mikecphoto / Shutterstock

© Diane Garcia / Shutterstock

Take a crash course in contemporary art at the Museum of Modern Art

NEW YORK // For art buffs, MoMA is heaven. For the uninitiated, it's a thrilling intro to all that is beautiful and addictive about modern art. MoMA's galleries scintillate with superstars: Van Gogh, Matisse, Picasso, Warhol, Lichtenstein, Rothko, Pollock, Bourgeois. Founded in 1929, the museum has some 200,000 artworks documenting the creative ideas and movements of the late-19th century through to those of today. MoMA's permanent collection spans a range of disciplines displayed across chronological segments: 1880s–1940s; 1940s–1970s; 1970s–present. Works rotate every six months: look out for iconic American art like Warhol's *Campbell's Soup Cans* and *Gold Marilyn Monroe*, Lichtenstein's *Drowning Girl* and Hopper's *New York Movie*. The Abby Aldrich Rockefeller Sculpture Garden is dotted with works by Matisse, Giacometti, and Picasso.

👉 SEE IT ! *Audio guides are free, available on a device from the museum in several languages or via the app or a phone browser.*

Fall silent at the Valley of the Gods' sculpted scenery

UTAH // Your 4WD shudders along the bumpy gravel road. Your destination? Blissful isolation, otherwise known as the Valley of the Gods. Here spreads a butte-filled desertscape, evoking Monument Valley with its pinnacles of sandstone and mushroom-shaped rocks.

You shield your eyes from the sun as you look for quirkily named rock formations like Seven Sailors, Lady on a Tub, and Rooster Butte. Sci-fi fans might feel a sense of déjà-vu – two episodes of the Doctor Who series were filmed in this arid realm. Most travelers complete the circuit by road in a day, but if you prep well and camp overnight, your rewards will be a starry canopy and perfect pin-drop silence.

👉 SEE IT ! *You'll need a 4WD to drive the Valley of the Gods, unless it's very dry; ask locally and allow an hour for the 17-mile loop, between Hwys 261 and 163. The closest town is Mexican Hat.*

© Ruben Martinez Barricarte / Shutterstock

© Real Window Creative / Shutterstock

130

See medieval marvels at tranquil Met Cloisters

NEW YORK // There are few places in NYC that feel less New York-ey than this peaceful assemblage of medieval French monasteries in Manhattan's far north. Sculptor George Grey Barnard bought ancient architectural fragments in Europe before WWI, transporting them to New York in pieces. They were acquired by John D. Rockefeller Jr who had the Cloisters built to house them in hilly, isolated Fort Tryon Park, eventually donating the collection to the Metropolitan Museum of Art; he also bought the Palisades cliffs across the Hudson River so the park would never lose its stunning views. The Cloisters are surrounded by gardens inspired by medieval manuscripts and filled with treasures – stained glass, ivory sculptures, precious metalwork. The highlight is the fantastical *The Hunt of the Unicorn* tapestries from the late 1400s.

🐾 SEE IT ! *Take the A train to 181st St Station and transfer to the M4 bus 165, taking it to the final stop.*

131

Muse majestic Arctic scenery from the 'End of the Road'

ALASKA // There's no visitor center and no comfortable coffee bar dispatching lattes. Instead, you must motor up a cold, windswept, lonely road, flanked by the occasional shack and 'palm trees' fashioned from whale baleen. The destination: Point Barrow, the northernmost extremity of the US, named for a British geographer and characterized – if you can get close enough – by a beach full of soft, sandy sinkholes. To the north lies the Arctic Ocean, shaded from slate gray to icy black and breaking on the pebbly shore (assuming the water isn't filled with ice-pack). Occasionally, you'll see a walrus carcass swelling on the beach.

From here it's a bone-chilling 1291 miles to the North Pole. Best not get out of the car – the local polar bears aren't particularly friendly.

🐾 SEE IT ! *Point Barrow is 10 miles north of the town of Utqiaġvik. To get there, take a tour or make friends with a local and cadge a ride.*

132

Stroll New Orleans' prettiest (and priciest) shopping strip along Royal Street

LOUISIANA // In the French Quarter, elegant Royal St feels a world away from its drunken neighbor, Bourbon St, just one block away. Vintage lampposts line the former Rue Royale, which is watched over by ornate wrought-iron balconies trimmed with flowers, ferns, and potted plants. The approach from busy Canal St leads past antique stores, art galleries, jewelry shops, and boutiques. There are plenty of places to spend some serious cash (like Moss Antiques if you're in the market for a Louis XV chandelier) as well as low-key spots to recharge (Cafe Beignet whips up its tasty namesake for eager customers). In the afternoon, the blocks between St Ann and St Louis streets close to cars, and jazz trumpeters, blues singers, and other roving performers take over. It's a great spot to survey the incredible talent found in New Orleans (don't forget to tip the musicians).

☛ **SEE IT !** *Both the Canal St and St Charles Ave streetcars intersect Royal St.*

© Anna Gorin / Getty Images

© Allyson Huntsman / Courtesy of The Menil Collection

133

Roam the extra-terrestrial plains at Craters of the Moon

IDAHO // Wandering through these lunar landscapes, you can't help but wonder – what's stranger, outer space or our own home planet? At this 400-sq-mile preserve in south-central Idaho, sweeps of sagebrush interrupt vivid seams of black and russet stone. The geological activity that puckered this land into the Great Rift of Idaho is truly ancient. Thousands of years ago, volcanic eruptions left behind lava fields, the casts of incinerated trees, and pyroducts (caves sculpted by molten lava). Embark on Tree Molds Trails or Broken Top Loop (after grabbing a permit to explore bat-filled Buffalo Cave). For a longer trek, the Wilderness Trail is a satisfying 8-mile round-trip. Feeling light-headed? It's not just the spectacular scenery: you're 5900ft above sea level, so take it easy along the park's paved walkways.

☛ SEE IT ! *In winter, Craters of the Moon's main hiking trails and the Loop Rd only open when snow permits.*

134

See artistic treasures that span the ages in the Menil Collection

TEXAS // When John and Dominique de Menil settled in Houston in the 1940s (fleeing war in Europe), it would forever change the city's cultural landscape. Longtime patrons of the arts, the de Menils assembled one of the world's most extensive private collections – and donated it to their adopted city. A staggering trove of paintings, sculptures, drawings, photographs, and rare books make up the 17,000-piece collection, spread across five buildings over 30 acres. The focal point is the Renzo Piano-designed main building, with exhibitions spanning the ages, from Ice Age carvings, via Cycladic figures from 2800 BCE and Benin bronzes, to more recent works by Pablo Picasso, Francis Bacon, Andy Warhol, and Kara Walker. Across the street, the Cy Twombly Gallery contains some of the most notable works of the eponymous abstract artist.

☛ SEE IT ! *The Menil Collection is about 3 miles southwest of downtown Houston; admission to all its galleries and programs is free.*

Enjoy splendid isolation amid the wilderness of Boundary Waters.

135

Paddle crystal-clear lakes in Boundary Waters Canoe Area Wilderness

MINNESOTA // Legendarily remote and pristine, Boundary Waters Canoe Area Wilderness (BWCAW) is an aquatic wonderland of glacial lakes, gurgling streams, and craggy, pine-forest-covered islands spread across more than one million acres. Nature lovers and paddlers of all skill levels make the pilgrimage to enjoy the 1500 miles of canoe routes, rich wildlife, and sweeping solitude. If you're willing to dig in and canoe for a while, it'll just be you and the moose, bears, and wolves that roam the landscape. It's possible to glide in for the day, but most people opt for at least a night of camping. And with over 2000 primitive campsites to choose from, you won't lack for options. Mesmerizing sunsets and mournful loon cries end the day, followed by a night filled with flickering stars – and occasionally the spectacular hues of the Northern Lights. With no discernible light pollution for many miles, Boundary Waters was named the latest addition to the International Dark Sky Sanctuary list in 2020.

☛ SEE IT ! *Off Hwy 1, Ely makes an ideal base for trip-planning and gear hire from top-notch outfitters like Piragis Northwoods Company.*

136

Find country music's beating heart at Ryman Auditorium

TENNESSEE // Built in 1892 to hold religious revivals, this soaring red-brick building later saw Helen Keller, Susan B. Anthony, and Booker T. Washington lecture here. Harry Houdini made an audacious on-stage water escape. Katharine Hepburn performed *The Philadelphia Story*. But most famously, as the Mother Church of Country Music, it was home to the Grand Ole Opry from 1943 to 1974, its stage seeing every star in the country firmament. It's now the Opry's winter home; the rest of the year brings performances of all stripes and juicy backstage tours.

☛ SEE IT ! *Both self-guided and special 'Backstage' tours are available; the Opry puts on shows November through January.*

137

Ride the river at Ocoee Whitewater Center

TENNESSEE // When the Olympics came to Atlanta in 1996, this greeny-brown stretch of the Ocoee River was narrowed to create a slalom course for the canoeing. Today, the National Forest Service release water into the course on certain summer days, turning it into an exhilarating whitewater playground. Whether there's water or not, the area is perfect for picnicking, hiking the rocky river gorge, and biking. It intersects the Tanasi mountain bike trails, with 30 miles of flowing singletrack set in a lush Appalachian valley just north of the Georgia line.

☛ TRY IT ! *The center is outside Ducktown and is open April through October.*

138

Take in the Yellowstone views at Inspiration Point

WYOMING // It's a little scary to stand on this platform, gazing down at the deep furrows of the Grand Canyon of the Yellowstone, knowing the original promontory snapped right off and tumbled into the abyss. Seriously, though, it's safe and sound, all newly renovated in 2018, with just slightly smaller panoramic views of the canyon and a sliver of silvery waterfall. Hike here from the North Rim Trail or drive right up and pop down a few stairs. Its ease of access makes it a popular spot, but no less stunning.

☛ SEE IT ! *The lookout is the last stop on the east end of North Rim Drive.*

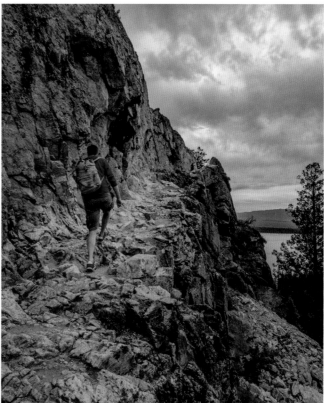

© Yorkshireknight / Shutterstock

Browse indie boutiques at Chelsea Market, then fuel up with a feast of gourmet goodies.

139

Indulge your gourmet side at Chelsea Market

NEW YORK // In a shining example of redevelopment and preservation, Chelsea Market was transformed from a former 1890s' factory into an indoor food and retail hub for today. For trivia buffs: it was the original home of the National Biscuit Company, Nabisco (yes, the one that invented and made Oreos). Located in the heart of New York City's Meatpacking District, Chelsea Market occupies an entire block; the funky red-brick building is nestled below the High Line and is a mere hop and a skip from the Whitney Museum. In other words, it's the perfect place to break up sightseeing with a bite at one of its food outlets. One of the first to open was The Lobster Place; head here for overstuffed lobster rolls and killer sushi. Or sniff out some cool finds at the retail stores, which range from well-known names such as Anthologie to the boutique offerings of unique local creators and designers. In 2018, Google purchased the premises in what was reported as being New York's second most expensive single-building deal ever (US$2.4 billion).

☞ SEE IT ! *Chelsea Market is at the southern end of the High Line, a few minutes' walk from 14th St subway (lines A, C, E and L).*

© 2021 Chihuly Studio / Artists Rights Society (ARS), New York

© Jim Schwabel / Shutterstock

140

Admire psychedelic artwork at Chihuly Garden and Glass

WASHINGTON // Stepping into the gallery, your eyes widen at the sight of spiral chandeliers and gigantic flowers. You've entered the vivid imagination of Dale Chihuly, whose glass-blown creations look simultaneously imposing and fragile. Every sculpture is crafted from brightly colored glass, which contorts into swirling flames and alien tentacles. Enrapturing crowds since it opened in 2012, Chihuly's gallery is segmented into shadowy and illuminated spaces, in which mirrors and tricks of the light showcase the sculptures' surreal beauty. But the art is most exquisitely presented in the gardens: delicate glass tendrils peep from the grass and dangle from flower beds, right at home among the native plantlife. Special events, separate from Chihuly's studio and work, see glass-blowers demonstrate their hypnotic craft.

☛ SEE IT ! *Chihuly Garden and Glass is at 305 Harrison St; take the Seattle Center Monorail from downtown.*

141

Sift for shark's teeth on Venice Beach

FLORIDA // Sorry, no canals here. But this relaxed Florida Gulf Coast town has its own rewards: warm green waters and soft sand begging for you to pitch a blanket; free beach yoga in the mornings; and, most of all, primo shark-tooth hunting. In fact, Venice bills itself as the 'Shark Tooth Capital of the World.' Amateur paleontologists should head to Caspersen Beach with a shovel and sifter (buy them at the bait shop by the pier). A couple hours of searching can net you handfuls of the shiny black teeth which wash up on shore by the millions every year, remnants of the era when Florida was beneath the sea. Serious shark toothers can hop on board a chartered dive boat – the big teeth are more common several miles out.

☛ TRY IT ! *The nearest airport is Sarasota, about 20 miles north. Find shark's teeth south of the Venice Jetty.*

© travelview / Shutterstock

© JHVEPhoto / Shutterstock

142

Savor the scene in Manhattan's Chinatown

NEW YORK // Mahogany ducks and strips of red pork belly in restaurant windows. Dim sum palaces where servers push carts of chicken feet and slippery rice rolls. Bakeries selling lurid-yellow egg tarts and hot milk tea. Stalls piled with hairy gourds and fat persimmons and dried scallops and fresh tofu. OK, so Manhattan's Chinatown isn't *only* about the food. There's history too. The area was settled by southern Chinese sailors, goldminers, and merchants in the 1870s, making it New York's original Chinatown, and it survived the Chinese Exclusion Act of 1882 and waves of gentrification and change; in the 1980s, migrants from Fuzhou swelled the population to some 100,000. Today, come for the smoky smell of pu'er tea, the click of mahjong tiles, the teeming markets of knockoff purses and perfumes and, of course, the food.

☛ EAT IT ! *Chinatown is south of Broome and east of Broadway; Mott and Canal are the main drags.*

143

Glimpse an eco-friendly future at Arcosanti

ARIZONA // Here in Arcosanti, where bald eagles wheel above and lynx and coyotes stalk the wilds, you can glimpse a low-carbon vision of the future. This eco-village in the semi-desert grasslands of Arizona was founded on architect Paolo Soleri's theory of 'arcology' (architecture and ecology). Soleri wanted to build a self-sufficient community, fed by large-scale greenhouses and powered by the fierce desert sun.

His project remains a work in progress, with no more than 100 inhabitants so far. Take a stroll among its form-cast concrete structures and vertically oriented buildings, designed to minimize urban sprawl. Join an hour-long tour to understand this small creativity community, peeping into the bronze foundry and ceramics studio along the way. Ready to move to this eco Eden? Book an overnight stay as a trial run.

☛ SEE IT ! *Take the I-17's exit 262 (Cordes Junction, 65 miles north of Phoenix).*

© wayfarerlife / Shutterstock

© Erika Goldring / Getty Images

144

Witness the fight for change at the Center for Civil and Human Rights

GEORGIA // You close your eyes and spread your hands flat on the table. Through headphones, you hear menacing shouts. You're listening to a recreation of sit-in protests during the American Civil Rights Movement, where college students non-violently occupied 'whites only' lunch counters. Even though a guide has warned you about the impending auditory assault, cold fear spreads in the pit of your stomach. This experience powerfully drives home the bravery of activists who confronted intense racial hatred in 1960s' Georgia, and is the centerpiece of the Center for Civil and Human Rights in Atlanta – birthplace of Martin Luther King Jr. The building's curved walls represent two hands clasping human dignity protectively, and the center connects the history of civil rights in the US with ongoing efforts worldwide.

☛ SEE IT ! *The center is at 100 Ivan Allen Jr Blvd, in downtown Atlanta near the Georgia Aquarium.*

145

Tap into diverse musical history at New Orleans' House of Blues

LOUISIANA // The honeyed sounds of a saxophone solo wash over you, while the rhythmic twangs of a bass guitar vibrate the floor. You're surrounded by voodoo-themed sculptures and downlit folk art in the Big Easy's buzzing French Quarter. Welcome to the House of Blues, which has become the city's unofficial 'Blues HQ'.

New Orleans blues is a distinctive phenomenon: this cocktail of Caribbean music and jazz, driven by piano and full-throated soulful vocals, is the city's soundtrack. But at the House of Blues, everything from bluegrass to pop to heavy metal has set crowds roaring. Our pick? Gospel Brunch on Sunday, where praiseful voices and soaring pianos provide the soundtrack to an overflowing buffet of waffles, biscuits, and slices of brisket. Hallelujah, another mimosa!

☛ SEE IT ! *House of Blues is at 225 Decatur St, on the southern flank of Nola's French Quarter.*

Enjoy eye-popping
Blue Ridge Mountain
views in Shenandoah
National Park.

146

Breathe fresh Appalachian air at Shenandoah National Park

VIRGINIA // What it lacks in size, Shenandoah makes up in photo ops: high meadows carpeted with wildflowers; deer grazing in mountain groves. Running north-south along a section of the Blue Ridge Mountains, it's a popular getaway for Washington, DC residents, who hike its slopes, explore its crumbling pioneer cemeteries, dip their toes in its waterfalls, and sleep in its charming lodges. The park's only road, Skyline Drive, is 105 miles of jaw-dropping scenery, with the Shenandoah River to the west and the gentle folds of the Piedmont region to the east. Start in the cute, antique shop-choked town of Front Royal on the north side, then stop at the Range View Overlook, taking in rugged Stony Man Mountain. Picnic at Pinnacle Peak, then spend the night playing board games with fellow guests at Big Meadows Lodge, built in classic National Parks style from stone and wood beams. The park's big hike is Old Rag Mountain, a steep 9-mile scramble with endless panoramic views from the summit.

☛ SEE IT ! *Front Royal is 70 miles west of DC; the south entrance at Rockfish Gap is 25 miles from Charlottesville.*

📷
Feel the vibe in the
Botanical Garden
in San Francisco's
Golden Gate Park.

147

Embrace the whimsical beauty of Golden Gate Park

CALIFORNIA // Think of Golden Gate Park as San Francisco 101: a beginner's guide to the City by the Bay. A stroll between its museums, landmarks, and gardens unravels SF's history – and shows its freak flag flying high.

Thank William Hammond Hall for landscaping these 1017 green acres in the 1870s. The feted engineer probably didn't foresee how culture and nature would coexist here for the next 150 years, and that it would become the USA's third-most visited park. Start with the de Young Fine Arts Museum and the ornately trellised Conservatory of Flowers. Find where beloved San Franciscans are mourned in the National AIDS Memorial Grove, and seek calm at 10 lakes, some of them offering pedalo hire. The Japanese Tea Garden and Botanical Garden – complete with the ruins of a Spanish monastery – also beckon to calm the soul. The flower children of the 1960s still dance on 'Hippie Hill' where Janis Joplin once strummed, joined today by lindy hop dance classes, hot yoga, and Segways galore. In this eye-popping park, you won't even bat an eyelid at the bison paddock, a short walk from surf-splashed Ocean Beach.

☛ SEE IT ! *Walk from Haight-Ashbury (east) or Inner Sunset (south). Grab a rental bike from stations around town for a DIY tour.*

African elephant Henry has watched over the National Museum of Natural History rotunda since 1959.

148

Walk with dinosaurs at the National Museum of Natural History

WASHINGTON, DC // Identifiable by its green dome, and one of the most visited of the Smithsonian museums, this place is a rite of passage for many visitors and kids who head here to view some of its 1.7 million objects. Wave to Henry, the elephant who guards the rotunda, then zip to the 2nd floor's Hope Diamond, a 45.52-karat bauble that's said to have cursed its owners, who included Marie Antoinette. The beloved dinosaur hall centers on 'the Nation's T. Rex'. Elsewhere, the giant squid, an exact replica of a North Atlantic right whale, live butterfly pavilion, and tarantula feedings provide additional thrills. Other highlights include Easter Island heads, mummies, and halls devoted to mammals and oceans, plus – because little things can pack a powerful punch too – don't miss the insect zoo. Then there's the latest dazzling addition, the fossil hall where 31,000 sq ft of space display 700 specimens that evoke ancient ecosystems and the evolution of life. The museum's vibrant temporary exhibition program should have something to tickle your interest. The butterfly pavilion has a separate admission cost but is free on Tuesdays.

☛ SEE IT ! *On select spring and summer days the museum stays open until 7:30pm. The nearest Metro station is Smithsonian.*

149

Ponder past shipwrecks from Point Sur

CALIFORNIA // A lighthouse beckons from the volcanic-rock cliffs. This historic light station overlooks a wave-battered stretch of Pacific coast and is now a landmark of Point Sur State Historic Park.

This has long been a dangerous place for ships: many vessels crashed on these sharp rocks, most famously the USS *Ventura* in 1875. The lighthouse was established in 1889, and its solitary keeper lived self-sufficiently from farmland to maintain and operate the tower's bulb, which once winked out across the ocean. It's the only such tower in California open to the public, so join one of the regular tours. They start just north of Point Sur Naval Facility (where Soviet submarines were tracked during the 1950s) and invite contemplation of a solitary lifestyle that is now lost in time.

☛ SEE IT ! *The park is 7 miles south of Bixby Creek Bridge, along the gorgeously scenic coast road of Hwy 1.*

© Lynn Yeh / Shutterstock

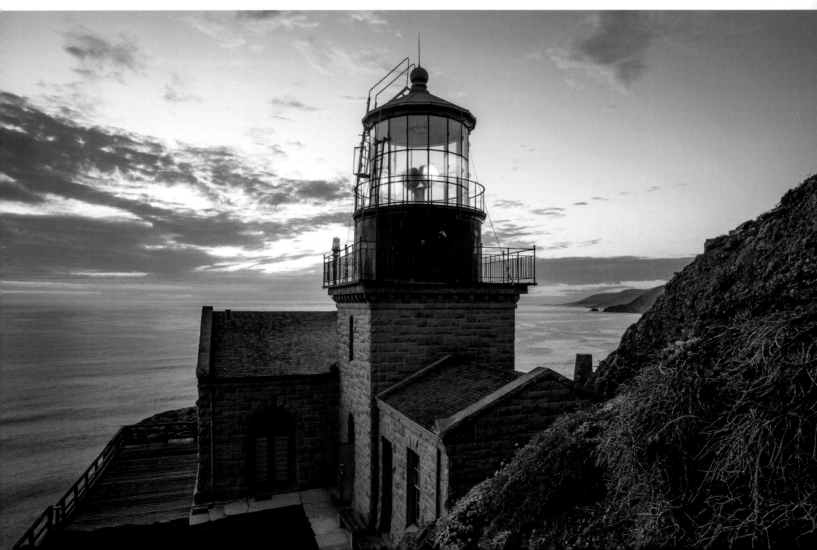

Whether you're on the water or strolling beside, San Antonio River Walk is a fun-filled journey.

150

Glide past the tree-lined banks of the San Antonio River Walk

TEXAS // When the San Antonio Spurs hold a victory parade after winning the NBA championship (as they last did in 2014), they choose to float past their fans along the San Antonio River Walk. Not surprisingly, this waterway is the city's most beloved feature – more admired than the Alamo or even its championship-winning basketball team. A slice of Europe in the heart of downtown, the River Walk comprises a scenic network of canals and pedestrian walkways that extend for more than 15 miles. The meandering waterside paths lie just below the downtown streets, meaning you'll never have to stop for traffic as you stroll past landscaped gardens and riverside cafes, or linger on stone footbridges that arch across the water. The winding cypress-lined paths get packed with crowds during the summer, but it's easy to find solitude outside the city center. The 8-mile Mission Reach expansion extends south to the King William District and beyond to the World Heritage-listed Spanish missions, while the 4-mile Museum Reach stretches north to the San Antonio Art Museum, the Pearl Brewery complex, and verdant Brackenridge Park.

☛ SEE IT ! *For an overview of the River Walk, hop aboard an eco-friendly river cruise operated by GO RIO.*

© Joshua Rainey Photography / Shutterstock

© Courtesy of the Harry S. Truman Library and Museum

© Let Go Media / Shutterstock

151

Grapple with postwar history at the Harry S. Truman Library and Museum

MISSOURI // Dedicated in 1957, the Truman Library and Museum caps a hill in Independence, Missouri, overlooking the Kansas skyline. Upgraded by a $25 million transformation, inside you'll find the life's work and final resting place of the 33rd US president.

The complex's brimming shelves hold thousands of clues to the challenges of the turbulent 1940s and '50s, including the famous 'The Buck Stops Here!' sign. There are documents, gifts from dignitaries, and a replica Oval Office – but the collection digs deeper than the presidency. Truman was the only US president to serve in combat during WWI, so exhibits on his training and active service are fascinating insights into the military experience. Make your way to the limestone pavilion, too: from here you can see Truman's office, in which he worked after the library's opening in 1957.

☛ SEE IT ! *The museum is located off US Hwy 24 in Independence.*

152

Pick up some snacks nearby and picnic on the grass in Bryant Park

NEW YORK // Stumbling upon a pocket of greenery in Midtown Manhattan is about as likely as finding water in the Mojave Desert. It's no wonder then that the grassy oasis of Bryant Park is so beloved by both working New Yorkers and out-of-towners. Despite its diminutive size, the park is a year-round draw, complete with European coffee kiosks, alfresco chess games, and summer film screenings. There's even a French-inspired, Brooklyn-made carousel, plus the Bryant Park Grill, well placed for a twilight cocktail. Fancy taking a yoga class, joining a painting workshop, or signing up for a birding tour? The park has a daily smorgasbord of quirky activities. Come Christmastime, the place becomes a winter wonderland, with holiday gift vendors and a shimmering ice-skating rink plunked in the middle.

☛ SEE IT ! *The 42nd St-Bryant Park subway station (B/D/F/M lines) is just steps from the park entrance.*

Find your inner balance while enjoying mindbending views over Arizona's Horseshoe Bend.

153

Embrace a sense of vertigo at Horseshoe Bend

ARIZONA // Gracing countless photographs, Horseshoe Bend looks as though it was sculpted by an unseen hand. As you gaze out over the sheer cliffs, your stomach somersaults: the river is 1000ft below you, carving a horseshoe shape through the rock.

Hundreds of millions of years ago, sand dunes covered this land. They eventually hardened into layers of Navajo sandstone (particular to this region of the US). A sudden abruption in the Colorado Plateau forced the river to take a new path, meandering around an impassable, unerodable escarpment. Centuries of action by wind and water revealed what you see today: a colossal cross-section of geological history.

A 1.5-mile round-trip on foot leads you from the parking lot along a sandy, gravelly trail. Then you see it: aquamarine waters circling the peninsula of rock as they make their way towards the Grand Canyon. If you can tear yourself away from this lofty overlook, a rafting trip allows an alternative view of the canyon.

☛ SEE IT ! *Find the trailhead south of Page off Hwy 89, just past Mile 545. Tread carefully at the top – there are no barriers.*

© Kushal Bose / Shutterstock

© Brett Winter Lemon / Courtesy of Floyd Country Store

154

View a bumper bat colony at Congress Avenue Bridge

TEXAS // Here is a heart-warming city tradition: reclining on a grassy lakeshore as dusk approaches, watching for the emergence of a million-plus Mexican free-tailed bats from their residence on the underside of a bridge, ready for a night's hunting. Lady Bird Lake, the dammed, green-edged stretch of Austin's Colorado River southeast of Congress Avenue Bridge, is normally a nicer spot than the bridge itself – until evening comes. It's then that the chittering bats, numbering 1.5 million in peak season (July and August) when their bat babies reach flying age, launch on their nightly insect-hunt. Fluttering out of bridge recesses in waves of black framed against the fading daylight, this is an astonishing natural display. They're hungry, they're on the loose, but thankfully they're not interested in you, so relax and enjoy the show.

☛ SEE IT ! *The bridge is a block south of the visitor center in Austin's Waller Creek District.*

155

Dance to old-time bluegrass at the Floyd Country Store

VIRGINIA // Tucked in the foothills of the Blue Ridge Mountains, the tiny town of Floyd isn't much more than an intersection between Hwy 8 and Hwy 221. In fact, the whole county only has one stoplight. Yet for over 100 years, the Floyd Country Store here has drawn visitors from near and far. You can buy overalls, locally made apple butter, or an ice-cream soda here, but most people come for the action-packed Friday Night Jamboree. That's when store shelves are pushed aside to make way for a dance floor, and mountain music lovers converge for a night of authentic Appalachian rhythms and communal good cheer. A live band, complete with fiddlers and fast-picking banjo players, fills the small stage, while young and old alike make the floorboards shake with high-powered clogging.

☛ SEE IT ! *Floyd is 20 miles southeast of I-81; there are also performances on weekend days.*

Snoqualmie Falls is as famous for its natural beauty as its cult TV cred.

156

Awaken the spirt of *Twin Peaks* at Snoqualmie Falls

WASHINGTON // Half the visitors to Snoqualmie come purely to see its plunging waterfall; the other half are drawn by an incurable obsession with the seminal 1990s TV series *Twin Peaks*, in which the waterfall played a cameo role (over the opening credits).

Whether you're here for natural beauty or a cult television drama, it's unlikely you'll be disappointed. The falls are considered spiritual by the Snoqualmie tribe and have given birth to a number of evocative Native legends. It's hardly surprising. Dropping 268ft, the wide cascade of water has a powerful allure, especially after heavy rain when it throws up a misty spray.

Perched above the falls, the Salish Lodge and Spa (*Twin Peaks'* Great Northern Hotel) invites aficionados to sample one of the series' most famous motifs: a slice of cherry pie and 'damn fine coffee', just watch out for eerie goings-on.

An outdoor observation deck lies just off the main road and provides access to a small parking lot and pretty park. A couple of trails lead off from here, revealing close-up views of the falls from different angles.

🡢 SEE IT ! *Snoqualmie is a 45-minute to one-hour drive from Seattle along I-90.*

© bigannie / Budget Travel

© Kenneth Keifer / 500px

157

Roam the Red Rock desert to its craggy climax at Cathedral Rock

ARIZONA // A second entry on this list for the rust-hued rocky desert encompassing the Arizona settlement of Sedona shows how startling the scenery hereabouts is. These rugged ramparts of rock loom out of their arid scrub-splashed surroundings like a gaggle of gossiping giants, and whilst their scale and setting is sublime, most magical is the shade these sandstone buttes turn around sunset when their ruddy coloring intensifies and glows. The rocks top out at 4697ft and you can make your way to the summit on a very steep but well-trodden 1.2 mile round-trip trail: allow the better part of an hour each way, plus time at the top for appreciating the superb views of the desertscape. It's no surprise that Cathedral Rock is one of the most camera-snapped attractions in all Arizona.

🖝 SEE IT ! *The trail to the top begins from the parking lot on Back O Beyond Rd, northeast of the rock.*

158

Hear the cannons fire at Castillo de San Marcos National Monument

FLORIDA // Cannon fire still roars across the marshes at this 17th-century masonry fort on the shores of Matanzas Bay. Completed by the Spanish in 1695, it's gone back and forth (peacefully) between owners five times: Spain to England to Spain (again) to the US to the Confederacy to the US (again). A hollow square with diamond-shaped bastions at each corner, it's built from local coquina stone, formed from ancient shells pressed together over millions of years. Wander the Plaza de Armas, the chapel, and the guard rooms, learning about the fort's long history, such as when it was a prison for Native Americans, including Chief White Horse of the Kiowa. Costumed interpreters fire cannons and muskets on weekends, the sound reverberating across the still blue water.

🖝 SEE IT ! *The fort anchors the eastern edge of St Augustine's Historic District.*

The green-swathed inner courtyard of the Isabella Gardner Museum reflects the tastes of its eponymous creator.

159

Wander in Isabella Stewart Gardner's world

MASSACHUSETTS // In a city rich with museums, this palazzo crammed with Dutch masters, medieval manuscripts, Islamic calligraphy, and Greco-Roman sculptures is surely one of the most memorable. It's the personal collection of eccentric heiress Isabella Stewart Gardner, who traveled the globe collecting works that spoke to her heart. She built the Venetian-inspired museum in Boston's then-marshy Fenway neighborhood and furnished it with tapestries and Persian carpets, all surrounding a lush interior courtyard. When she died in 1924, her will stipulated the museum not be altered. It hasn't been, though in 1990 thieves made off with 13 never-recovered works, including a Vermeer, a Degas, and a Rembrandt; the crime remains unsolved. Visiting the museum is like exploring Gardner's mind, with works arranged to inspire, not edify.

☛ SEE IT ! *Take the T's Green Line E to the Museum of Fine Arts stop, or the Orange Line to the Ruggles stop.*

160

Witness the fearsome march of progress at the Hoover Dam

NEVADA // From the 726ft-high Hoover Dam, views across the yawning Black Canyon are staggering. This Art Deco-style structure was built to contain floods and harness hydroelectric power; simultaneously, it stands as a monument to human endeavor and to great hardship.

When it was completed in 1936, the dam was considered daring and highly experimental. This was the largest concrete structure of its time, built with untried techniques at an immense human cost. Depression-era workers toiled in 120°F temperatures to construct this colossus, and around 100 lives were lost to flash floods, suicide, heat, or falling from height.

In spite (or perhaps because) of disregard for human suffering, the dam was completed well ahead of schedule. Other forms of life suffered, too, with many fish species which once thrived here now listed as endangered. One thing is certain: humankind's effect on the natural environment is truly sobering.

☛ SEE IT ! *Tours begin at the Hoover Dam Parking Garage & Visitor Center.*

161

Be a kid again at California's Disneyland Resort

CALIFORNIA // Florida's the big one, but California's the original. Rocket through Space Mountain, soar over London on Peter Pan's Flight, wander Sleeping Beauty Castle, climb Tarzan's Treehouse, take a selfie with Elsa, and slurp a Mickey-shaped ice cream before ending the day with the fireworks show. The 1955 park was joined in 2001 by Disney California Adventure Park, with Golden State-themed areas like Grizzly Peak and Hollywood Land. Yes, the crowds and lines are a drag, but it's worth it to experience such total commitment to childhood fantasy.

SEE IT ! *Disneyland is in Anaheim, about 30 miles southeast of downtown Los Angeles.*

162

Conquer the Coastal Trail on foot, bike or horseback

CALIFORNIA // The Coastal Trail is the American outdoors lover's next big thrill. Poised to connect Oregon with Mexico along the ravishing 1200-odd miles of California's coast through a path network to suit hikers, bikers, and horse riders alike, and running as close to the ocean as possible throughout, the trail is as ambitious as it is alluring. At around 60% complete, it's soon set to deliver on its tantalising promise – and has already improved access to a superlative shoreline, from the northern redwood forests to the sun-kissed bays of the south.

TRY IT ! *Prairie Creek Redwoods State Park has some beautiful coast-meets-forest sections.*

163

Admire Art Deco craftsmanship at the Chrysler Building

NEW YORK // Sparkling like a crown jewel in the New York City skyline, the Chrysler Building is neither the tallest nor the oldest skyscraper in town, but it can lay claim to being one of the loveliest. The 77-story tower is an Art Deco masterpiece, guarded by stylized eagles of chromium nickel and topped by an iconic seven-tiered spire reminiscent of the rising sun. Inside, the lobby is a lavish ensemble of dark wood, elaborately veneered elevators, sculpted marble, and a vibrant 1930 ceiling mural depicting the golden promise of industry and modernity.

SEE IT ! *It's a short walk to the subway at Grand Central-42nd St.*

© Lissandra Melo / Shutterstock

© CHOONGKY / Shutterstock

164

Unwind in nature at the US National Arboretum

WASHINGTON, DC // It's hard not to imagine a few forest nymphs and centaurs popping out of the woods here. One of the greatest green spaces in Washington, DC unfurls across almost 450 acres of meadowland, sylvan theaters, and a pastoral setting that feels somewhere between bucolic Americana countryside and a classical Greek rural idyll. Highlights include the National Bonsai & Penjing Museum (exquisitely sculpted mini-trees), the National Herb Garden (over 650,000 specimens are housed in the collection), and the otherworldly Capitol Columns Garden (studded with Corinthian pillars that were once part of the Capitol building). As you wander past azaleas, daffodils, maple, and magnolia, you'll be sure to spot a wedding or three; it's a favorite for marriage photos. And it's easy to see why.

☞ SEE IT ! *The Arboretum is 4.5 miles northeast of The Mall. There are two entrances: at 3501 New York Avenue NE, and at 24th & R Streets NE.*

165

Scramble the heights of Hudson Highlands State Park Preserve

NEW YORK // Southern New York doesn't typically conjure images of vast forests, craggy mountaintops, or sweeping views over the Hudson River. But this is exactly what you'll find some 50 miles north of the Big Apple – a journey from burgeoning metropolis to pristine wilderness that can be transformative. Take a train from Grand Central, rolling along a scenic stretch of the Hudson before arriving at quaint Cold Spring, an easy walk from the park's entrance. Within, over 70 miles of trails crisscross an 8000-acre patch of forests, shores, and summits. You can tackle a challenging 4.5-mile climb up Breakneck Ridge, or an easy-going riverside walk to Little Stony Point, with its tiny sandy beach. Another non-contiguous section of the park lies further south, which encompasses a small stretch of the 2190-mile-long Appalachian Trail.

☞ TRY IT ! *It's a 90-minute train ride from NYC's Grand Central Terminal to Cold Spring (Metro-North line).*

Santa Monica State Beach offers surfing, swimming, sunning, selfie-taking – and beach volleyball.

166

Frolic on golden sands at Santa Monica State Beach

CALIFORNIA // West of the downtown area, all of LA's wondrous menagerie converges on Santa Monica State Beach. These 3.5 miles of sun-splashed sand stretch from Will Rogers State Beach south to Venice Beach. Surfers and swimmers are a dime a dozen here, and you're sure to see sun-buffed locals competing at beach volleyball. On a busy day, you can watch breakdancers gyrate across the sand while Insta-famous locals look on through mirrored sunglasses. The north side is superb for kids, with a playground full of swings and slides, plus the nearby pier – complete with irresistibly retro carousel. Settle in at picnic spots dotted along the shore, or sign up for beach butler service at Perry's Café to luxuriate in shade and refreshments brought right to the sand. Just south of the pier you can work up a sweat on the rings, swings, and parallel bars of the Original Muscle Beach, or partake in cerebral pursuits like the first-come, first-served chess table. To explore the coast further, rent a bike to pedal along the Marvin Braude Beach Trail.

SEE IT ! *Metro Line E links Santa Monica to downtown Los Angeles.*

167

See history-making documents at the National Archives

WASHINGTON, DC // It's hard not to feel a little in awe of the big three documents in the National Archives: the Declaration of Independence; the Constitution; and the Bill of Rights. Taken together, it becomes clear just how radical the American experiment was. The archival bric-a-brac of the Public Vaults exhibition makes a flashy, but fun, rejoinder to the main exhibit (pick up the red phone and hear presidents dealing with the events of the day). The David M. Rubenstein Gallery explores the evolution of rights in the United States from its earliest days through to the present. Among its vast collection of photographs, documents, videos, and interactive displays, the most coveted artifact is one of four surviving originals of the 1297 Magna Carta.

☛ SEE IT ! *Reserve tickets online for a small fee and use the fast-track entrance on Constitution Ave.*

168

Re-energize at Fall Creek Falls

TENNESSEE // The air is crisp at Fall Creek Falls State Park. This realm of virgin hardwoods hugs the edge of the Cumberland Plateau, its 29,800 acres freshened by meandering creeks and myriad waterfalls.

At its heart is one of the tallest waterfalls in the eastern USA: Fall Creek Falls, which drops gracefully from a 256ft-high rocky shelf. Along 56 miles of walking trails, you can reach other cascades like modest Piney Falls and broad, churning Cane Creek, or hike around the lake shore. Golf and shaky bridges at the Canopy Challenge Course complete the park's family-friendly options.

These towering forests of beech and oak are also home to dozens of bird species. You'll hear red-headed woodpeckers drilling the trees, and spot turkey vultures hovering above. Stick around to experience the soundtrack of songbirds: you can plant a tent or rent one of 20 overnight cabins. Time a trip between March and October, when migratory birds like warblers and vireos flit through.

© CampSmoke / Shutterstock

☛ SEE IT ! *The park is 115 miles southeast of Nashville, between Spencer and Pikeville.*

169

Explore the power of print at Powell's City of Books

OREGON // This awesome independent bookstore, housed in a former car dealership, makes reading, well, cool. The building itself fills an entire Portland block – that's 68,000 sq ft, or nine rooms over three floors, with 3500 sections packing in one million books. The store was started in Chicago by Michael Powell in 1970. Then, Walter, his father, started up a branch that stocked second-hand books in Portland. These days, Powell's sells both used and new, hardcover and paperback titles. Ask about the series of in-store book readings.

☛ SEE IT ! *Powell's has two stores in Portland and one in nearby Beaverton.*

170

Wander Kahanu Garden and sacred Piʻilanihale Heiau

HAWAIʻI // At this incomparable site on Maui, an ancient temple is clasped by tropical gardens. Piʻilanihale Heiau is the largest temple in the Hawaiʻian Islands. Its first basalt block was laid in CE 1200, and the walls of this great complex offer a glimpse into traditional Hawaiʻian culture before European settlers arrived. Stroll the 294-acre Kahanu botanical garden surrounding the temple. Among sugarcane and banana trees you'll see Hawaiʻi's staple food all around: the garden has the world's largest collection of breadfruit tree species.

☛ SEE IT ! *Find the garden and temple down 'Ulaʻino Rd, off the gloriously scenic Hana Hwy. Guided tours illuminate the site's history.*

171

Revel in iconic architecture at Chicago's Millennium Park

ILLINOIS // Your reflection – and that of Chicago skyline– distorts and bounces on the sculpture's silvery surface. You're standing directly in front of the Windy City's emblem: Sir Anish Kapoor's *Cloud Gate*, also known as 'the Bean'.

This gleaming artwork is one of several gems strewn around Millennium Park, a former industrial wasteland transformed into Chicago's leading attraction, a mosaic of public art, world-class architecture, and landscaped gardens. The Frank Gehry-designed Jay Pritzker Pavilion takes center stage with its arresting steel bandshell, a venue for free concerts each summer. Jaume Plensa's *Crown Fountain* grabs your attention with its entertaining digital displays, while Lurie Garden lures birds and butterflies to its flower beds and ornamental grasses. Then there's the McCormick Tribune Ice Rink, visited each year by 100,000 spinning skaters.

After touring the architectural highlights, drink in skyline views from the snakelike BP Bridge or the Nichols Bridgeway (designed by Renzo Piano). The entire plaza drapes across a parking garage and railway station, making Millennium Park a colossal rooftop garden with lofty views: the perfect intro to Chicago.

☛ SEE IT ! *Take Metra Rail to Millennium Station and walk to the entrance at Michigan Avenue & Washington St.*

172

Embrace sensory overload in SF's Chinatown

CALIFORNIA // The crimson-and-green tiered former Chinese Telephone Exchange stops you in your tracks, just one of numerous striking buildings in San Francisco's Chinatown. As you navigate the busy streets, incense billows from doorways, jade ornaments wink from storefronts, and Peking ducks glisten in restaurant windows. Established in the 1840s, this is the largest Chinatown outside Asia: crane your neck at Sing Chong Building, see places of worship like 1854 Old St Mary's, and finish with a mai tai at delightfully seedy Li Po Cocktail Lounge.

SEE IT ! *Chinatown Alleyway Tours and Chinatown Heritage Walking Tours offer guided walks.*

173

Stay out late hitting the music halls on Frenchmen Street

LOUISIANA // Lined with quality jazz clubs, New Orleans' Frenchmen St is one of the best places in America to hear live music. A three-block stretch through the Marigny has a few classy sit-down joints (dinner-music spots like Snug Harbor, The Maison, or Three Muses), but Frenchmen is best known for its loud and brassy music halls, where fiery jazz bands light up the crowds and everyone packs the dance floor. You'll also find groups playing on the street, with nearly as much talent on the sidewalks as there is on the stages.

SEE IT ! *Catch the Riverfront streetcar line south along Canal St or along the waterfront.*

174

Absorb combat history at the WWII Museum

LOUISIANA // If it weren't for Higgins boats, WWII might have ended very differently. These flat-bottomed amphibious landing craft, developed in the bayous near New Orleans, played a critical role moving Allied soldiers onto Normandy's beaches during the 1944 D-Day invasion. In recognition of this weighty contribution, NoLA was the natural choice to house the vast Smithsonian-affiliated National WWII Museum. Exhibits capture the battlefronts via film footage, photos, oral histories, and immersive experiences (such as aboard a submarine during an attack).

SEE IT ! *The St Charles Streetcar stops two blocks away.*

© Tallmaple / Shutterstock

175

Venture skyward on the trail up Pikes Peak

COLORADO // Even from a distance, this 14,115ft-high colossus exerts an irresistible pull. Snow-cloaked and framed by vivid evergreens, Pikes Peak is the easternmost of Colorado's Fourteeners (mountains that tower above 14,000ft). As you huff uphill, you think to yourself: 'I should have gone the easy way' – reaching the top via cog railway or driving the Pikes Peak Hwy (about a five-hour round-trip from Colorado Springs). Instead, you're one of the half-million hikers who embark on the lung-busting 13.5-mile Barr Trail to the summit each year. Even the great American explorer Zebulon Pike, for whom the mountain is named, never made it this far. But when author Katharine Lee Bates arrived at the top, she was inspired to write the original draft of *America the Beautiful*; gaze out at the mountainous panorama to understand why.

 SEE IT ! *Start walking before sunrise to ensure plenty of daylight for the descent.*

176

Cool off at Delaware Water Gap National Recreation Area

NEW JERSEY / PENNSYLVANIA // Protected since 1965, the Delaware Water Gap National Recreation Area's 109 sq miles flank the Delaware River and spread across the states of New Jersey and Pennsylvania.

The 100 miles of walking trails found here take the visitor into thick woodland, past spray-producing waterfalls and across meadows carpeted with rhododendrons. Christmas ferns grow to huge sizes, framing bike paths like the meandering McDade Recreational Trail. Whether you're hiking or biking, you should make time to stop at the swimmable beaches and leafy picnic spots along the way. There are numerous places to launch a canoe, too – allowing you to watch skittering salamanders and strutting water birds up close.

SEE IT ! *Go in summer or fall for great weather. Note that roads like Blue Mountain Lakes Rd and Skyline Dr close from January until the snow melts in spring.*

© Janine Kaufman / Shutterstock

© Photo Spirit / Shutterstock

Meander past marvellous masterworks at Washington, DC's National Gallery of Art.

177

View a world of masterpieces at the National Gallery of Art

WASHINGTON, DC // Two buildings. Hundreds of masterpieces. Infinite enjoyment. The only problem here is where to start. Grab a map from reception, plan your journey, and take your time. The Neoclassical West Building (a sight in itself) showcases European art through to the early 1900s: peruse works by da Vinci, Manet, Monet, and Van Gogh. The extraordinary IM Pei-designed East Building is worth visiting for the architectural thrill

alone – though exhibits are fabulous too. It displays modern and contemporary art: don't miss Pollock's *Number 1, 1950 (Lavender Mist)*; Picasso's *Family of Saltimbanques*; and the massive Calder mobile specially commissioned for the entrance lobby. An underground walkway connecting the buildings is made extraordinary by Leo Villareal's light sculpture, *Multiverse*.

You could easily spend a full day here,

especially as there are several in-house cafes. Consider joining one of the regular volunteer-led tours or taking advantage of the free 'Director's Tour' audioguide, which introduces the gallery's highlights. There's also a dedicated audioguide for kids.

☛ SEE IT ! *The National Gallery hosts both a film program and classical concerts (Sundays, fall through spring).*

© John Hoffman / Getty Images

© makasana photo / Shutterstock

178

Plunge into a marine paradise at SoCal's classic La Jolla Cove

CALIFORNIA // La Jolla has it all: palm trees, soft sand, and gentle waves. But its true treasures lie beneath the surface – this dainty San Diego cove is an ecological reserve teeming with marine life. With snorkel in place, enter a sapphire realm where bright orange Catalina goldfish flit past, sea stars lurk on the rocks, and forests of kelp sway gently; it's also a superb spot to see leopard sharks. Back on dry-ish land, the lifeguarded beach is popular with families and is great for swimming (though chillier than other San Diego beaches). Just north you can join a boat tour of seven wave-lashed caves, set within a 75-million-year-old sea cliff. But La Jolla isn't just a playground for humans: it's also frequented by harbor seals and sea lions. The 1930s-built children's pool is now a splash zone for these frolicking pinnipeds.

☞ TRY IT ! *The cove is off Coast Blvd. Keep your distance from the sea lions.*

179

Rocket down the natural waterslide at Sliding Rock Recreation Area

NORTH CAROLINA // Located in the Pisgah National Forest, Sliding Rock is a favorite summer playground. You'll wind up freezing and with a sore butt, but it's so worth it for the exhilarating whoosh down this 60ft natural waterslide. Some 11,000 gallons of (cold) water gush over a slick granite rockface every minute, as swimsuit-clad visitors hurtle down and into the (very cold) 8ft-deep pool at the bottom; wear shorts to spare your bottom the indignities of rock rash. The rock's open year-round, with lifeguards overseeing the fun daily from May to September (think twice about entering the water when they're not on duty). Combine it with a visit to the picturesque Looking Glass Falls, 2 miles down the road, where swimmers splash around in front of a 60ft bridal veil of a cascade.

☞ SEE IT ! *Sliding Rock is 7 miles off the Blue Ridge Parkway, outside the town of Brevard and 40 miles from Asheville.*

© James R. Martin / Shutterstock

© Stephen Moehle / Shutterstock

180

Sample good vibes at Ben & Jerry's Ice Cream Factory

VERMONT // If you've ever spooned Chunky Monkey greedily into your mouth, you'll want to tour the factory HQ of Ben & Jerry's. The feel-good ice cream brand, founded by Ben Cohen and Jerry Greenfield in 1978, now stirs up nearly one million pints per day. Surrounded by cow-filled pastures, the factory runs regular tours that give insights into Ben & Jerry's community-building efforts, while revealing a few recipe insights into signature flavors like Cherry Garcia and Phish Food. From a glassed-in room you can watch ice cream being made in mammoth quantities, before you finally get a little sample of the sweet stuff. You'll probably want to order something more substantial from the scoop shop before you tour the 'Flavor Graveyard' of now-retired ice creams.

SEE IT ! *The factory is at 1281 Waterbury-Stowe Rd, just north of I-89. Book ahead for the design-your-own Flavor Fanatic Experience.*

181

Hike through flower bedecked meadows on the Skyline Trail

WASHINGTON // Of Mt Rainier National Park's 260 miles of trail, the finest 5.5 are on the Skyline, navigating a loop between aptly named Paradise (5400ft) and rugged Panorama Point (6227ft), where snow can linger into July.

The terrain is a vivid mix of dwarf forest, brawny mountains, photogenic waterfalls, and impressionistic flower meadows, all at their best in August. Whistling marmots stand sentry on rocky outcrops, and heather, lilies, lupine, and cinquefoil add to an intense color palate.

On the trail's higher reaches, you can get a closer appreciation of the giant volcanic hump of Rainier and the ice-blue mass of the Nisqually Glacier (one of 25 on the mountain). The views south over the Tatoosh Range extend to Mt Adams and Oregon's Mt Hood.

SEE IT ! *The trail starts and finishes at Paradise, 18 miles west of Mt Rainier's Nisqually entrance and 2.5 hours by car from Seattle.*

© Jim McIsaac / Getty images

© Traveller70 / Shutterstock

182

Root, root, root for the home team at Yankee Stadium

NEW YORK // You can't sit in the original seats where fans once watched Joe DiMaggio or see the dugout where Lou Gehrig was photographed drinking a beer – this Yankee Stadium opened in 2009, replacing the 1920s original. But the new stadium tries to make up for the lack of history with amenities like ultra-luxe suites (for those willing to shell out $500 plus), bar areas, and a baseball-themed kids playspace. Its most important quality, though, is its home-run-friendliness: something about the park's design seemed to cause a sudden uptick in home runs. Whether you're a true-blue baseball fan or not, it's hard not to feel the *Take Me Out to the Ballgame* spirit while you're perched on the bleachers, hotdog in hand, the smell of freshly mown grass and spilled beer in your nose, the batter stepping up to home plate.

☛ SEE IT ! *The Yankees play April through October. Daily, hour-long stadium tours leave every 20 minutes or so.*

183

Summon your frontier spirit at South Pass City

WYOMING // The hardscrabble frontier is perfectly conserved at this ghost town where, during the late 19th century, a community of gold rush fortune-seekers established South Pass City. Today, well-preserved buildings show the spartan conditions of this erstwhile mining community. It's also a cornerstone of women's suffrage in the USA. South Pass City is where a woman named Esther Hobart Morris was appointed the town's Justice of the Peace. The assumption was that Morris would fail, making a mockery of the women's suffrage movement. But she rose to the occasion: she arrested her own violent husband, as well as the previous judge, and none of her rulings were ever overturned. You can see her cabin near the old Carissa Mine, and marvel at the grit that paved the way to equal rights in this lonely, arid place.

☛ SEE IT ! *Visits to South Pass City Historic Site are possible from May through September.*

184

Appreciate the Rockefeller's art and NYC atmosphere

NEW YORK // You know the NYC festive season has truly begun when they light the Christmas tree in front of Rockefeller Plaza, part of this 22-acre mixed-use complex built in Art Deco style during the Great Depression. It's now home to some of America's great public art: most iconic are Paul Manship's gilded *Prometheus*, above the lower plaza; and Lee Lawrie's globe-shouldering bronze *Atlas*, in front of the International Building. And don't miss the Top of the Rock observation deck, NBC Studio Tours, and the seasonal ice-skating rink.

☛ SEE IT ! *Rockefeller Center sprawls between 48th and 51st streets.*

185

Have a 1950s-style beach vacation on Anna Maria Island

FLORIDA // Don't expect the Spring Break wildness of the Panhandle or the see-and-be-seen vibe of Miami. This sleepy, sun-dazed barrier island is all about the slower pleasures. Rent a faded mid-century beach cottage and wake early to watch seabirds wheeling over the aquamarine waters. Spend a few hours reading on a blanket in the powdery sand, have a grouper sandwich at a local seafood shack, then stroll north to Bean Point for views over Tampa Bay. Evening's big excitement is a double-scoop ice cream cone and watching the sun set from the porch.

☛ SEE IT ! *The island's three communities are, south to north, Bradenton Beach, Holmes Beach, and Anna Maria village.*

186

Find inner peace at the Chapel of the Holy Cross

ARIZONA // Standing out in Sedona's Red Rock desert like an extension of the land itself is this extraordinary Roman Catholic chapel completed in 1956. Emulating Frank Lloyd Wright's architectural tendencies, the building employs a wall of glass to maximize the magnificent views, whilst the exterior walls and cross blend into their surrounds as naturally as the spectacular sandstone formations between which the building nestles. The spiritual healing spreads beyond the chapel – supposedly, there are energy vortexes out here radiating Earth's energy.

☛ SEE IT ! *The chapel is 4 miles south of Sedona; take Hwy 179 to Chapel, then Chapel Rd to the very end.*

© fdevalera / Getty Images

187

Sail around enormous icebergs at the Columbia Glacier

ALASKA // Spilling forth from the Chugach Mountains, the big daddy of all the glaciers in Prince William Sound is also one of the world's fastest moving ice torrents – though, like many Alaskan glaciers, the Columbia is rapidly retreating, having peeled back by an estimated 20 miles since 1980.

But even by Alaska's gigantic standards, the Columbia's statistics are impressive: it covers 400 sq miles and measures up to 1800ft at its greatest depth. Speed-wise, it's still the Usain Bolt of glaciers, covering a zippy 98ft a day, although in recent years it has shown signs of slowing. How close you can get to it depends on the Columbia's calving activity. Up to 13 million tonnes of ice can break off the face every day, discharging huge icebergs into the surrounding sea and causing potentially hazardous conditions.

☛ SEE IT ! *You'll need to book a day trip out of Valdez, either in a boat or on a kayaking excursion.*

© Joel Rogers / Getty Images

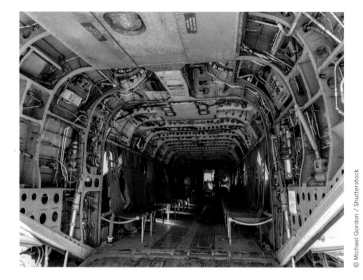

© Michael Gordon / Shutterstock

© Patrick Orton / Getty Images

188

Imagine galaxies far, far away at the US Space & Rocket Center

ALABAMA // Did you dream of being an astronaut as a child? There's still time to kind of make it happen: the US Space & Rocket Center has a G-Force simulator and even full training programs to test whether you have what it takes to explore outer space.

Opened to the public not long after the Apollo 12 Moon landing in 1969, this Smithsonian-affiliated museum has one of the largest collections of equipment covering space travel anywhere on earth. Among its 1500 cosmic items are spacesuits, entire rockets and engines, and capsules that astronauts trained in before they were launched into the stars. Start your kids early at the space-themed play areas, then take a walk through a replica of the International Space Station.

🖝 SEE IT ! *Find the center at One Tranquility Base, a 10-minute drive west of Huntsville.*

189

Thunder down Vail Mountain's snow-kissed trails high in the Rockies

COLORADO // Just the mention of Vail reduces snow-lovers to awed silence. The mountain is a world-leading winter sports paradise, and the third-largest single-mountain resort in the USA. Its 195 trails thread across 5317 skiable acres, accessed by more than 30 lifts. Board the high-speed gondola from Vail Village, followed by the Mountaintop Express, and you're soon tackling the resort's longest ski run, Riva Ridge, where you'll soar along 4 miles of uninterrupted piste, finding a hypnotic rhythm as you cruise between blue (easy) and black (advanced) sections of the trail. Timed your trip for summer instead? Gondola One is still your access point, but ski trails are now mountain-bike trails with glorious views: do look down.

🖝 SEE IT ! *Skiing doesn't come cheap, so consider an Epic Pass if you're coming for more than a long weekend as it'll give you access to resorts across the US and beyond.*

190

Dive into the inviting waters of Barton Springs Pool

TEXAS // Even during the hottest summer days in Texas, you'll find relief in the cool, sparkling waters of Barton Springs Pool. True to its name, this much-loved swimming spot is fed by natural springs and the water temperature always hovers around 68°F – ideal for year-round swimming in sunny Austin. The massive 900ft-long pool spreads across 3 acres, with a shallow end that's perfect for kids and an 18ft deep end with a diving board that sees plenty of cannonballing. Draped with century-old pecan trees, the grassy banks that descend down to the pool make a fine setting for a picnic and become a social scene in themselves, especially during the busy summer months. At other times, you'll have plenty of space to frolic in the water; you'll even see folks swimming laps in February.

SEE IT ! Barton Springs Pool lies at the heart of 350-acre Zilker Park in South Austin; you can also splash about in the scenic Barton Creek nearby.

191

Contemplate golden hour at James Turrell Twilight Epiphany Skyspace

TEXAS // Standing beneath a grass-covered mound, you gaze heavenward through a viewing hatch. LED lights bathe the 72-sq-ft aperture in color while the sky transitions from night to peachy dawn, or from daylight to the dusky lavender of approaching sunset.

Sound strange, or even spiritual? Artist James Turrell wanted to devise an installation to highlight how the earth rotates, while simultaneously creating a space for viewers to ponder our tiny place in the universe. Turrell completed this concrete, steel, and stone structure in 2012; ever since, visitors have arrived at dawn or dusk to admire how his light sequence frames the changing sky. It's a meditative experience – well worth setting your alarm for.

☛ SEE IT ! *Skyspace is free to visit, located on the campus of Rice University at the Suzanne Deal Booth Centennial Pavilion, with parking a short walk away. Arrive an hour before sunrise or 15 minutes before sunset.*

Now numbering almost 2000, the sea lion colony at San Fran's Pier 39 is here to stay.

192

Visit San Francisco's sea lion squatters at Pier 39

CALIFORNIA // If you think you've seen San Francisco's most ostentatious sunbathers at parks or Baker Beach, think again. The most attention-grabbing residents are the city's sea lions, who flap their flippers, bicker and bark from their colony on the docks of Pier 39.

It started with just a few rogue animals who arrived at the pier shortly after 1989's Loma Prieta earthquake. When more began hauling themselves out onto the docks, locals gave way to these protected mammals and, to the astonishment of residents in the Marina neighborhood, the sea lions just kept coming. Despite the sighs of yacht owners who had to give up their valuable slips, the Marine Mammal Center ruled that this was the sea lions' home now. These marine squatters have remained here ever since, and their numbers are now approaching 2000. The sea lions chose well: there's shelter from predators, rich food supplies from the bay, adoring fans who arrive to snap their picture – and it's one way to get around SF's notoriously high real estate market.

☛ SEE IT ! *After you've admired the colony, learn more about local marine life and conservation at the Sea Lion Center.*

193

Taste freedom at Independence Historical Park

PENNSYLVANIA // Dubbed 'America's most historic square mile', Independence Park is hallowed ground for patriots. The USA's founding history lives and breathes in this Philadelphia district. See the Liberty Bell, the famously cracked bronze emblem of American independence. Next, join one of the regular tours of Independence Hall (now a Unesco World Heritage Site), where the Declaration of Independence and US Constitution were debated and signed. Finally, take a break on a shaded lawn to watch costumed actors bring the history to life.

☛ SEE IT ! *The park extends between 6th & 2nd streets and Walnut & Arch streets. Head to the Independence Visitor Center for more info.*

194

Hear sweet sax at Minton's Playhouse, birthplace of bebop

NEW YORK // Let soulful sounds wash over you. Minton's Playhouse is one of the birthplaces of jazz, and to this day it hosts jazz-and-dinner nights to a smart, suited crowd. Founded by Henry Minton in 1938, it became an incubator for the distinctive sound of Harlem. It's the birthplace of bebop, a fast-tempo, improvisation-heavy flavor of jazz. Famous alumni include Duke Ellington, Louis Armstrong, Dizzy Gillespie, and Ella Fitzgerald. Contemporary talent captures the same spirit, and the 1940s-style dining room completes the lost-in-time ambience.

☛ SEE IT ! *Minton's is at 206 West 118th St. Browse events on their calendar and book well ahead for the dining experience.*

© Bob Pool / Shutterstock

195

Watch breaching whales from Lime Kiln Point State Park

WASHINGTON // Whale-watching usually requires a boat trip and a pricy ticket, but from a 41-acre state park on the rocky west coast of San Juan Island, you can view orcas, humpback, and gray whales as they breach in Haro Strait, the deep channel that separates the US from Canada. This is reputedly one of the best places in the world to whale-watch from the shoreline and the word is out. In peak season from May to September, the view areas are often packed with hopeful picnickers. To meet the demand, locals staff a small interpretive center containing displays on the lives and habits of the world's largest marine mammals.

Still preserved on the site is the park's original raison d'être, a restored lime kiln along with a handsome lighthouse built in 1919.

☛ SEE IT ! *From May to October, San Juan Transit shuttles visitors from the ferry landing in Friday Harbor to the park entrance.*

© Grindstone Media Group / Shutterstock

197

Get connected at the Museum of International Folk Art

NEW MEXICO // Florence Dibell Bartlett had a noble vision: to appeal to people's common sense of humanity by showcasing diverse cultures side by side. This wealthy donor's dream is realized at Santa Fe's Museum of International Folk Art. Barlett funded the original building and its 2500-item collection (still displayed in a wing named after her). That number has since grown to 130,000, including dioramas, masks, tapestries, tiles, and clothing – it's now the world's largest collection of folk art and an inspiring place to revel in the richness of human cultures.

☛ SEE IT ! *The museum is 2 miles south of downtown Santa Fe. Come in July for the International Folk Art Market.*

196

Speed like a demon at NASCAR Racing Experience

FLORIDA // Does watching a NASCAR driver screech around the circuit make you think, 'hey, I could do that'? If so, come on down to Daytona Beach. At the Daytona International Speedway (the Notre Dame of NASCAR), the NASCAR Racing Experience is an insider's peek into the South's second-favorite entertainment (after football). Nervous beginners might opt for three laps around the track in the passenger seat. But true speed enthusiasts can slip on a driver's suit and helmet and shell out for track time in 16-minute increments. Yes, passing slower drivers is allowed. If NASCAR is your passion and money's no object, the Advanced Experience is a day-long rush of adrenaline, with coaches by your side to help you achieve your fastest speeds. Built in 1959, the Speedway is home of the Daytona 500, NASCAR's biggest event.

☛ SEE IT ! *The Speedway is adjacent to Daytona International Airport in the eastern Florida city of Daytona Beach.*

198

Carve through fresh powder in the Aspen Highlands

COLORADO // Boarders and skiers thunder across 1000 acres of fluffy snow at this locally loved winter sports zone. The white stuff is abundant and light here, and more than 100 trails weave across a vertiginous ski area. The unrivalled highlight? The Highland Bowl, which has some of the best advanced skiing in the USA. Note that this high-altitude area is for powder-pros only, and you'll have to hike most of the way. Blue-sky views from the roof of the mountains are well worth the exertion – while the descent through virgin snow is unforgettable.

☛ TRY IT ! *A free snowcat can take you one-third of the way to the Highland Bowl's 12,392ft summit.*

The Library of Congress Great Hall is a suitably grand entrance to the home of some truly great (and small) books.

199

Immerse yourself in history and books at the Library of Congress

WASHINGTON, DC // The world's largest library awes in both scope, design and history. We're talking 838 miles of bookshelves with around 160 million items: 32 million books; 3.5 million recordings; 13.7 million photographs; 5.5 million maps; 6.7 million pieces of sheet music; and 61 million manuscripts. All in more than 470 languages. The collection's smallest publication is a 'book' of *Old King Cole* that is the size of the period at the end of this sentence. Visitors can't see the collections, but there's plenty to keep you entertained in the centerpiece, the 1897 Jefferson Building. Gaze at the Great Hall's stained glass, marble, and mosaics of mythical characters, then seek out the Gutenberg Bible (c.1455), the reading room viewing area, and Thomas Jefferson's actual round library, an important part of the institution's legacy (Jefferson sold his personal collection of 6487 books after the British had destroyed the Capitol – including the congressional library – in 1814).

The cafe on the sixth floor of the James Madison Memorial Building offers great views of the city.

☛ **SEE IT !** *Free tours of the Jefferson Building take place between 10.30am and 3.30pm on the half-hour.*

200—
299

200

Gulp golden nectar at Anchor Brewing Company

CALIFORNIA // In the dizzy heights of Potrero Hill, arguably San Francisco's prettiest (and most fog-free) neighborhood, you'll find one of the USA's oldest breweries inside a landmark building. Anchor has been pouring amber ale since 1896: you can inhale the hoppy tang on a guided tour among big copper vats, and sip a flight of Anchor beers at the end. Too educational? On the opposite side of Mariposa St is Anchor Public Taps, an industrial-style tasting room where you can mingle with locals, tropical IPA in hand.

🐖 SEE IT ! *Ride-shares or rental bikes are best for reaching Potrero Hill. Book ahead to join a 45-minute tour.*

201

Find spirits of the past in Terlingua Ghost Town

TEXAS // A 19th-century boomtown, Terlingua's mercury mines closed in the 1940s: the town dried up and blew away like a tumbleweed, its buildings falling into ruins. Since the 1980s, some of the old abodes have been reclaimed by guides, artists and others who relish the backcountry solitude. Amid the parched, mountain-backed scenery, vestiges of the old town remain, along with sparks of new life – like La Posada Milagro, a guesthouse made of repurposed abandoned buildings, and the once-derelict Starlight Theater, now a restaurant and live music joint.

🐖 SEE IT ! *Terlingua is just off the FM 170, about 35 miles west of Big Bend National Park and 83 miles south of the town of Alpine.*

202

Grab a fishing rod and road-trip the Gunnison River

COLORADO // Carving through western Colorado on its way to the San Juan Mountains, the Gunnison River is most spectacular where it reaches the Black Canyon. At 2000ft, this is one of the world's deepest gorges, the result of millions of years of erosion. Reservoirs have tamed the Gunnison to lower levels, but the landscape remains thrillingly dramatic: take the rim roads for a self-drive tour past fearsome black cliffs. Rent fishing gear, too: the area between Crystal Dam and Smith Fork is designated Gold Medal Water: pure, clear and teeming with trout.

🐖 SEE IT ! *Speak to the National Park Service about access to fishing spots via the steep, winding East Portal Rd.*

© AlexeyKamenskiy / Getty Images

203

Unwind in New York's less-famous but equally splendid Prospect Park

NEW YORK // Central Park has the name-recognition, but Brooklyn's Prospect Park is just as magical – perhaps even more so. It's a 526-acre urban arcadia of emerald meadows and sun-dappled woodland, all sprinkled with 19th-century ornamental bridges, pagodas, and picnic shelters, and edged by Brooklyn's only lake. The park's big sights are the zoo, the skating rink (a biking, skating and water-play area in summer), the Beaux Arts-style boathouse, and the bandshell. On Saturdays, half of Brooklyn seems to come out with their tote bags to buy kale and goat cheese at the Grand Army Plaza farmers market. The park's designer, the venerable Frederick Law Olmsted, envisioned it as a place where people of all classes could gather, relax, and refresh themselves. Today you can go pedal-boating on the lake, fire up one of the public barbecue grills, toss a frisbee on the Long Meadow, or ride the splendid 1912 carousel, complete with hand-carved horses.

☞ SEE IT ! *Many subway stops are convenient to the park's various entrances, including Grand Army Plaza and Prospect Park.*

© littleny / Getty images

Completed in 1849, Monticello is the only US home to be designated a Unesco World Heritage Site.

204

See both sides of Monticello, home of president and slave-owner Thomas Jefferson

VIRGINIA // The USA's third president spent 40 years building this sprawling plantation whose centerpiece is a meticulously symmetrical Neoclassical house inspired by the Italian architect Palladio. Visitors flock to marvel at Jefferson's ingenuity: he laid out the central hall for natural air-con; designed the Great

Clock in the entrance (driven by weights, it rings a Chinese gong on the hour); and devoted much of his garden to experiments with plant breeding. But Monticello is just as much about the enslaved people who built and worked the plantation, including Sally Hemings, with whom Jefferson had six children. The

Slavery at Monticello Tour illuminates the lives of generations of enslaved people, including a visit to Hemings' living quarters.

————————————

☛ SEE IT ! *Monticello is just outside the college town of Charlottesville at 931 Thomas Jefferson Pkwy.*

Showcasing the work
of some of the globe's
finest street artists,
Wynwood Walls is
public art perfected.

205

See an eye-popping array of street art on the Wynwood Walls

FLORIDA // Once a district of empty storefronts and derelict warehouses north of downtown Miami, Wynwood is now a vibrant showcase for America's best collection of street art. Since the project began in 2009, more than 50 artists from 16 countries have added their work to the Wynwood Walls, including renowned painters like Shepard Fairey (best known for his 'Hope' posters with Obama's portrait), OSGEMEOS (twin brothers from Brazil), French painter Invader, Japanese artist Lady Aiko and Portuguese Alexandre Farto (aka Vhils), who 'carves' rather than paints – at times even using a jack-hammer to create realistic portraits on concrete walls. Unlike in many gallery paintings, the street art contains a topical and political edge.

☛ SEE IT ! *There's street art all over Wynwood , though the epicenter is at NW 2nd Avenue, between 25th and 26th Streets.*

© Chie Inoue / Shutterstock

© Perry de Graaf / Getty Images

206

207

Help launch a career at the Apollo Theater

NEW YORK // The Apollo is an intrinsic part of Harlem history and culture. A leading space for concerts and political rallies since 1914, its venerable stage hosted virtually every major Black artist in the 1930s and '40s, including Duke Ellington and Billie Holiday. Decades later, the Apollo would help launch the careers of countless stars, from Diana Ross and Aretha Franklin to Michael Jackson and Lauryn Hill. More recently, Bruno Mars performed here for a televised special. Today, its thriving program of music, dance and special events continues to draw crowds and applause. The Apollo's most famous event is the long-running Amateur Night, which takes place on Wednesdays, February through November. The wild and ruthlessly judgmental crowd is as fun to watch as the performers.

🖝 SEE IT ! *The theater is on West 125th St, a few minutes' walk from the subway station of the same name.*

Socially distance in the Arctic National Wildlife Refuge

ALASKA // Beyond the bragging rights gained by visiting one of the most remote regions of the world, the Arctic National Wildlife Refuge lures the curious and brave with its boundless wilderness and surprisingly diverse wildlife. This 'Serengeti of the north' is home to dozens of land mammals, including grizzlies, musk ox, Dall's sheep and the second-largest herd of caribou in North America. Over 20 rivers cut through the region, several suitable for multiday paddles, and it's home to the four highest peaks of the Brooks Range. Cocooned in Alaska's northeast corner, the refuge has long been touted for its oil potential, though President Biden slapped a moratorium on drilling activity in 2021. Visiting is a challenge. There are no facilities of any kind and millions of mosquitoes will treat you as an acceptable source of food.

🖝 SEE IT ! *To get deep into the refuge, you'll need to charter a plane. Inquire at the Morris Thompson Visitor Center in Fairbanks.*

208

209

Feel the power of nature at Niagara Falls

NEW YORK // You get three mighty waterfalls in one at Niagara Falls, nature's most impressive watery display in North America. Two of the cascades, the American and the Bridal Veil, are entirely on the US side of the Niagara River, while the third, the Horseshoe, is mostly across the border in Ontario. The best views might be on the Canadian side, but to enjoy the full experience of this thundering spectacle you need to see it from both sides – something made pleasingly easy by the country-connecting, excellent-view-providing Rainbow Bridge.

🖝 SEE IT ! *The falls straddle the US-Canadian border just a few miles north of Buffalo, NY.*

Delight in Antelope Canyon's sublime swirls of rock

ARIZONA // This slot canyon resembles an exquisitely carved cathedral. Located on the Navajo Reservation, the upper and lower canyons are respectively nicknamed the Crack and the Corkscrew – which captures their shapes, if not their geological poetry. To Navajo people, the upper canyon is Tsé Bighánílíní, 'where water runs through rocks'. It's an accurate description: this sensuous sandstone was carved over time by the action of rain water. Colors are soft in winter and vivid in summer, when photographers clamor to capture shafts of high-noon light.

🖝 SEE IT ! *A few miles east of Page, the canyon is accessible by tour only. The best light is from April to September; it's quieter at other times.*

210

Delve into filmmaking lore at the MoMI

NEW YORK // Hollywood takes all the credit, but American movie-making actually started in Astoria, Queens in the 1920s. This would be a footnote in cinematic history were it not for the Museum of the Moving Image (MoMI), whose astonishing 130,000-piece collection is set in the very same complex where movies were once made. Galleries showcase historical curiosities, cutting-edge video art, and 19th-century optical toys, with interactive displays revealing the science behind the art. You can also catch an indie flick – there are over 400 screenings a year.

☛ SEE IT ! *Take the M/R subway line to 36th St Station.*

211

Kayak the secluded straits of Cedar Keys

FLORIDA // There's something about places reachable only by water that tickles the imagination. Rent a boat or slip into a kayak to reach Cedar Keys National Wildlife Reserve's 13 uninhabited islands – home to 250 bird species and 10 kinds of reptiles – and enter a steamy, much older-feeling Florida. Highlights include Seahorse Key's whitewashed 1854 lighthouse, where Seminole prisoners were held before being sent west along the Trail of Tears; and the eerie, Spanish-moss-shrouded 19th-century Atsena Otie cemetery. Sunscreen and bug spray are essential.

☛ SEE IT ! *Access the refuge via Cedar Kay, connected to the mainland by causeway, where you can rent boats.*

212

Experience the power of design at CAC

ILLINOIS // Design influences how we feel and how we behave, and the mission of the Chicago Architecture Museum (CAC) is to unpack this hidden power. Exhibits lead visitors through architectural history: pore over the city's skyline with the help of a 3-D model, and learn about the technology that brought it into being. The center also unlocks cultural histories around Chicago via guided experiences: Art Deco-themed walking tours or architecture cruises. Bonus: there's an excellent shop selling coffee-table books and Chicago hot-dog ornaments.

☛ SEE IT ! *This colossal gallery is at 111 East Wacker Dr. The nearest CTA station is Millennium.*

© Tom Harris / Courtesy of the CAC

213

Learn a thing or two at Harvard University

MASSACHUSETTS // America's oldest university was nearly 150 by the time the US became a country, and boy is it still proud of its heritage. Harvard offers visitors a glimpse into its history- and prestige-steeped campus with free tours around the historic red-brick buildings of Harvard Yard. Rub the foot of the John Harvard statue for luck, but beware: undergrads pee on the statue as a graduation rite.

The university has several excellent museum collections. Top of the list are the freakily realistic hand-blown glass flowers at the Harvard Museum of Natural History, and the extensive exhibits on Native American culture at the Peabody Museum of Archaeology and Ethnology. Just outside campus is Harvard Square, where street musicians perform and punk-rock teens still gather, despite decades of gentrification.

☛ SEE IT ! *Harvard is in Cambridge, across the river from Boston. Take the Red Line T to Harvard station.*

© Roman Babakin / Shutterstock

214

Be roused to battle inequality at the National Memorial for Peace and Justice

ALABAMA // Sorrow and strength emanate from this sobering monument in Montgomery. Its 800 steel slabs are shaped like coffins, one for every county where a racial terror lynching took place. Each is etched with the names of the victims and the date of their murder.

Research by the Equal Justice Initiative revealed hundreds of undocumented lynchings in the American South, and this thought-provoking memorial, the first of its kind in the USA, honors the 4400 lives brutally stolen.

Other monuments around this 6-acre site commemorate activists who challenged racial hatred and division, like Dana King's sculpture of the women of the Montgomery bus boycott. As you walk around, contemplate stirring words from Toni Morrison and Martin Luther King Jr inscribed into black marble – and realize how the fight for justice goes on.

☛ **SEE IT !** *It's a 15-minute walk from Montgomery's Legacy Museum to the memorial.*

FOR THE HANGED AND BEATEN.
FOR THE SHOT, DROWNED, AND BURNED.
FOR THE TORTURED, TORMENTED, AND TERRORIZED.
FOR THOSE ABANDONED BY THE RULE OF LAW.

WE WILL REMEMBER.

WITH HOPE BECAUSE HOPELESSNESS IS THE ENEMY OF JUSTICE.
WITH COURAGE BECAUSE PEACE REQUIRES BRAVERY.
WITH PERSISTENCE BECAUSE JUSTICE IS A CONSTANT STRUGGLE.
WITH FAITH BECAUSE WE SHALL OVERCOME.

Take sober stock of past injustice – and the battles to come – at the National Memorial for Peace and Justice.

Buckle up and fly through the air on Hagrid's Magical Creatures Motorbike Adventure – Nimbus 2000 not required.

215

Cast a spell at the Wizarding World of Harry Potter

FLORIDA // Nowhere in the world is more magical than the extraordinary Wizarding World of Harry Potter. It's so authentic that in one sense it leaves little to the imagination. Alan Gilmore and Stuart Craig, art director and production designer for the films, collaborated closely with the Universal Orlando Resort engineers to create what is without exception the most fantastically realized themed experience in Florida. The details tickle the fancy at every turn, from the screeches of the mandrakes in the shop windows to the groans of Moaning Myrtle in the restrooms. Poke along the cobbled streets and impossibly crooked buildings of Hogsmeade, sip frothy Butterbeer, munch on Cauldron Cakes and mail a card via Owl Post, all in the shadow of Hogwarts Castle, while keeping your eyes peeled for magical happenings. The Wizarding World of Harry Potter is divided into two sections, each with rides and shows: Hogsmeade sits in Islands of Adventure (and includes Hagrid's Magical Creatures Motorbike Adventure, where visitors buckle in and 'fly' through the Forbidden Forest); Diagon Alley is in Universal Studios.

☛ SEE IT ! *Get a park-to-park ticket to hop on the wonderful Hogwarts Express from one section to the other. But first find Platform 9¾!*

216

Fathom immigrant experiences at the Tenement Museum

NEW YORK // If you were a Jewish immigrant coming from Russia in 1890 or an Italian in 1905 or a Dominican in 1963 or a Chinese immigrant from Fujian in 1997, chances were high you ended up – at least for a while – on the Lower East Side. Life was hard and often heartbreaking, with no running water, poor ventilation, and cramped conditions, and the Tenement Museum aims to preserve and share the experience of these immigrants, with tours of two preserved 19th-century tenement buildings.

☞ SEE IT ! *The Lower East Side Tenement Museum is at 103 Orchard St and is open for tours only; book ahead online.*

217

Look for gunslingers' ghosts at the Old Tucson Studios

ARIZONA // Nicknamed 'Hollywood in the Desert,' the Old Tucson Studios date back to 1939 when Columbia Pictures built an 1860s replica of a Wild West town. Workers erected more than 50 buildings – including a bank, saloon, jail, ranch house and other essential backdrops – which were featured in *Gunfight at the OK Corral*, *Little House on the Prairie* and hundreds of other movies and TV series. It was later transformed into a Wild West theme park, complete with staged shoot-outs, thundering stagecoach rides, stunt shows, and dancing saloon girls.

☞ SEE IT ! *It's a 13-mile drive west of Tucson along the scenic West Gates Pass Rd to reach Old Tucson Studios.*

218

See primeval Appalachian views at Linville Falls

NORTH CAROLINA // Gazing out over the thundering Linville Falls from a rocky overlook along the Erwins View Trail is like peering back through the centuries. An old-growth forest of eastern hemlocks, white pine and Carolina rhododendron frame the Linville River as it plunges in three tiers over the steep-walled Linville Gorge – sometimes called 'the Grand Canyon of the Southern Appalachians.' Only trails provide access to these dramatic cascades, along a twisting, curving waterway aptly called 'the river of cliffs' by the Cherokee.

☞ SEE IT ! *Stop at mile marker 316 on the Blue Ridge Parkway; the Erwins View is one of several trails to access the Linville Falls.*

© Kris Davidson / Lonely Planet

The road less traveled in Antelope Island State Park: plenty of bison and pronghorns.

219

Roam with the bison on Antelope Island State Park

UTAH // Bighorn sheep, coyotes, and bobcats roam the prairie grass on this island in the middle of the Great Salt Lake, but the stars of the show are the majestic lumbering bison. The 600 here make up one of America's biggest publicly owned herds; they were brought to the area in the late 1800s and originally used for hunting. Each October they're rounded up for veterinary exams – which makes for quite a spectacle. Their home, the largest of the 10 islands in the lake, is a magnet for hikers, cyclists, and nature photographers. It has 19 miles of hiking trails, an 8-mile scenic driving loop, and a blindingly white beach at Bridger Bay. The lake's high salt content makes it similar to the Dead Sea – jump in and bob around like an empty bottle, then dry off in the sun and watch a silvery rime of salt appear on your skin. Stop off at Fielding Garr Ranch, built in the late 1840s by early Mormon pioneers and allegedly haunted by the ghost of a grave robber exiled here in the 1860s. The island's an official International Dark Sky Park – at night the Milky Way looks close enough to touch. Pitch a tent for leisurely stargazing.

☛ SEE IT ! *Antelope Island is 42 miles northwest of Salt Lake City. There are three rustic campgrounds for overnighters.*

220

Soak up the sunny glamour of South Beach

FLORIDA // 'SoBe' is the South Florida of your reality-TV dreams. Retro architecture is a backdrop to the beautiful and gym-built, who sun themselves on its white sands, dine on sushi in its celebrity-chef restaurants, and drink caipirinhas in its nightclubs. The historic district has the world's largest collection of Art Deco architecture – stroll Ocean Drive to gawk at pastel buildings in styles like Streamline Moderne. For a true SoBe experience, spend the night in Gianni Versace's mansion, the Villa Casa Casuarina, now a luxury hotel.

☛ SEE IT ! *SoBe is on a barrier island connected by causeways to Miami.*

221

Watch giant bears feast at Brooks Falls

ALASKA // Every year in early summer, hundreds of brown bears emerge from hibernation and make their hungry way to Brooks Falls, a small but iconic waterfall in Katmai National Park, to feast on thousands of salmon which also embark on a journey at this time of year, making their way up Brooks River to spawn in Brooks Lake. The consequence of this natural coincidence is quite a sight to behold – formidable 1000lb brown bears pawing giant salmon straight out of the river, some even catching the jumping fish clean in their jaws.

An outdoor deck next to the falls gets you spine-tinglingly close to these massive animals. At the peak of the salmon run, there might be eight to 12 bears here, two or three of them wading atop the falls themselves.

☞ SEE IT ! *You can fly with Alaska Airlines from Anchorage to King Salmon, from where air-taxis offer the 20-minute floatplane flight out to Brooks Camp.*

Enjoy a Zen moment amid the maple trees, tinkling waterfalls, and koi-filled ponds of Portland Japanese Garden.

222

Seek serenity in Portland Japanese Garden

OREGON // Wandering this 12-acre refuge of koi ponds, rock gardens, and meticulously tended moss, ferns, maples, and flowering shrubs, you might think you're in Kyoto. Designed by Osaka-born professor of landscape architecture Takuma Tono in the mid-1960s, it's considered one of the most authentic Japanese gardens outside Japan.

Stroll the paths and bridges, admiring the carefully asymmetric design and stopping for pictures at the iconic Heavenly Falls. Then visit the teahouse, made in Japan and reassembled here by artisans, before meandering through the mossy woods to the Cultural Village for Japanese performances and traditional arts demos. In late March, Portlanders flock to see

the cherry blossoms bloom a delicate and ephemeral pink. The gardens are built into a hillside in Washington Park, with its rose garden, amphitheater, and zoo.

☛ SEE IT ! *Washington Park is accessible by MAX train or TriMet bus 63; there's a free summer park shuttle to the gardens.*

223

Walk in the footsteps of freedom fighter Harriet Tubman

MARYLAND // Born enslaved in Maryland's Dorchester County, Harriet Tubman fled north aged 27. But rather than live out her days in quiet freedom, she returned over a dozen times to rescue some 70 family members and other fugitive escapees. The Harriet Tubman Underground Railroad National Historical Park brings her story to life via 36 sites, explorable on a self-guided driving tour. Highlights include her childhood home, Brodess Farm; and Mount Pleasant Cemetery, where Harriet met with others to plan escapes on the Underground Railroad.

☛ SEE IT ! *Start your historical journey perusing multimedia exhibits at the visitor center, off Route 16 in Church Creek.*

224

Play Robinson Crusoe at Cayo Costa State Park

FLORIDA // It's easy to leave the modern world behind at Cayo Costa State Park, a 2500-acre island of beaches, dunes, and wind-carved woodlands that lies an hour's boat ride from Florida's Southwest Gulf Coast. You can look for turtle tracks along the 9 miles of powdery shoreline (four sea turtle species nest on the island), kayak the mangroves in search of snowy egrets and manatees, or simply bask in the idyllic solitude after exploring the island trails. Extend your stay by overnighting at the campground (simple cabins also available).

☛ SEE IT ! *Captiva Cruises offers ferry service to the park from Punta Gorda, Pine Island, Fort Myers, Sanibel Island, and Captiva Island.*

225

Revel in contemporary views at the Whitney

NEW YORK // Since reopening in 2015, the Whitney Museum of American Art has done nothing but delight – and create discussion – among the hordes who head here. Anchoring the High Line's southern reaches, the stunning Renzo Piano-designed building provides 63,000 sq ft of space for an unparalleled collection of US art. The light-filled galleries display works by all the modern greats: Edward Hopper, Jasper Johns, Georgia O'Keeffe, Mark Rothko. In addition to rotating exhibits on American art luminaries, the Whitney Biennial is held in odd-numbered years.

☛ SEE IT ! *The Whitney is in Manhattan's Meatpacking District and overlooks the High Line.*

© Ed Lederman / courtesy of the Whitney Museum of American Art

© FiledIMAGE / Shutterstock

© cindylindowphotography / Shutterstock

226

Read until you drop at The Last Bookstore

CALIFORNIA // Housed in an echoing old bank building with shelves of new and used books arranged higgledy-piggledy against towering columns, SoCal's biggest bookstore feels like the set for a steampunk fantasy film, where you can browse titles deliberately left un-alphabetized to encourage lucking into your new favorite thriller or memoir. Bibliophiles spend happy hours wandering this two-level space with a coffee shop, a stage for bands, a 'book tunnel' (exactly what it sounds like), sculptures fashioned from paperbacks, a record store, nooks of mismatched couches, a graphic-novel alcove called 'Dungeon Dungeon,' gallery rooms and more. Though it may not actually be LA's last bookstore, it's certainly one of the few thriving indie booksellers in the country, thanks to its cheeky, welcoming vibe and crazy-good prices.

☛ SEE IT ! *The bookstore is in downtown LA on South Spring St.*

227

Ponder past injustice at the Salem Witch Trials Memorial

MASSACHUSETTS // When most people hear the word 'Salem', they immediately think of witches. In 1692, nearly 200 people in the town were accused of witchcraft, and 20 were tried and executed, most by hanging – tragic victims of fear and superstition. Though simple in design, the Salem Witch Trials Memorial makes a poignant setting in which to contemplate the terrible dangers posed by lies and hysteria. In a small park next to an old burial ground and backed by a low stone wall, 20 granite benches lie shaded beneath locust trees. Each bench is inscribed with the name of a victim – 14 women and six men – along with the date and method of their execution. Holocaust survivor and Nobel Laureate Elie Wiesel dedicated the memorial on the 300th anniversary of the trials.

☛ SEE IT ! *The Rockport/Newburyport train line runs at least hourly from Boston's North Station to Salem Depot, 30 min.*

From ocean life to meteorites, the American Museum of Natural History covers so much more than just giant dinos.

228

Discover a T. rex at the American Museum of Natural History

NEW YORK // Founded in 1869, this hugely popular museum contains a veritable wonderland of over 34 million artifacts. Its large and airy Fossil Halls showcase nearly 600 specimens, including crowd-pleasers such as an apatosaurus, titanosaurus, and fearsome Tyrannosaurus rex. For the astronomical enthusiast, the cutting-edge Rose Center for Earth and Space is the, er, star of the show. From October through May, the museum is home to the Butterfly Conservatory, a vivarium holding a fluttering 500-plus butterflies from all over the world. There are also plentiful animal exhibits (the stuffed Alaskan brown bears and giant moose are popular), galleries devoted to gems and minerals, and an IMAX theater. The Milstein Hall of Ocean Life contains dioramas exploring marine ecologies, weather, and conservation, as well as a beloved replica of a blue whale suspended from the ceiling. Similarly aloft is a 63ft-long canoe that was carved in the 1870s and which features designs from different Native American peoples of the Pacific Northwest. And don't miss the astonishing Willamette Meteorite, a 15.5-ton hunk of metallic iron that fell to earth in present-day Oregon thousands of years ago. A massive museum expansion, the Richard Gilder Center for Science, Education and Innovation, was slated for opening in 2022.

☛ SEE IT ! *The AMNH sits next to 81st St station, west across Central Park from its artistic sibling, the Met.*

© YinYang / Getty Images

© Jeff Whyte / Shutterstock

229

230

Wonder at the mystery of Chaco Culture National Historical Park

Gape at mountains and deserts aboard the Palm Springs Aerial Tramway

NEW MEXICO // Deep in the arid Colorado Plateau lies one of America's most impressive ruins. In the 9th century CE, Ancestral Puebloans began building miles of roads and huge ceremonial 'great houses' – complexes including hundreds of rooms and circular underground chambers called *kivas* – as well as amassing hoards of turquoise, shell jewelry and ceramics. But in the 13th century, they stopped coming. No one knows why. The site's remoteness means you can wander the ruins largely alone, hiking sandstone cliffs and exploring far-flung petroglyphs.

CALIFORNIA // In just ten minutes, you can go from scorching desert heat to chilly alpine heights, where temperatures are up to 40°F cooler. Going strong since 1963, the Palm Springs Aerial Tramway takes riders on just such a dramatic, rotating 2.5-mile ascent that passes through five vegetation zones, from dusty Sonoran valley floor to pine-scented Mt San Jacinto State Park. Once at the 8516ft-high mountain station, you can hike to your heart's content along 50 miles of trails, or enjoy a first-rate meal with a view at one of several restaurants.

☞ SEE IT ! *The park's in far northwest New Mexico. Follow the NPS' careful directions to avoid getting lost on the dirt roads.*

☞ SEE IT ! *Palm Springs is roughly 100 miles west of Los Angeles. Buy tickets online well ahead of time.*

Mars? No, it's Hunt's Mesa in otherwordly Monument Valley.

231

Explore red-rock landscapes with a Native American guide in Monument Valley

ARIZONA // A famous Diné (Navajo) poem ends with the phrase 'May I walk in beauty.' This wish is easily granted at the Monument Valley Navajo Tribal Park in northeastern Arizona. After crossing many miles of barren landscape, you're suddenly transported to a fantasyland of brick-red spindles, sheer-walled mesas, and grand buttes – the park's iconic sandstone towers thrusting up to 1200ft skyward. Long before the land became part of the Navajo Reservation, the valley was home to Ancestral Puebloans who migrated from the site some 700 years ago. When the Navajo arrived a few centuries later, they called it 'Valley Between the Rocks.'

The most famous formations are conveniently visible from the rough 15-mile dirt road looping through Monument Valley Navajo Tribal Park. But for a deeper experience, you can head into the backcountry with a Navajo-led tour on foot, horseback, or by vehicle. You'll see rock art, natural arches and coves such as the otherworldly Ear of the Wind, a bowl-shaped wall with a nearly circular opening at the top.

☞ SEE IT ! *Monument Valley straddles the Arizona-Utah border, just off Hwy 163. Guided tours depart from the visitor center on Monument Valley Rd.*

© Khairil Azhar Junos / Shutterstock / 'Returning the Chains' — A sculpture at the Whitney Plantation

© 400tmax / Getty Images

232

Learn about the lives of enslaved people at Whitney Plantation

LOUISIANA // America's South is home to dozens of historic plantations, though only one focuses exclusively on the lives of enslaved people. The Whitney Plantation flips the script on the typical antebellum home tour, focusing not on the 'big house,' but on the many Black people who lived and died in bondage. The tour starts in the tiny Antioch Baptist Church, which was built by freed African Americans and contains 40 realistic casts of enslaved children spread among the church pews. Afterwards, visitors see the cabins in which the enslaved lived, a rusting jail, and the sunbaked sugarcane fields where so many toiled under the whip. Powerful memorials personalize the staggering human toll, including a sculpture of a Black angel embracing a dead infant amid the names of 2200 enslaved children who perished between the 1820s and the 1860s.

☛ SEE IT ! *The Whitney Plantation is 45 miles west of New Orleans.*

233

Discover the source of Texan pride at the Alamo

TEXAS // For proud Texans, the much-fabled Alamo, in the heart of downtown San Antonio, is not so much a tourist attraction as a place of pilgrimage. Inside a fortified frontier post, a few hundred Texas freedom fighters battled and died defending the site from thousands of Mexican troops. The 1836 sortie, against overwhelming odds – led by the likes of Davy Crockett, William Travis, and James Bowie – still stirs the feisty independent spirit of locals and underdog-lovers alike.

Built as a mission church by the Spanish in the 1750s, the main building is now known as the Shrine. Beyond that, various exhibition areas tell the story of the 13-day siege, while staff give walking tours and absorbing historical overviews.

☛ SEE IT ! *The Alamo is at the center of San Antonio. It's just two blocks to restaurant-lined River Walk, the city's other famed attraction.*

© Victoria Ditkovsky / Shutterstock

© Stephan Schlachter / Shutterstock

Win an emperor's ransom at a Caesars Palace baccarat table

NEVADA // Ancient Rome gets the Las Vegas fantasyland treatment, via 1960s Hollywood, at the legendary Caesars Palace. Replicas of Roman sculptures adorn the corridors, gaming rooms, and outdoor areas – there's even a full-size copy of Michelangelo's *David* made of Carrara marble. The luxurious trappings make a fine backdrop to win (or lose) some serious cash at one of 185 gaming tables, followed perhaps by a visit to the high-end boutiques of the Forum Shops. Nearby, the Colosseum is a high-tech version of ancient Rome's famous arena (without the gladiator fights). Frank Sinatra was a regular performer back in the '60s and '70s, while these days big-name stars from Sting to Usher take the stage. Out front are the spritzing fountains that motorcycle daredevil Evel Knievel made famous during an ill-fated leap across their 141-feet span in 1967.

☛ SEE IT ! *The casino is on the west side of The Strip (Las Vegas Blvd).*

Enjoy kaleidoscopic folk art at Philly's Magic Gardens

PENNSYLVANIA // Artist Isaiah Zagar has dedicated much of his life's work to the creation of enchanting mosaic-filled murals around his longtime neighborhood in South Philly. Zagar's work adorns over 200 buildings, though his greatest masterpiece is Philadelphia's Magic Gardens, a folk-art fantasia of murals made from mirror and ceramic shards, bottles, and found objects such as bicycle wheels and urinals. A community-led effort to preserve Zagar's artwork kicked off in 2002 when the property's owners threatened to destroy it. The non-profit Philadelphia's Magic Gardens was created, allowing Zagar to continue with a project that now extends over practically every inch of the neighboring building and its basement (only visitable on a tour). Inside, you'll also find a gallery showing work by other mosaic- and folk-artists.

☛ SEE IT ! *Some 15 minutes' walk southwest of Independence National Historical Park, the Magic Gardens offer weekend walking tours.*

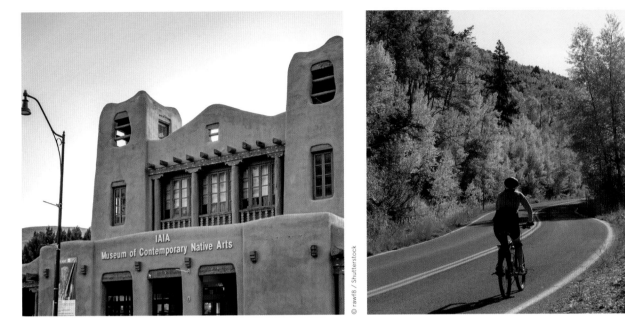

© rawf8 / Shutterstock

© AspenGal / Lonely Planet

236

Discover rising Native talents at Santa Fe's MoCNA

NEW MEXICO // In the heart of downtown Santa Fe, the Museum of Contemporary Native Arts stages extraordinary exhibitions by top native artists from all across the US. Wide-ranging, cutting-edge installations dispel any stereotypes about the limits of Native American art, and MoCNA doesn't shy away from challenging topics: shows have explored the murder of indigenous girls and women, dystopic futures of native peoples, and indigenous resistance, alongside ambitious retrospectives of celebrated artists like Rick Bartow, Linda Lomahaftewa, and Dan Lomahaftewa. Outside, browse the powerful sculptures of the Chiricahua Apache artist Allan Houser. The permanent collection contains some 9000 pieces representing hundreds of tribes, making it the planet's largest repository of contemporary Native American art.

🖝 SEE IT ! *Exhibitions aside, the museum hosts film screenings, craft workshops, gallery talks, and other happenings.*

237

Gape at grand peaks on a Continental Divide drive

COLORADO // Scenic drives are a dime a dozen in the Colorado Rockies, but few can compete with the dramatic vistas afforded at nearly every hairpin turn on the road up to Independence Pass. Setting out from Aspen, you'll ascend over 4000ft on the 18-mile drive, passing the remains of Independence, a 19th-century gold-mining boom settlement turned ghost town. Once you reach Independence Pass, you can loosen your white-knuckle grip on the steering wheel and take a short walk out to a lofty viewpoint plunked at 12,095ft. There your eye can wander across the harsh, windblown wilds out to a horizon packed with the chiseled peaks of the Sawatch Range. For more winding road adventures, continue your journey over the Continental Divide to the pretty, aptly named town of Twin Lakes, some 17 miles on.

🖝 SEE IT ! *Reach Independence Pass along Hwy 82, which is generally open from late May to early November.*

238

Sing along at the thigh-slapping Grand Ole Opry

TENNESSEE // The modern brick building amid the suburban sprawl of Nashville's Music Valley doesn't look like much, but it's home to one of the most storied parts of country music history. The Grand Ole Opry, a country music stage show, began in 1925 as a radio program. After a long stint at downtown's Ryman Auditorium, it moved here in the 1970s. Catch a delightfully corny performance, with bluegrass banjos, romantic duets, comedy skits, and more. Everyone who's anyone has played here, from Johnny Cash to Emmylou Harris to Garth Brooks to Taylor Swift.

☛ SEE IT ! *Shows are Tuesday, Friday and Saturday, plus Wednesday in summer. In winter the Opry moves to the Ryman Auditorium.*

239

Encounter big bones at Waco Mammoth National Monument

TEXAS // This excavation site offers a fascinating a window into Ice Age history. Regular tours lead you along a woodland trail to an atrium where the bones of Pleistocene mammoths protrude from the soil. From a raised platform, you can see the huge skulls and curving tusks of a herd of these extinct giants, thought to have drowned in a flood some 68,000 years ago. Seeing their tremendous remains, it's easy to picture herds of these shaggy mammals stampeding across the plains of Texas.

☛ SEE IT ! *This protected site lies roughly halfway between Dallas and Austin; a great way to break up a long drive.*

240

Hear the wail of electric guitars at Buddy Guy's Legends

ILLINOIS // Though born in July, the great bluesman Buddy Guy likes to think of September 25 as a kind of second birthday. On that day, in 1957, he left his native Louisiana and took a train to Chicago. There he found fame, and his powerful style of guitar playing became synonymous with the Chicago blues scene. He also opened Buddy Guy's Legends, doing his part to keep the blues alive as he'd promised Muddy Waters before Waters' death in 1983. At Legends, you can hear top blues artists from across the country – as well as the legend himself if he's not out touring.

☛ SEE IT ! *Performances happen nightly at Buddy Guy's Legends in the Loop.*

© George Silk / Getty Images

© fdastudillo / Getty Images

241

Be greatly inspired by the Muhammad Ali Center

KENTUCKY // The heavyweight boxer known as 'the Louisville Lip' was one of Kentucky's favorite sons, and this interactive museum traces his historic career and epic life. Born Cassius Clay in Louisville in 1942, Ali began training in local gyms aged 12. After converting to Islam, he refused to fight in the Vietnam War and was convicted of draft evasion, losing years of his career for his beliefs. The museum is centered around these beliefs – the 'six core principles' that shaped Ali's life: confidence; conviction; dedication; giving; respect; spirituality. Step into the ring and shadowbox with Ali, watch videos of his famous fights, learn about his opposition to the Vietnam War and his commitment to the Civil Rights Movement, and share your own story in the recording booths.

 SEE IT ! *The museum is in downtown Louisville, connected to other attractions by a pedestrian bridge.*

242

Peer back in time at the Oregon Caves National Monument

OREGON // As you watch the candlelight dance on the cavern walls and scan the glittering stalactites shimmering overhead, it's easy to imagine you've slipped back into the 19th century – the year 1874, to be more precise. That's when a hunter named Elijah Davidson chased a bear into a shadowy opening hidden beneath the Siskiyou Mountains, and became the first documented person to lay eyes on an extraordinary cave system formed of marble. Candlelight tours take you back to the cave's earliest discovery, then wind the clock back another million or so years to the formation of this rare geological wonder. Over many millennia, acidified groundwater seeped through cracks to carve underground channels and create myriad formations, such as cave popcorn, pearls, moonmilk, classic pipe organs, columns, and stalactites.

☛ SEE IT ! *The caves are off Hwy 46 in southern Oregon; reserve ahead for one-hour candlelight tours, which are offered once per day.*

© ferrantraite / Getty Images

© Galyna Andrushko / Shutterstock

243

244

Catch a world-class performance at the Lincoln Center

Gen up on geology at Grand Staircase-Escalante National Monument

NEW YORK // The stark Modernist temples of this 16-acre complex house some of Manhattan's most important artistic companies (the New York Philharmonic; the New York City Ballet; the Metropolitan Opera), as well as a theater, two film-screening centers and the Juilliard School for performing arts. Built in the 1960s, the campus replaced the San Juan Hill tenement neighborhood (gleefully bulldozed by 'master builder' Robert Moses) – a predominantly African American area where exterior shots for the movie *West Side Story* were filmed. In addition to being a controversial urban planning move, Lincoln Center was relentlessly criticized for its conservative design, fortress-like aspect and poor acoustics. For its 50th anniversary, Diller Scofidio + Renfro and other architects gave the complex a critically acclaimed freshening up.

UTAH // Prettier than the backdrop to any Western movie, the Grand Staircase-Escalante National Monument has towering sandstone cliffs, dramatic slot canyons and hidden waterfalls. Incredibly remote, this vast wilderness never draws crowds. In fact, it was the last place in the contiguous United States to be mapped. The first half of its unusual name refers to the 150-mile-long geological strata that begin at the bottom of the Grand Canyon and rise, in stair steps, 3500ft to Bryce Canyon and Escalante River Canyon. The striped layers of rock reveal 260 million years of history. There are fabulous scenic drives past lunar-like landscapes, and rewarding hiking trails that take in serpentine canyons, desert wildflowers and shimmering pools that will feel like a mirage after tramping through the parched landscape.

🐛 SEE IT ! *Daily 75-minute tours explore the Metropolitan Opera House, Revson Fountain, Alice Tully Hall and more.*

🐛 SEE IT ! *The park HQ is in Kanab, off Hwy 89. High-clearance 4WD vehicles allow you the most access, since many roads are unpaved.*

Dive into the Underwater Museum of Art

FLORIDA // Visiting most museums is simply a matter of showing up and paying the admission price. Not so at the Underwater Museum of Art, located in 58ft of water off the Florida panhandle. You'll have to be a certified Open Water Diver and hire an operator to reach the site, but once there, you'll enter an enchanting seascape, with over two dozen oversized sculptures dotting the sandy sea bed. The project, launched in 2018, marries art with conservation, as the works will eventually create an artificial reef and marine habitat.

☛ SEE IT ! *The dive site is a mile offshore from Grayton Beach State Park. Emerald Coast Scuba runs dive trips.*

Feast your way around Chinatown in Queens

NEW YORK // Dwarfing its counterpart in Manhattan, the vast Chinatown in Queens is the best place in New York for anyone in search of authentic, rare and deliciously affordable Asian food. The intersection of Main St and Roosevelt Ave in downtown Flushing is the heart of the neighborhood, with nearby markets and restaurants bursting with exotic fare. A good place to start is the New World Shopping Center, with a magnificent food court on the lower level. Aside from culinary curiosities from China, you'll also find Korean, Thai and Vietnamese dishes. Don't miss the hand-pulled noodles served at Lan Zhou Noodles.

☛ EAT IT ! *Take the 7 subway line to Flushing Main St.*

Take in the sea views at Portland Head Light

MAINE // Grab a paintbrush, a yoga mat or a canine companion and make your way to the dramatically set Portland Head Light. The oldest of Maine's 52 functioning lighthouses (commissioned by President George Washington in 1791) overlooks a rocky headland fronting island-dotted Casco Bay, and makes a fine backdrop to sun salutations, seascape painting or just strolling the cliffside paths. The surrounding Fort Williams Park hides ruins of a late-19th-century fort, along with WWII bunkers and gun emplacements that still dot the rolling lawns.

☛ SEE IT ! *The lighthouse is a 5-mile drive (around $20 by taxi or ride share) from Portland. Bring a picnic.*

© Adam Olson / Getty Images

248

Hear the thunder of the calving Hubbard Glacier

ALASKA // Alaska is stuffed with mind-boggling natural wonders, but you still might need to double-take the first time you lay eyes on the Hubbard, the world's longest tidewater glacier and North America's largest calving river of ice. Stirred by strong riptides which cause chunks the size of 10-story buildings to break off its 8-mile-wide face, the Hubbard is a dramatic and dangerous proposition: submerged icebergs often shoot spectacularly to the surface without warning. It's also one of the few Alaskan glaciers that's advancing rather than retreating.

☞ SEE IT ! *The glacier is 30 miles north of Yakutat, where you can arrange tours. Many cruise lines include Hubbard in their itinerary.*

© CSNafzger / Shutterstock

© Malachi Jacobs / Shutterstock

249

Shred some powder at Jackson Hole Mountain Resort

WYOMING // Some say you haven't truly skied until you've tackled the 4139ft of vertical descent on these epic slopes. With an annual average of 459in of snowfall and some of the world's most challenging terrain, this luxurious resort draws serious shredders from around the world. Experts tackle the bowls, chutes, and glades of Rendezvous Mountain and the infamous Corbet's Couloir, sometimes called 'America's scariest ski slope.' Not to worry – there are intermediate runs and a handful of easy slopes as well. Summer brings plenty of action too, with a bike park, disc-golf course, climbing wall, ropes course, and a *via ferrata*, where mountaineers cling to metal chains bolted on the rockface. An aerial tram gives 360-degree views over the jagged teeth of the Rockies.

☞ SEE IT ! *The Resort is in the town of Jackson Hole, which has its own airport, inside Grand Teton National Park.*

250

Get your groove on at the Blue Moon Saloon

LOUISIANA // As the unofficial capital of Cajun Country, Lafayette has some fabulous places to hear live music. None, however, quite compares to the inviting back-porch setting of the Blue Moon Saloon. Opened in 2001 as a guesthouse and live music venue, the 18th-century Acadian-style house hosts a packed calendar of Louisiana bands playing Cajun, Creole, Zydeco, and swamp pop, plus roots groups from around the globe. Talented local artists like Cedric Watson, a four-time Grammy nominated singer, fiddler, and accordion player, tap into old-style French songs in regular appearances – it's almost impossible not to shimmy along. Beneath tin ceilings, dancers swirl across the wooden floorboards, while tucked-away backyard furniture make fine spots to take a break from the action.

☞ SEE IT ! *The Blue Moon is 140 miles west of New Orleans; you can also bunk in for the night in a hostel bed or a private room.*

© K I Photography / Shutterstock

© John Brueske / Shutterstock

251

Take in the waters at Hot Springs National Park

ARKANSAS // America's smallest national park, Hot Springs is all about a very tranquil pursuit: bathing. People have flocked to the area's geothermal pools for thousands of years, believing the water has healing powers. The buildings of Bathhouse Row were built between 1892 and 1923 in a variety of splendiferously flamboyant architectural styles. Today, two of the eight original spas are in use: the Roman Gothic-style Buckstaff Bathhouse; and the Spanish Colonial Revival-style Quapaw Baths. Check out the visitor center in the Fordyce Bathhouse before submitting to the bliss of a soak and a rubdown. Rejuvenated, hike some of the park's 26 miles of trails before doing it all again. As the park is located in downtown Hot Springs, you've got your pick of local restaurants and bars for evening refreshment.

 SEE IT ! *Hot Springs is 55 miles southwest of the Arkansas capital, Little Rock.*

252

Leave a love note on the Roseman Covered Bridge

IOWA // Bucolic countryside and picture-postcard towns are part of Madison County's charm, but it's the Roseman Covered Bridge that everyone comes to see. Built in 1883, the barn-red bridge with wooden floorboards and white plank rails evokes a bygone era, and it's easy to feel like you've slipped into the past amid the forested banks and quiet country lanes. There's an obvious romance to the 107ft-long bridge – particularly if you've read Robert James Waller's blockbuster, tear-jerking novel *The Bridges of Madison County*, or seen the subsequent film starring Meryl Streep and Clint Eastwood. On foggy nights, the bridge takes on a more mystical aura, especially when recalling the strange events of 1892: cornered by a sheriff's posse on the bridge, a county jail escapee let out a scream – and disappeared into thin air.

SEE IT ! *The bridge, off Elderberry Ave, is roughly 50 miles southwest of Des Moines.*

253

Explore artistic variety at the Barnes Foundation

PENNSYLVANIA // In the first half of the 20th century, collector and educator Albert C. Barnes amassed a remarkable trove of artwork by the likes of Cézanne, Degas, Matisse, Renoir, and Van Gogh. Alongside them he set beautiful pieces of folk art from Africa and the Americas – an artistic desegregation that was shocking at the time, and which is still followed today via careful juxtaposition of colors, themes, and materials. Even more remarkable: you've likely never seen any of these works before because Barnes' will limits reproduction and lending.

☛ SEE IT ! *From downtown Philly, SEPTA buses 7, 32, 33, 38 and 48 pass by the museum.*

255

Enjoy avant-garde art at atmospheric Dia Beacon

NEW YORK // When the Dia Foundation opened one of the world's largest museums in the blue-collar, economically depressed town of Beacon, success seemed unlikely. But the ambitious $50 million project defied the odds, transforming an old box-printing factory beside the Hudson River into a renowned destination for contemporary art. Today, the 300,000-sq-ft exhibition space showcases monumental works by the likes of Richard Serra, Dan Flavin, Louise Bourgeois, and Gerhard Richter, and its temporary shows draw art lovers from across the globe.

☛ SEE IT ! *Metro-North trains make the trip from NYC's Grand Central Terminal to Beacon in one hour 40 minutes.*

254

Gaze across Grand Teton glories at Jenny Lake Overlook

WYOMING // This is the paradigmatic, the iconic, the absolute classic Rocky Mountains view: a mirror-like gray-green lake ringed by firs and, beyond, the craggy, snow-capped mountains, their peaks doubled by their watery reflections. Located in Grand Teton National Park, Jenny Lake is named after the Shoshone woman who helped plan the 1870s expedition to map this part of Wyoming. Stand at the overlook gazing across to the glacier-carved Cascade Canyon and watching tour boats glide across the water. Visit as part of the 8-mile Jenny Lake Loop Trail.

☛ SEE IT ! *The overlook is on a one-way turnout off Jenny Lake Rd; you can walk here from the visitor center.*

256

Step into a rainbow at the Blanton Museum of Art

TEXAS // America's most striking artworks are often found in surprising places. When famed abstract artist Ellsworth Kelly completed his most monumental work, *Austin*, it opened not in New York City or Los Angeles, but on the campus of the University of Texas, at the Blanton Museum of Art. Kelly's masterpiece – a sanctuary-like space illuminated by a kaleidoscope of geometric stained-glass windows – is but one piece of the Blanton's stellar 19,000-strong collection, which runs from European masters to renowned Latin American artists.

☛ SEE IT ! *The museum is just north of downtown Austin, about 1.5 miles north of the Congress Ave Bridge.*

257

Discover the natural riches of Downieville and the Lost Sierra

CALIFORNIA // In ages gone by, prospectors schlepped up from Sacramento to this northeast corner of the Sierra Nevada in search of gold. Downieville, set where the Downie River meets the North Yuba River, was one staging post for these forty-niners, and the town flourished, gaining a population of 5000. But the gold petered out and so did the people. More than 150 years later and the town, population 200-ish, is at the heart of a rekindling of interest in what is known as the Lost Sierra. And that is thanks to the efforts of local people and a community group, the Sierra Buttes Trail Stewardship, which has been rebuilding the trails the prospectors left in these granite mountains. The tough trails are intended for everybody: hikers, mountain bikers, motorcyclists and horse riders. They link small towns such as Downieville, Graegle and Quincy via clear alpine lakes and pine forests to create recreational treasure.

☛ SEE IT ! *Downieville is about 100 miles from Sacramento or 90 miles west of Reno.*

© Eleni Mavrandoni / Shutterstock

© GiuseppeCrimeni / Shutterstock

258

259

Get cinematic thrills at the Santa Cruz Beach Boardwalk

Contemplate lost lives at the Vietnam Veterans Memorial

CALIFORNIA // If you've seen Jordan Peele's creepy 2019 horror film *Us*, you may want to tread carefully when visiting the Santa Cruz Beach Boardwalk. While you're unlikely to encounter murderous, wait, no spoilers, in the spooky Fright Walk, you will discover an atmosphere of glorious Americana that has made the West Coast's oldest beachfront amusement park so appealing to filmmakers. The smell of cotton candy mixes with the salt air, which is punctuated by the squeals of kids hanging upside down on carnival rides. Famous thrills include the Giant Dipper, a 1924 wooden roller coaster; and the 1911 Looff carousel. Both are National Historic Landmarks – and favorite vampire hangouts judging by the 1987 classic *The Lost Boys*. During summer, you can catch free movies as well as live rock concerts.

WASHINGTON, DC // The opposite of DC's white, gleaming marble, the black, low-lying Vietnam Veterans Memorial cuts into the earth, like a scar wrought by the Vietnam War. A wall of granite tapers from a height of 10ft down to 8in, and bears the names of the war's 58,000-plus casualties, listed in the order they died. Rank is not provided on the wall – privates share space with majors. Seeing your own image among the names on the polished reflective wall is meant to bring past and present together. It's a muted but remarkably profound monument, where visitors leave mementos such as photos of babies and notes ('I wish you could have met him, Dad'). It's subtle and moving – and all the more surprising as Maya Lin was only 21 when she designed it, after winning a nationwide competition in 1981.

☛ SEE IT ! *From late May through early September, the Santa Cruz Electric Shuttle connects downtown Santa Cruz with the beach.*

☛ SEE IT ! *It's a 20-minute walk from Foggy Bottom-GWU metro station; or take the Circulator Bus, which loops around the Mall.*

© Michael Warwick / Shutterstock

© f11photo / Shutterstock

260

261

Feel like a flower child at hippie haven Haight Street

CALIFORNIA // An entire movement of flower children, anarchists, and artists can be traced to a single intersection in San Francisco: the corner of Haight and Ashbury streets. In the swinging '60s, The Haight's infamous Psychedelic Shop was a community hub – and free-love vibes endure to this day. Take time to breathe it all in (the scent of incense, we mean). Amble between tie-dye clothing shops, marijuana dispensaries, homemade jewelry boutiques, and anarchist bookstores. The atmosphere is unashamedly retro, though street art adds modern flair. Along the way, look out for the neighborhood's famous fishnet-clad legs, which dangle provocatively from the window of Piedmont Boutique. If San Francisco is a capital of quirk, then Haight St is its fluttering heart.

☛ SEE IT ! *Start at the corner of Haight St and Central Ave, continuing along The Haight to Golden Gate Park.*

Pay homage to the birth of the nation at Independence Hall

PENNSYLVANIA // The birth of the USA occurred within the walls of a modest 18th-century Georgian building in Philadelphia. It was here in Independence Hall (then known as the Pennsylvania State House) that the Declaration of Independence was debated, drafted, and signed in 1776, which was followed 11 years later by the adoption of the US Constitution. Apart from pivotal moments in America's foundation, the building served many other purposes over the years. In the early 1800s, the artist Charles Willson Peale opened America's first public natural history museum (admission 25 cents) on the second floor. Years later, Abraham Lincoln's body lay in state following his assassination in 1865; some 300,000 mourners paid their respects. Less illustriously, the basement served as the city dog pound in 1830.

☛ SEE IT ! *Visits are by guided tour only. Reserve online to avoid long waits during the peak summer months.*

262

Find movie magic in the Museum of Western Film History

CALIFORNIA // If you've ever wanted to be in many places at once, travel up to the high desert country in the eastern Sierra Nevada and stroll through the Alabama Hills. The parched, rocky landscape backed by snow-covered peaks has served as the setting for Wild West frontier towns, as well as more remote outposts in Mexico, India, China, Afghanistan – and even outer space. Over 400 movies were shot here, and the fascinating collection at the Museum of Western Film History captures the region's glory days on the silver screen.

☛ SEE IT ! *The museum is in Lone Pine, a 200-mile drive north of Los Angeles via scenic highways 14 and 395.*

263

Enter the land of sweets at Dylan's Candy Bar

NEW YORK // Near the heart of Midtown Manhattan, you can leave the urban jungle behind and step into a technicolor wonderland of towering lollipop trees, Grizzly Bear-sized chocolate rabbits, and a shimmering rainbow-hued wall of jelly beans dispensing a dizzying variety of fruit flavors. Inspired by Willy Wonka, founder Dylan Lauren (daughter of fashion mogul Ralph Lauren) stocks over 7000 types of confectionery, including one-of-a-kind treats like Belgian chocolate-dipped cake pops or cookies-and-cream popcorn. The upstairs cafe has heavenly milkshakes and ice-cream sundaes if you need an instant sugar rush.

☛ SEE IT ! *Nearby subway stations include Lexington Ave/59th St.*

264

Follow the herd at Assateague Island National Seashore

MARYLAND // Wild horses still gallop across dunes and over secluded beaches on Assateague, a 37-mile-long barrier island between Maryland and Virginia. The freely roaming horses (said to be descendants of survivors from a shipwrecked Spanish galleon) are sometimes hard to spot – your best bet is to stroll one of three separate half-mile hiking trails. Better yet, pitch a tent and spend the night. You can also go kayaking, catch a ranger talk, or make like a pony and frolic in the waves. From November to March, you'll likely have the beach all to yourself.

☛ SEE IT ! *A bridge links the island to Maryland's Eastern Shore; it's a 140-mile drive from Washington, DC.*

© bonandbon / Shutterstock

© Steve Lagreca / Shutterstock

265

See where diplomacy and luxury collide at Sunnylands

CALIFORNIA // Publisher, philanthropist, diplomat: Walter Annenberg wore many crowns. The fabulously wealthy scion of a media empire and his wife Leonore were one of America's 'first families' of the 20th century, and entertained seven US presidents, royalty, Hollywood celebrities, and heads of state at Sunnylands, their 200-acre winter retreat. The estate's 25,000-sq-ft, art-filled main home is a 1966 Mid-Century-Modernn masterpiece by A. Quincy Jones. Sometimes called the 'Camp David of the West,' it has served as the backdrop to political gatherings and summit meetings between many world leaders. Outside, the magnificent designed gardens were inspired by Impressionist paintings; paths meander past thousands of arid-landscape plants. The grounds also support a bird sanctuary, attracting over 130 species.

☛ SEE IT ! *Sunnylands is 10 miles southeast of Palm Springs; book online far in advance for a guided tour of the house.*

266

Listen for moose on a multi-day hiking trip in Isle Royale National Park

MICHIGAN // Covered with dense forests of birch and spruce, and lying in a remote corner of Lake Superior, Isle Royale seems the embodiment of a pristine national park. Lumbering moose crash through the lowland swamps, while bald eagles soar overhead. Yet despite nature's apparent bounty, the island was heavily logged in the 1800s and later transformed into a summer haven for wealthy families from Chicago – there was even a nine-hole golf course near the northeast shoreline. Today, the trees have grown back, wolves once again roam the forests, and 99% of the island is designated as wilderness. Not surprisingly, Isle Royale makes a fabulous setting for outdoor adventures. Its 165 miles of trails are accessible by foot or boat only, and there are limitless possibilities for reconnecting with nature.

☛ SEE IT ! *Four ferries and one seaplane provide service from Houghton or Copper Harbor, Michigan; or Grand Portage, Minnesota.*

267

See the groundbreaking designs of Frank Lloyd Wright at Taliesin

WISCONSIN // Architects from across the globe make the pilgrimage to prairie-filled southwestern Wisconsin, where Frank Lloyd Wright created his most comprehensive collection of works. Taliesin was Wright's lifelong residence, as well as his studio and architectural school. The 37,000-sq-ft home and surrounding 800-acre estate include buildings that span his prolific career, from the earliest designs (the Unity Chapel from 1886) to his final works (the 1953 River Terrace). Tragically, Taliesin was also the sight of a horrific mass murder, when Wright's mistress Mamah Borthwick and six other people were killed by an axe-wielding madman in 1914.

☛ SEE IT ! *Taliesin, some 120 miles west of Milwaukee, offers a range of guided tours.*

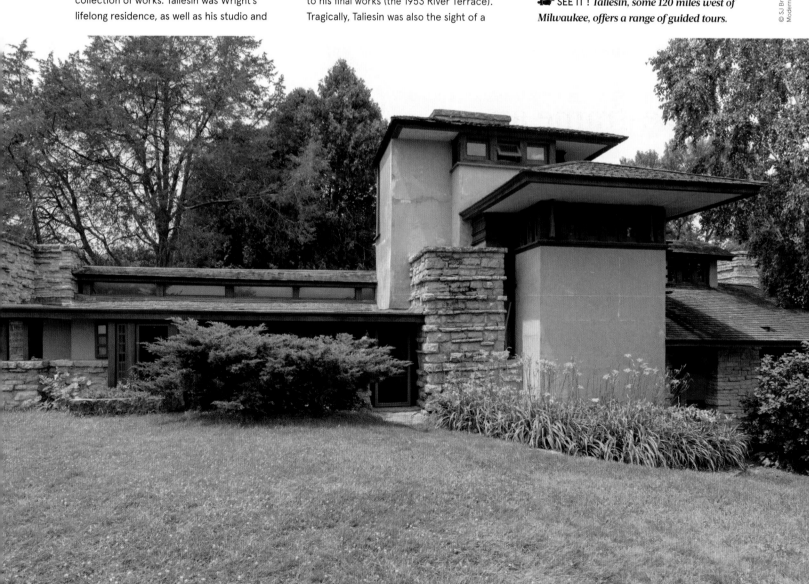

268

269

Freeze-frame an iconic view of the Mendenhall Glacier

Ascend to Paradise in Mt Rainier National Park

ALASKA // Going to Juneau and not seeing the Mendenhall is like visiting Rome and skipping the Colosseum. The most famous of Juneau's glaciers, and the city's most popular attraction, slides 13 miles downhill from its source, the Juneau Icefield, and has a half-mile-wide face. It ends at Mendenhall Lake, which is overlooked by a slick visitor center offering splendid views of the ice tongue.

Well set up for activities, the area is strafed with hiking trails. However, the most novel way to experience the Mendenhall is by glacier trekking: stepping into crampons, grabbing an ice axe, and roping up to walk on ice that's over 1000 years old. Several local companies offer excursions. Go there soon: climate change means the glacier is retreating.

WASHINGTON // Heaven *is* a place on earth when you head to Mt Rainier National Park, where serpentine trails meander through alpine flower meadows in the shadow of a glacier-encrusted stratovolcano.

This high-mountain nirvana was named by the daughter of park pioneer James Longmire who allegedly exclaimed 'paradise!' on visiting the 5400ft-high meadows for the first time in 1885. It's since spawned a lodge (built in 1916 and now considered a historic landmark), a museum-worthy visitor center, and a reputation for being one of the snowiest places on earth, with average annual dumps of 640in.

In summer, hikers use Paradise as an access point for numerous above-the-tree-line trails, while mountaineers consider it base camp for strenuous Mt Rainier summit attempts.

SEE IT ! *The easiest access to the glacier is via a 'blue bus' operated by M & M Tours, which picks up from the cruise-ship dock in Juneau.*

SEE IT ! *You'll need your own vehicle: access the park on SR706 via the Nisqually entrance and drive 18 miles to the Paradise parking lot.*

270

Bike an old railway track on the Virginia Creeper Trail

VIRGINIA // We can all agree that the best part of biking is the downhill, right? Well, it's all downhill on this southwest Virginia trail along a former logging railway. Rental companies shuttle riders to Whitetop Station where the ground's often snowy well into spring. Fly downhill through forests blooming with mountain laurel, arriving 17 miles later in the town of Damascus. Then continue on level terrain, riding through pastureland and barn-dotted farm fields to Abingdon. Say hi to the old steam locomotive that once chugged the route, now parked at the trailhead.

👉 SEE IT ! *Bike shops in Damascus will shuttle you to Whitetop and pick you up in Abingdon.*

© Mark A Joseph / Shutterstock

271

Gawk at the grandeur of Grand Central Terminal

NEW YORK // Grand Central Terminal (often referred to as 'Grand Central Station') is a magnificent ode to the humble commute, with marble floors and ticket counters, and a neck-craning celestial ceiling painted with constellations. Opened in 1913, the Beaux Arts building's numerous artworks make it well worth a visit. Most notable are the four-sided brass clock atop the information booth, and winged Mercury in the *Glory of Commerce* sculpture on the facade. Slurping a platter of oysters beneath the vaulted roof at the Grand Central Oyster Bar has been a classic NYC experience since the station opened.

👉 SEE IT ! *Enter at 89 East 42nd St at Park Ave.*

© Life In Pixels / Shutterstock

© Michael Ochs Archives / Getty Images

© f11photo / Shutterstock

272

Get funky at the Stax Museum of American Soul Music

TENNESSEE // In the aptly named 'Soulsville USA' neighbourhood, the site of the former Stax Records recording studio is now a museum to soul music. In the 1960s, this place was *the* spot for up-and-coming Memphis soul artists, recording Otis Redding, Booker T. and the MGs (above), Sam & Dave, and Wilson Pickett – among other luminaries. In 15 years, it scored more than 167 songs on the Top 100 pop chart and 243 hits on the Top 100 R&B chart. It went bankrupt in the 1970s, but in 2003 the space was revived as a museum through grassroots efforts. Visit to admire Isaac Hayes' shag-carpeted, 24-karat-gold-trimmed 1972 Superfly Cadillac, pray at a recreated Delta church, and boogie on the dancefloor from the late, much-lamented *Soul Train* TV show. For soul aficionados, this is truly hallowed ground.

☞ SEE IT ! *The museum is at the corner of McLemore Avenue in south Memphis, and opens Tuesday through Sunday.*

273

Be charmed by Charleston's Historic District

SOUTH CAROLINA // Gardenia-scented cobblestone alleys, quaint 18th-century churches, rowhouses painted in crayon-box colors – is there anywhere more romantic than this costal South Carolina city? Historically important for its roles in shipping, the slave trade, and the Civil War, Charleston's past – good and bad – is on display in its Historic District. Visit the gracious sea captains' manses of the Battery; gaze out to Fort Sumter where the first shots of the Civil War rang out; and explore sites dedicated to the history of the enslaved people who worked, lived, and were sold here. The city is also one of the US's top food destinations – tuck into everything from Nouvelle Southern to French to sushi, and don't miss the dishes of the Gullah people, African Americans from the Lowcountry with a distinct culture and language.

☞ SEE IT ! *The Historic District runs from the southern part of the Charleston peninsula up to Calhoun St.*

Three times each day, the unique Burke Brise Soleil sunshade unfurls its moving 'wings' over the Milwaukee Art Museum.

274

See architecture take flight at Milwaukee Art Museum

WISCONSIN // Standing on the edge of Lake Michigan with the sun high over Milwaukee, you might think you've stumbled upon some futuristic Jurassic world. Stretching out before you are what looks like the bone-white appendages of a graceful pterosaur about to take flight, its 217ft-long wings slowly unfurling toward the sky. Renowned Spanish architect Santiago Calatrava created this elegantly innovative design, better known as the Burke Brise Soleil, to serve as

a monumental sunscreen above the vaulted halls of the Milwaukee Art Museum. The drama continues inside in a cathedral-like reception hall with a mesmerizing view over the lake. Apart from architectural theatrics, the museum is famed for its encyclopedic collection of artwork that spans the ages – in all over 31,000 pieces, spread across three different buildings, including a 1957 Brutalist structure designed by Eero Saarinen. Allow a good few hours to properly see

the collection, with its stellar array of old European masters, German Expressionist paintings, iconoclastic creations by outsider and folk artists, rare works by photographers like Man Ray, and numerous pieces by Georgia O'Keeffe (who was born in Wisconsin).

👉 SEE IT ! *The museum anchor's Milwaukee's downtown lakefront. Calatrava's 'wings' open and close at 10am, noon, and 5pm.*

275

Visit an enduring American icon at the Liberty Bell Center

PENNSYLVANIA // 'Proclaim liberty throughout all the land unto all the inhabitants thereof' reads the inscription on the famous 2080lb bell, originally cast for the Philadelphia State House in 1752. According to legend, it was rung on July 8, 1776, for the first public reading of the Declaration of Independence. But it wasn't until the 1830s that it was actually called the 'Liberty Bell' – initially by abolitionists seeking to end the abominable practice of slavery, and later by those fighting for other causes, including women's suffrage and civil rights.

☞ SEE IT ! *A glass-walled building off Market St protects this icon of Philadelphia; see it from outside or join the queue to file past.*

276

Hike forests and beaches at Cape Cod National Seashore

MASSACHUSETTS // A frequent summertime resident, John F. Kennedy was a big admirer of Cape Cod's natural beauty. In 1961, he set aside more than 40,000 acres to create the Cape Cod National Seashore, a treasure of unspoiled beaches, iconic lighthouse, salt marshes, upland forests, and wild cranberry bogs. The 8-mile Great Island Trail (one of many memorable walks) takes in dunes, coastline and clifftop views – a fine setting for contemplating the words of Thoreau (another Cape Cod fan): 'A man can stand there and put all of America behind him.'

☞ SEE IT ! *Beat the traffic by taking a passenger ferry to Provincetown from Boston or Plymouth.*

Gaze across NYC at Top of the Rock

NEW YORK // Sometimes you just have to change your perspective in order to realize the beauty all around you. Such is often the case with the trip from sidewalk to 70-story viewing platform at Rockefeller Center's Top of the Rock. There, the skyscraper-dotted cityscape of NYC spreads before you, broken only by narrow ribbons of blue to east and west (the East River, the Hudson) and the vibrant green rectangle of Central Park unfurling off to the north. The views are magical around sunset when the city transforms from day to glittering night.

☛ SEE IT ! *Take the B/D/F/M to 47th–50th Sts-Rockefeller Center. For cocktails with a view, head to the Rockefeller's 65th-floor Bar SixtyFive.*

© Joe Daniel Price / Getty Images

Admire the skills of ancient builders at Montezuma Castle

ARIZONA // Built into sheer limestone cliffs above the Verde Valley, Montezuma Castle National Monument shows the remarkable engineering skills of the Sinagua people. Dating back to the 12th century, the five-story structure contained about 50 rooms, and its setting in a natural alcove protected it from the elements. Today it's one of the US's best-preserved cliff dwellings. Nearby, you can explore more Sinagua ingenuity at Montezuma Well, a natural limestone sinkhole containing water that was diverted into the fields by a stone-lined irrigation canal.

☛ SEE IT ! *The site is around 95 miles northeast of Phoenix, a short hop from the I-17.*

© Traveller70 / Shutterstock

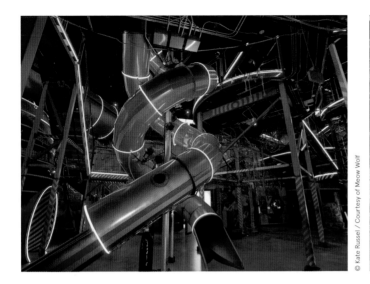

© Kate Russel / Courtesy of Meow Wolf

© Orange Grove / Shutterstock

279

Immerse yourself in a fantastical new world at Meow Wolf

NEW MEXICO // If you've been hankering for a trip to another dimension but have yet to find a portal, the House of Eternal Return by Meow Wolf could be the place for you. The premise here is quite ingenious: visitors get to explore a recreated Victorian house for clues related to the disappearance of a Californian family, following a narrative that leads deeper into fragmented bits of a multiverse (often via secret passages), all of which are unique, interactive art installations. Created by the Santa Fe art collective Meow Wolf in an old bowling alley (donated by *Game of Thrones* author George RR Martin), the space is large enough that you could spend several hours here – or visits – trying to crack the code to the safe at the top of the stairs, reading every detail of Mom's diary, or finding inspiration yourself in the makerspace at the entrance. Weekend nights see live-music shows at the heart of this compelling imaginary world.

☛ TRY IT ! *Meow Wolf is 4 miles southwest of downtown Santa Fe. The Santa Fe Trails bus route 2 stops nearby.*

280

Peer into the ooze at La Brea Tar Pits and Museum

CALIFORNIA // Sometime during the last Ice Age, thousands of mammoths, dire wolves, saber-toothed cats, giant sloths, and other prehistoric creatures met a sticky end in this gooey asphalt bog. The tar preserved their bodies and the city of Los Angeles grew up around the pits. Excavations began in the early 1910s and are still ongoing. Today the pits are a combination tourist attraction, museum, and working paleontological dig next to modern-day Wilshire Boulevard. See life-size model animals attempt to escape the bubbling black lake, learn about extinct megafauna at the museum, and watch scientists sift through the muck. The Mid-Century-Modern-style observation pit opened in 1952 and is a touchstone for generations of Los Angeles schoolchildren. It's all set in Hancock Park: check out prehistoric LA vegetation in the Pleistocene Garden or let the kids climb giant sloth statues. The famous (and famously stinky) Lake Pit is a remnant of 1800s asphalt mining.

☛ SEE IT ! *The museum, part of Museum Row on the stretch of Wilshire Boulevard known as 'Miracle Mile', is open daily.*

281

Uncover Seattle's weird side at the *Fremont Troll*

WASHINGTON // Long known for its wry contrarianism, Fremont is Seattle's wackiest neighborhood: its unofficial motto is 'freedom to be peculiar'. For proof, look no further than its quirky sculptures epitomized by the *Fremont Troll*, a 13,000lb steel and concrete rendering of a troll crushing a VW Beetle in its hand that resides beneath the Aurora Bridge. The troll was the winner of a 1989 Fremont Arts Council competition to design thought-provoking community art, and is one of a half-dozen surreal pieces that enliven the neighborhood.

☛ SEE IT ! *Fremont is a highly walkable neighborhood served by regular buses from downtown Seattle.*

282

Ski across powder-filled meadows in the Royal Gorge

CALIFORNIA // Set against the forest-covered backdrop of the Sierra Nevada, the Royal Gorge is a wondrous destination for Nordic ski lovers. In fact, this is America's largest cross-country resort, with some 87 miles of groomed track crisscrossing 6000 acres of terrain. It has great skating lanes and diagonal stride tracks, and welcomes snowshoers. Plus there are some 19 miles of dog-friendly trails you can head out onto with your canine best friend. Nine strategically placed warming huts ensure you can spend the whole day outside.

☛ TRY IT ! *The resort, part of Sugar Bowl, is about 45 miles west via I-80 from Reno, Nevada.*

283

Admire architectural excellence at the SC Johnson Campus

WISCONSIN // In 1936, the head of SC Johnson company asked architect Frank Lloyd Wright to create its new HQ in Racine. The result was a masterpiece, an innovative building with custom-made modular furniture, an open office plan, and extraordinary design details like the tall, flared lily-pad-like columns in its Great Workroom, and 43 miles of Pyrex glass-tube windows that let in soft, natural light. Next door, Wright's SC Johnson Research Tower is another masterstroke, one of the tallest structures ever built on the cantilever principle.

☛ SEE IT ! *SC Johnson Campus lies 30 miles south of Milwaukee; guided tours are offered Wednesday through Sunday.*

The steam-powered ride to Silverton offers breathtaking Rocky Mountain vistas.

284

Take in majestic mountain views from the Durango & Silverton Railroad

COLORADO // In the southern Rockies, steam-powered locomotives rumble through the San Juan mountains just as they have for over 140 years. The 45-mile Durango & Silverton Narrow Gauge Railroad follows the sparkling Animas River as it winds through breathtaking scenery. You crisscross the river five times, taking in views of old stagecoach roads, rolling farmlands, former mining camps, and towering peaks, some of which reach over 14,000ft. With only wilderness beyond the train tracks, keep your eyes peeled for wildlife, including deer, moose, bighorn sheep, even the odd black bear or mountain lion, while eagles and hawks soar overhead.

Ringed by snowy peaks and steeped in tawdry mining town tales, Silverton makes an impressive arrival point. It's a two-street town, but only one is paved: Greene St is where you'll find most businesses; still unpaved, notorious Blair St – renamed Empire – was home to thriving brothels and boozing establishments during the silver rush.

☛ SEE IT ! *The train runs year-round, though in winter it goes only as far as Cascade Canyon (a 26-mile trip), where you can have a fireside lunch or take a frosty stroll along the riverbanks.*

285

Spy raptors filling the sky at Cape May Point State Park

NEW JERSEY // Anchoring the southern end of the 141-mile-long Jersey Shore, Cape May Point State Park protects a vibrant landscape of rolling dunes, coastal marshland, forested islands, and one very photogenic 1859 lighthouse. Several trails lead through the diverse habitats of the 190-acre park, which draws birdwatchers during the spring and fall migrations. In fact, over 400 species pass through including thousands of hawks soaring high overhead each day. You can get a bird's eye view of the land- and seascape by climbing 199 steps to the top of the 157ft lighthouse.

☛ SEE IT ! *NJ Transit buses serve Cape May from NYC (journey time is three to five hours).*

286

Ponder the power of architecture inside the Robie House

ILLINOIS // 'I am the greatest,' Frank Lloyd Wright sometimes sang to himself while entertaining his guests. Though bereft of humility, the great American architect did not lack for talent, as evidenced in masterpieces like the Robie House. Dating from 1910 and recently renovated, it's one of the best examples from the Prairie School. Iconic Wrightian elements include cantilevered roof eaves, oak ceiling trim, geometrical furnishings, art glass doors with stylized forms from nature and an exterior that emphasizes horizontal lines, so evoking the prairies.

☛ SEE IT ! *Robie House is in southern Chicago; take Metra Electric Line (ME) to 59th St.*

287

Sniff out hints of the past in Little Italy

NEW YORK // Back in the late 19th and early 20th centuries, this chunk of Lower Manhattan was a genuine Italian village – grocers selling mozzarella and *salsicce*, nonnas yelling at kids in Neapolitan dialect, pushcart vendors humming *O Sole Mio*. But Italian immigration declined, and the once-vibrant Little Italy shrank to the three-block area you see today. There are a handful of red-sauce restaurants, a few groceries, and plenty of souvenir stores selling shirts with slogans like 'Fuhgeddaboudit.' It's a fun stop for the nostalgia, the architecture, and the popular Feast of San Gennaro street festival in late September.

☛ SEE IT ! *Find Little Italy on Mulberry between Broome and Canal.*

© Leonard Zhukovsky / Shutterstock

288

See art and architecture blend in the Kimbell Museum

TEXAS // Some architects treat the Kimbell Art Museum as a sacred space, making a pilgrimage to Fort Worth to admire one of the greatest achievements by Modernist luminary Louis Kahn. Sculpted vaulted ceilings, elegant courtyards, and abundant use of natural light create a memorable setting for one of America's best little art museums. The 350-piece collection contains some real big-hitters: Michelangelo's first known painting, *The Torment of St Anthony*; and masterpieces by Caravaggio, Rembrandt, Van Gogh, Matisse, Cézanne, and Gauguin.

☞ SEE IT ! *The Kimbell Art Museum lies in Fort Worth's Cultural District, about 2.5 miles west of downtown.*

© Sylvain Sonnet / Getty Images

289

Descend below in Mammoth Cave National Park

KENTUCKY // The longest known cave system in the world is an eerie fairyland of immense stalactites, frozen waterfalls of stone, subterranean rivers, and echoing chambers the size of train stations. Humans first entered the caves around 4000 years ago and have since used them for shelter, to mine saltpeter for gunpowder, as a tuberculosis hospital, and as a church. Descend into the gloom on a guided National Park Service tour, walking or – for adventurous visitors – crawling and slithering through sinuous water-carved passages.

☞ SEE IT ! *Cave City is the park's not-very-impressive access town; Nashville and Louisville airports are under 100 miles away.*

290

Watch dancing droplets at the Fountains of Bellagio

NEVADA // The best free show in Vegas happens every night of the week and it stars – water. Dancing fountains may seem like a tough sell in Sin City, but the Bellagio resort takes things to a whole other level on its 8.5-acre lake fronting The Strip. Over 1200 jets fire up to 460ft in the air, the spray swirling and spinning in perfect time to songs by the likes of Frank Sinatra and Tiësto. Synchronized lighting adds to the artistry; at times the fountains look like dancing fire against the night sky.

☞ SEE IT ! *The show happens every 15 to 30 minutes from 3pm to midnight.*

Ice-cream colors and clean lines define Miami's historic Art Deco and MiMo gems.

291

Be awestruck by Miami's Art Deco Historic District

FLORIDA // Sporting a color palette as bright and bold as the candy shop of your dreams, this exuberant Miami neighborhood is a perfect backdrop for the beautiful blond sands of South Beach. Over 800 examples of Art Deco architecture, by far the USA's most extensive collection of edifices from this period, grace streets here, many so spruced up they look like the last lick of paint was yesterday. Strictly speaking, the historic buildings are also Mediterranean Revival (predating the Art Deco period, but reaching its zenith around the same time during the 1920s and '30s) and MiMo, or Miami Modernist (post-WWII to the '60s) and the variety of designs showcased is stunning.

The middle of the district holds many of the most iconic structures. Near the intersection of Ocean Drive and 11th St, admire the Congress Hotel, showing perfect symmetry in its three-story facade and reminiscent of 1930s grand movie palaces. A block north, the highlight of several nautical-themed hotels is The Tides, with its porthole-topped entranceway and reception desk imprinted with fossilized sea creatures.

☞ SEE IT ! *The district is bounded by Ocean Dr and Washington Ave, running roughly south-north between 5th and 23rd streets.*

© Nicolas Kipourax Paquet / Getty Images

© Brian Yarvin / Shutterstock

292

Lose all sense of scale at Canyonlands National Park

UTAH // Your eyes struggle to adjust as you stare out from Grand View Point Overlook. You know you're in Utah's largest national park, but these russet canyons and arid plains could just as easily be Mars.

The Colorado and Green rivers carve through this kingdom of burnished cliffs and rocky spires, slicing Canyonlands into distinct regions. The Island in the Sky is as serenely beautiful as its name suggests. Hiking trails here are short, not too steep, and well-marked with cairns, so even idle walkers can revel in conquering these glorious heights. Our picks? The Mesa Arch Trail, or the appropriately named Grand View Point. Down in The Needles, more energetic routes (some covering 60 miles) thread deep into the desert, while The Maze's 4WD-only roads entice wilder souls.

☛ SEE IT ! *Drive half an hour west from Moab, the gateway town to several Utah parks.*

293

Cycle through sun-dappled forests along the GAP

MARYLAND // It took more than 20 years to complete one of America's finest trails linking Cumberland, Maryland, with Pittsburgh, Pennsylvania, along an abandoned railway line where coal-laden freight trains once rumbled. Built section by section with the help of local volunteer groups, the 150-mile-long Great Allegheny Passage (GAP) was deemed a smash success when its final stretch opened 2013. The smooth trail (made of packed crushed limestone) courses through verdant forests, past rolling farmlands, and along wooden bridges above rushing rivers and sunlit streams – with spooky tunnels carved into the mountains breaking up the bucolic scenery. The grade is gentle (never more than 2%), and towns along the way make handy spots for a meal or a place to rest your head (and legs).

☛ TRY IT ! *Near the trailhead, the Cumberland Trail Connection rents bicycles and provide shuttle service anywhere from Pittsburgh to DC.*

Zip to the top of Seattle's emblematic Space Needle

WASHINGTON // Whether you're from Tampa or Timbuktu, your take-home image of Seattle will probably be the Space Needle, a streamlined, modern-before-its-time tower built for the 1962 World's Fair. Now the city's defining symbol, the needle anchors the Seattle Center, and over a million annual visitors ascend to its flying saucer-like observation deck. The reason? Awesome 360-degree Washington State views, a wine bar with a glass floor, and an all-glass observation deck with inclined benches providing vertical-drop vistas of Seattle far below.

TRY IT ! *It's easy to hoof it from downtown Seattle or you can take the mile-long super speedy monorail.*

© Matteo Colombo / Getty images

Discover wonderful whiskey at Jack Daniel's Distillery

TENNESSEE // Is there a more famous whiskey on the planet? There is certainly no better-selling one, for JD has topped the list for years, trouncing even the Scots – something of an irony, given it's made in an officially 'dry' county. Come on down to little Lynchburg to see what all the fuss is about. Folks here have been dripping grain-infused limestone spring water through charcoal then aging it in oak barrels since 1875, making this the nation's oldest distillery – and it's great fun to explore. Some tours are dry, but others include tastings of Tennessee's finest.

SEE IT ! *Lynchburg is 82 miles southeast of Nashville via I-24.*

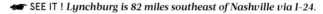

© Paul McKinnon / Shutterstock

Consider complex racial history at the Lincoln Memorial

WASHINGTON, DC // At the west end of the National Mall, Honest Abe sits gazing calmly and a bit imperiously at all comers. The marble statue to the USA's 16th president is ensconced in a Neoclassical temple, with the words of the Gettysburg Address and Lincoln's second inaugural address carved on the walls. Look for the engraving on the steps marking the spot where Martin Luther King Jr. delivered his 'I Have a Dream' speech. The lower level is a museum of Lincoln's life and the history of the memorial.

🖝 SEE IT ! *The memorial, at 2 Lincoln Memorial Circle NW, is open 24 hours a day.*

Tour volcano-sculpted wonders in Waimea Canyon

HAWAI'I // This 3000ft-deep canyon of lava rock is one of Kaua'i's most staggering natural formations. It's dubbed the 'Grand Canyon of the Pacific' but the landscape is infinitely more varied, with red-tinged valleys, tropical forests, and numerous waterfalls.

Waimea was formed by the collapse of volcanic Mt Wai'ale'ale. The drive here is truly special, with roadside lookouts that gaze across pinkish peaks. Lace up your hiking boots for a closer encounter: the three-hour Canyon Trail leads you past 800ft Waipo'o Falls.

🖝 SEE IT ! *To drive Waimea's western rim, begin at the visitor center and follow Waimea Canyon Dr, which flows into Koke'e Rd after 8 miles.*

298

Sip Oscar-worthy wines at the Francis Ford Coppola Winery

CALIFORNIA // Winemaking has deep roots for film director Francis Ford Coppola. His grandfather made wine in the family's New York apartment, and as an Italian-American he never saw a dinner table without *vino* on it. The movie mogul and his wife Eleanor made wine for several decades before opening Francis Ford Coppola Winery in 2010, and it has a bit of everything: an upstairs tasting room; a museum of moviemaking memorabilia; a modern Italian-American restaurant. And the bocce courts and swimming pools make it a family-friendly delight.

☛ SEE IT ! *Near Geyserville in Sonoma County, the winery is 75 miles north of San Francisco, off Hwy 101.*

© Stass Gricko / Getty Images

Courtesy of Francis Ford Coppola Winery

299

Explore geothermal wonders at Lassen Volcanic NP

CALIFORNIA // The dry, smoldering, treeless terrain within Lassen Volcanic National Park stands in stark contrast to the cool green conifer forest that surrounds it. That's in summer. In winter, tons of snow ensure you won't get too far inside its borders without some serious gear. Still, entering the park from the southwest entrance is to step into another world. The lavascape offers a fascinating glimpse into the earth's fiery core, marked by roiling hot springs, steamy mud pots, noxious sulfur vents, fumaroles, lava flows, cinder cones, craters, and crater lakes.

☛ SEE IT ! *Lassen is about 50 miles east of Redding; the park's eight campgrounds open from late May through October.*

300—
399

300

Ponder America's past at the National Museum

WASHINGTON, DC // The impressive US icons contained within the free National Museum of American History on the National Mall range from the original Star-Spangled Banner flag to Julia Child's kitchen to the lunch counter from the 1960 Greensboro Civil Rights sit-in. This is no fusty repository of pottery shards and books under glass, but a vibrant, dynamic experience. Examine a Revolutionary War gunboat, check out an 1831 steam locomotive, and click your heels in delight when you see Dorothy's ruby slippers from *The Wizard of Oz*.

☛ SEE IT ! *Part of the Smithsonian Institution, the museum is at 1300 Constitution Ave NW.*

© Feng Cheng / Shutterstock

301

Educate yourself on Civil Rights history at Ole Miss

MISSISSIPPI // Live oak trees garlanded with Spanish moss, verdant lawns leading up to grand antebellum homes, and vibrant squares full of chit-chatting college students: wandering through the campus of the University of Mississippi feels like strolling onto a movie set – one that depicts a certain stereotype of the Deep South. If it all feels oddly familiar, that's because you've probably seen the film – or at least some version of it over the years that revolves around Civil Rights – as Ole Miss played a starring role when it comes to social justice. On October 1, 1962, James Meredith, accompanied by his courageous adviser, NAACP state chair Medgar Evers, marched through a violent mob of segregationists to become the first African American student to register for classes at the University of Mississippi. Riots ensued and the Kennedy administration had to call in 500 federal marshals and the National Guard to ensure his safety. When the iconic school was desegregated by Meredith's actions, it was inevitable that the rest of Mississippi – and in some ways, the entire South – would follow. Tragically, Evers was assassinated in 1963 by a white supremacist.

☛ SEE IT ! *The university lies in the town of Oxford, some 85 miles southeast of Memphis.*

© Barbara Noe Kennedy / Lonely Planet

Swap four wheels for four (or eight) legs at Stockyards National Historic District – and don't forget your Stetson!

302

Hit a honky-tonk in Fort Worth's Stockyards

TEXAS // Fort Worth definitely lives up to the nickname of 'Cowtown'. Each morning and afternoon, Stetson-wearing cowboys climb into the saddle and drive a herd of longhorn cattle up the dusty streets of town. During the great open-range cattle drives of the late 19th century, Fort Worth was known as the place 'where the west begins', and more than 10 million head of livestock tramped here along the Chisholm Trail. Today, the Stockyards National Historic District is a living connection to that past, its collection of low-slung buildings evoking the Wild West. You'll find vintage saloons, Western-wear stores, steakhouses, and the massive Cowtown Coliseum indoor rodeo, with nightly events. Its undeniably touristy, but authenticity still shines through in places like Billy Bob's Texas, a former cattle barn turned honky-tonk with indoor bull riding, live music, and a boot-scuffed dance floor that draws country-loving crowds at weekends. There are also live cattle auctions inside the 1902 Fort Worth Livestock Exchange building, and local history at one-room Stockyards Museum, with displays on shoot-outs, outlaws, trick riding, and butchery.

🐄 **SEE IT !** *Trinity Metro buses 12 and 15 connect the Stockyards with downtown Fort Worth.*

303

Try fine farmhouse cheddar at Plymouth Artisan Cheese

VERMONT // The cows outnumber people in the bucolic countryside of rural Vermont. Black-and-white Holsteins and doe-eyed Jerseys gaze over rolling pastures that seem little changed by the passage of time. Unsurprisingly, this is one of the best places in the US to find authentic, farmhouse cheeses. Plymouth Artisan Cheese has been around since 1890, making it America's second-oldest still operating cheesemaker. The small-batch operation produces an exquisite raw-milk cheddar that's hand-dipped in wax, just as it has been for over 130 years.

☞ EAT IT ! *Plymouth Artisan Cheese lies just off scenic VT 100, about 150 miles northwest of Boston.*

304

Scan the skies for UFOs at Marfa Lights Viewing Area

TEXAS // Near the Chinati Mountains in west Texas, mysterious orbs of light suddenly appear then disappear over the desert landscape. Whether ghosts, alien spacecraft, or obscure atmospheric phenomenon, the lights – in shades of white, yellow, red, and blue – have mystified onlookers for well over a century. The cowboy who first reported them in 1883 thought they were Apache signal fires; more recent eyewitnesses suppose reflections of distant car lights (though no roads traverse the lights' location). Once you see them, it's easy to become obsessed, as actor James Dean found while filming *Giant* in the area.

☞ SEE IT ! *The viewing area lies 9 miles east of Marfa on Hwy 90.*

305

Enjoy plants and art at Cheekwood Estate and Gardens

TENNESSEE // When you're all honky-tonked out, head for some more genteel pleasures at this Georgian-style limestone mansion in suburban Nashville. Built in the 1930s with the proceeds of the Maxwell House coffee fortune, it's filled to bursting with paintings, decorative arts, sculpture, silver, textiles, books, and more. The lovely surrounding botanical gardens capture a dozen different themes: sniff out the fragrant Herb Study Garden; delight in the turtle pond at the Children's Garden; or sprawl with a novel in the Literary Garden.

☞ SEE IT ! *Cheekwood is in the Belle Meade neighborhood, 8 miles southwest of downtown Nashville.*

306

Be inspired by the desert at the Georgia O'Keeffe Museum

NEW MEXICO // Georgia O'Keeffe was a woman of passions, but her greatest love affair of all was with the sun-bleached landscape of northern New Mexico. She eventually bought a ranch in the village of Abiquiú, on the Chama River, and made the high desert her muse: silvery mesas; bleached cow skulls; enormously oversized desert flowers. See hundreds of her pieces at this Santa Fe museum, or book ahead to visit Ghost Ranch, her Abiquiú home. Her most famous pieces are in other museums, but this rambling adobe building is still special.

☞ SEE IT ! *The museum is in central Santa Fe, just northwest of the central plaza.*

© PnPy / Shutterstock

© Andrew F Kazmierski / Getty Images

307

Go supersonic at the Intrepid Sea, Air & Space Museum

NEW YORK // Docked on a bustling stretch of the Hudson River waterfront, the USS *Intrepid* is a living testament to the horrors unleashed during WWII. The colossal aircraft carrier survived both a bomb and kamikaze attacks, and it tells its tale through videos, historical artifacts, and frozen-in-time living quarters. The flight deck features fighter planes and military helicopters; you can also take a peek inside the guided-missile submarine *Growler* (not for the claustrophobic) and a decommissioned Concorde plane. Hands-on exhibits include a number of simulators (such as the G Force Encounter) allowing you to enjoy the virtual thrill of flying a supersonic jet plane, and headsets in the Space Shuttle Pavilion (a vast hangar housing the *Enterprise*, NASA's first space shuttle orbiter from the 1970s) that enable you to experience the life of an astronaut in space.

☛ SEE IT ! *It's a 15-minute walk to the nearest subway (42nd St-Port Authority Bus Terminal); the M42 bus takes you straight there.*

308

Take the global perspective at the United Nations HQ

NEW YORK // Assuming there's not a nuclear disarmament meeting or something, you can actually visit the General Assembly Hall and Security Council Chamber at UN Headquarters in NYC, part of the one-hour tour into the world of international diplomacy. You can also visit the gardens (home to Henry Moore's peace-themed *Reclining Figure*), browse exhibits, lunch alongside ambassadors at the Delegates Dining Room, and pick up a souvenir at the bookshop. Even non-philatelists might get a kick out of sending a postcard with a UN stamp. There are several special-interest tours too, including a children's tour complete with a visit to a real refugee tent; a women's focus tour; and a Black history tour. There's a silent meditation held every Thursday at noon in the Meditation Room – om for world peace.

☛ SEE IT ! *Guided tours run Monday to Friday; book ahead and bring photo ID. The visitor center is open daily, except January and February.*

© Sean Pavone / Shutterstocky

© lembi / Shutterstock

309

Have a picnic amid the oak trees in Forsyth Park

GEORGIA // If you stand on the corner of Bull and Gaston streets in Savannah's historic district and look south, you can't help but feel the magnetic pull of Forsyth Park. Gnarled oak trees draped with Spanish moss line the elegant walkways, leading you to a lovely Parisian-inspired 1858 fountain. Although a fine place to contemplate nature's quiet grandeur, there are many other inviting spots found in the 30-acre park, including a Garden of Fragrance for blind visitors, tennis courts and playgrounds, and lush grassy lawns perfect for a picnic – especially after browsing the temptations at the farmers market held on Saturdays.

☛ SEE IT ! *Free shuttle buses go to Forsyth Park via Whitaker and Drayton streets.*

310

Admire the totem poles of Saxman Native Village

ALASKA // There is no finer manifestation of coastal Alaska's indigenous culture than the intricately carved totem poles at Saxman Native Village, south of Ketchikan, adorned with ravens, killer whales, and carved countenances from Native mythology. The totems are spread across a tree-lined park abutting a small Tlingit village. There are 24 in total, most rescued from abandoned settlements around southeast Alaska and restored or re-carved in the 1930s. Among them is a replica of the Lincoln Pole (the original is in Juneau), carved in 1883 to commemorate the first sighting of white people using a picture of Abe as a reference.

☛ SEE IT ! *The park is 3 miles southeast of Ketchikan and accessible on foot or by bus.*

Take a tour of the twinkling night sky at McDonald's astronomer-led Star Parties.

311

Survey distant galaxies with McDonald Observatory's high-powered telescopes

TEXAS // Far from the light pollution of big cities, west Texas boasts some of North America's clearest and darkest skies, making it the perfect spot for an observatory. Some of the world's largest telescopes are perched on the 6791ft peak of Mt Locke; they're so enormous you'll spot them long before you arrive. Operated by astronomers from the University of Texas, the McDonald Observatory is an active research center that also runs guided tours and frequent stargazing events. After sunset, several times a week, the observatory shows off its favorite planets, galaxies, and globular clusters at popular Star Parties, where astronomers guide up to a thousand visitors in some heavy-duty stargazing. Using powerful laser pointers, they give you a tour of the night sky, and you'll get to use some of the telescopes to play planetary detective. You can also come for a daytime tour that includes solar viewing, where you get to stare at the sun without scorching your retinas.

→ SEE IT ! *With good lodging options, Fort Davis is the best base for visiting the observatory, 30-minutes' drive northwest.*

© Kris Davidson / Lonely Planet

312

Get high Colorado-style at the Maroon Bells

COLORADO // One of Colorado's most striking vantage points lies along the shores of Maroon Lake. There, rising above you, are the iconic pyramid-shaped twin peaks of North Maroon (14,014ft) and South Maroon (14,156ft). You don't even need to crane your neck to admire the view – on calm days their snow-striped forms shimmer on the mirror-like surface of the water. Though it's an appealing setting for photography – or even a bit of Bob Ross-esque landscape painting – most people come here to get active. The surrounding wilderness offers wonderful hiking, with nine passes over 12,000ft and six fourteeners (over 14,000ft). Some jut into jagged granite towers, others are more slope-and-curve, nurturing a series of meadows. A four-hour round-trip walk takes you to the high-alpine Crater Lake, marvelously surrounded by sculpted summits. For a bit more altitude, you can press on to Buckskin Pass (12,462ft) – from the narrow granite ledge you can see mountains erupt in all directions. Maroon Bells is also a great spot for horse riding, while avid (masochistic?) cyclists make the 11-mile uphill ride here from Aspen.

🔫 TRY IT ! *The Maroon Bells RFTA Shuttle provides easy access from Aspen.*

© Kong_Setthawaut / Shutterstock

© Pung / Shutterstock

313

Pace past the cellblocks at Eastern State Penitentiary

PENNSYLVANIA // A formidable edifice of Brobdingnagian walls and castellated towers, this was once the most notorious jail in the USA and, arguably, the world. When built in 1829 it was a pioneering prison that would become a model for hundreds of others: an early exponent of the separate incarceration system which, odd as it might now seem, was groundbreaking in focusing on reform rather than just being a place for punishment. The gloomy Gothic look was intended to instil fear in those considering committing future crimes; see what you think exploring its echoing corridors and cellblocks today. Its best-known incumbent during 142 years of operation through to 1971 was gangster Al Capone, who famously lived a life of prison luxury during his time inside. Displays give insights into the current prison system and, to brighten the mood, there are interesting art installations throughout.

 SEE IT ! *The prison is a short walk west of Philadelphia's Fairmount metro station.*

314

Relive momentous history at Pearl Harbor

HAWAI'I // On Sunday, December 7 1941, the Japanese bombed the then-neutral USA's base at Hawai'i's Pearl Harbor. The attack killed 2403 people, wounded a further 1178, wiped out 188 aircraft, sank four battleships, and precipitated American entry into WWII. This poignant national memorial tells the tragic tale.

The main sight is the USS Arizona Memorial. Accessible only by boat, it straddles but doesn't touch the submerged hull of the *Arizona*, one of the battleships wrecked on that fateful day. But there is much more to this site. A visitor center and the interactive displays of two excellent museums bring to life the Road to War and the Attack & Aftermath through photos, films, illustrated graphics, and taped oral histories. Most remarkably of all, as the 80th anniversary took place in 2021, there are still a handful of Pearl Harbor veterans you could catch on your visit, answering questions and signing autographs.

SEE IT ! *Bus routes 20 and 42 run to Pearl Harbor from downtown Honolulu.*

© Douglas Klug / Getty Images

© thinair28 / Getty Images

315

Spot wonderful wildlife around Channel Islands NP

CALIFORNIA // Channel Islands National Park is a Unesco Biosphere Reserve and a National Marine Sanctuary too, and such protection is warranted. While these islands might lie just 90 miles from Los Angeles, the USA's second-biggest city, nature here remains pristine and unique. The park covers five of the archipelago's eight islands: San Miguel; Santa Rosa; Santa Cruz; Santa Barbara; Anacapa. Endemic species number well over 100 on what is nicknamed 'California's Galápagos'. The flora and fauna includes spotted skunk, deer mouse, Channel Islands fox, one-of-a-kind subspecies of oak and pine, and a cornucopia of marine life. Nor is the backdrop bad: a raw, end-of-the-world landscape where you can camp, hike, scuba dive, and whale-watch.

☛ SEE IT ! *Access is by boat from Ventura or Oxnard.*

316

Find perpendicular paradise at Smith Rock State Park

OREGON // Out of a verdant pocket of Oregon's High Desert sprout craggy ramparts of basalt, shooting 600ft or more above Crooked River. To say the mountains of State Rock State Park are steep is an understatement: they are invariably immediately, giddyingly vertical or overhanging. The park is often heralded as the cradle of modern American sport climbing – there are several thousand routes here, including over a thousand bolted ones. So challenging are ascents that hard-core climbers from across the planet gravitate to the park, but those inclined to vertigo can try less precipitous canyon-country pursuits like scrambling, hiking, mountain biking, or horseback riding. And keep eyes peeled for golden eagles, prairie falcons, and beavers.

☛ SEE IT ! *The park is off Hwy 97, 9 miles north of Redmond.*

317

Go for a spin on Santa Monica Pier Carousel

CALIFORNIA // From your whirling vantage point, the palm-lined boulevards and sparkling Pacific Ocean soon become a blur. You're clinging to a shiny steed on Santa Monica Pier Carousel, one of 44 horses (or, if you're lucky, a goat or rabbit) that rotate merrily on this 1920s landmark. The carousel spins inside the period Hippodrome, a stone's throw from Santa Monica beach, and is your perfect introduction to Los Angeles' beloved beachfront escape, all for the retro price of just $2 per ride.

☛ TRY IT ! *Santa Monica is linked to LA's downtown via Metro line E. If driving, the pier marks the end of Route 66.*

© Thomas Barrat / Shutterstock

318

Scramble to the very top of Maine in Baxter State Park

MAINE // For a wilderness escape, it's hard to think of a better place than Baxter State Park. In the heart of the vast Maine North Woods, the wind whips around mountain peaks, black bears root through the underbrush, and hikers walk for miles without seeing another soul. The scale is daunting, with a 210,000-acre footprint encompassing sheer cliffs, mirror-like lakes, gurgling streams and 215 miles of trails. Baxter's 5267ft Mt Katahdin is the park's crowning glory: it's Maine's tallest mountain and the northern end of the 2190-mile Appalachian Trail.

☛ SEE IT ! *Baxter's main southern entrance is at Togue Pond, 18 miles north of the town of Millinocket.*

© Cavan Images / Getty Images

Death Valley, a great place to spot wildlife, wildflowers – and the pot-draped roadsign for Teakettle Junction, en route to Racetrack Playa.

319

Look for life in the sand dunes of Death Valley National Park

CALIFORNIA // The ominous name might bring to mind Wild West ghost towns, broken-down pioneer wagon trains, and tumbleweed blowing past skulls across parched land, but Death Valley is actually full of life. Spring wildflowers daub the dunes with a painter's palette of colors, adrenaline-seekers zoom across cracked salt flats, and shy desert wildlife lives by starlight. This is also a land of superlatives, holding the US records for hottest temperature (134°F), lowest point (Badwater, 282ft below sea level) and largest national park outside Alaska (more than 5300 sq miles). And if you've come for the dramatic scenery, you won't be disappointed. Early morning is the best time to visit Zabriskie Point, with its spectacular views across ethereally glowing, golden badlands eroded into waves, pleats, and gullies. By sunset or moonlight, the Mesquite Flat Sand Dunes, which rise up to 100ft, are especially magical. For the most dramatic panorama, make the 14-mile roundtrip hike up to Telescope Peak. From its 11,049ft perch, the views plummet to the desert floor, as far below you as two Grand Canyons deep.

☛ SEE IT ! *The national park is 140 miles northwest of Las Vegas. Furnace Creek Visitor Center, off Hwy 190, is a useful gateway.*

320

Hike wild trails in Big Bend Ranch

TEXAS // Lying in one of the most remote corners of Texas, Big Bend Ranch State Park is 486 sq miles of mountain-filled desert. With limited infrastructure, exploring can be a challenge, but the rewards are ample: solitary hikes through slot canyons and up to rocky viewpoints by day, followed by an evening watching the sky fill with stars from backcountry campsites. There's just one paved road through the park, the dramatic Route 170, which curves along the Rio Grande past striking geological formations. In the interior, gravel roads lead to sparkling springs, hidden waterfalls, and El Solitario, an eroded volcanic dome and 8-mile-wide caldera formed over millions of years.

☛ SEE IT ! *A key access point is Barton Warnock Visitor Center, located 95 miles south of Alpine.*

321

Connect East and West at the National Museum of Asian Art

WASHINGTON, DC // Welcome to the National Museum of Asian Art, the stunning collections of Charles Lang Freer and Arthur M. Sackler, spread over two connected galleries and containing beautiful Japanese silk scrolls, smiling Buddhas, rare Islamic manuscripts, and Chinese jades. Freer designed his gallery to connect East and West, ancient and modern. He also built a partnership with American painter James Whistler, collecting over 1000 of his remarkable artworks; Whistler's blue-and-gold Peacock Room showcases a Chinese porcelain collection.

☛ SEE IT ! *Located on the southern side of the Mall, the two-galleries-in-one are connected underground.*

322

Beat Florida's heat at Wekiwa Springs

FLORIDA // In the Sunshine State, a hammock is not just a device for suspended relaxation but a stand of tropical trees, many of which flank the watery Eden of Wekiwa Springs State Park. Here, you can hike, bike, and then cool off by plunging into a swimming hole or paddling down the serene Wekiva River. Being so close to busy downtown Orlando makes the park's greenery all the more refreshing for the soul. At the springs, water temperatures stay a constantly lovely 72°F, and tree-shaded surrounds seduce picnickers. You can float along Wekiva River for 10 tranquil miles or more, alighting at islands or shady banks and eventually reaching other reserves.

☛ TRY IT ! *The park is 16 miles north of central Orlando via I-4, Hwy 434 and Wekiwa Springs Rd.*

323

Pedal past dunes and forest on Sleeping Bear Heritage Trail

MICHIGAN // Cyclists (and walkers and runners) get pumped up about this 22-mile route, the Sleeping Bear Dunes National Lakeshore's only biking trail: the mostly paved path navigates a beguiling expanse of this Lake Michigan reserve. Colossal sand dunes halfway along the reserve's length are the show-stealers, but a mix of dreamy forests, quaint townships, and Great Lakes waterfront inject variety into what's most easily traveled as a leisurely day's pedal. The gentle run allows maximum appreciation of all the majestically blue water, tawny sand, and greenery. And should you tire of biking, there's hiking and kayaking too.

☛ TRY IT ! *Begin the route in Empire, near Philip A. Hart Visitor Center.*

© Gestalt Imagery / Shutterstock

© Alexander Davidovich / Shutterstock

324

Book your seat for a thrilling ride on the Cumbres & Toltec Scenic Railroad

COLORADO/NEW MEXICO // This stateline-crossing train trip is a fantastic engineering feat that tackles the majestic 10,022-ft Cumbres Pass by rail and steam power. Traversing the mountains between Antonito, Colorado and Chama, New Mexico, this narrow-gauge thrill ride is the surviving 64-mile tract of tracks laid by Denver & Rio Grande Western Railroad in 1880. Steam locos wheeze you up pine- and aspen-cloaked hillsides, revealing vistas of plain and peak, in what is North America's longest and highest narrow-gauge steam run. The heart-in-mouth highlight is the chug along the Toltec Gorge, where trains edge a 600ft rock face high above Rio de los Pinos. Allow a plodding but picturesque six hours for a complete Antonito-Chama adventure.

☛ SEE IT ! *Trains run from both Antonito and Chama, round-trip to midway stop Osier; or one-way the whole way, returning passengers to their start point by coach.*

325

Have fun on and off the water at Emerald Bay State Park

CALIFORNIA // Lake Tahoe is a place that lives up to its reputation, and Emerald Bay State Park, an inlet and surrounding hills and woods tucked into the lake's southwest corner, is the icing on Tahoe's sumptuous cake. This 1533-acre park has to be California's finest non-coastal water experience. Steep conifer-carpeted shores provide amphitheater-like views at this tear-shaped lake extension, whilst center-stage is the lake's only island, Fannette, a tree-dotted speck of land, reachable by boat across water that shimmers between cloverleaf green and light jade depending on the angle of the sun. Equally eye-catching is lavishly turreted Vikingsholm Castle, one-time summer home of heiress Lora Knight. Vikingsholm and lovely Eagle Falls cascade are accessible by pretty hiking trails.

☛ SEE IT ! *Driving the lakeshore clockwise from South Lake Tahoe on Hwy 89, you reach parking first for Eagle Falls and then Vikingsholm.*

© CSNafzger / Shutterstock

© Kris Davidson / Lonely Planet

326

Follow powder-hound celebs to seriously swanky Sun Valley Resort

IDAHO // Occupying one of Idaho's more stunning natural locations, Sun Valley is a living piece of ski history. It was the first purpose-built ski resort in the US and opened in 1936 to much fanfare, thanks to both its luxury showcase lodge and the world's first chairlift.

The ski area and adjacent town of Ketchum were popularized early on by celebrities led (as ever) by Ernest Hemingway, with Clark Gable, Gary Cooper, and several Kennedys in hot pursuit. It has maintained its love affair with swanky Hollywood clientele ever since. Not surprisingly, the place is squeaky clean, easy on the eye – and pricey. Notwithstanding, it offers a diverse range of skiing and is well-endowed with plenty of non-snowy activities like hiking, fishing, hunting, and spirit-reviving hot springs.

TRY IT ! *Friedman Memorial Airport is located 12 miles south of Ketchum in Hailey. It has daily service to most western-states hubs.*

327

Stop by Hemingway House to hear some of Key West's most colorful stories

FLORIDA // One of a dozen Americans to scoop the Nobel Prize in Literature, Ernest Hemingway ranks hands-down among the USA's most highly regarded writers. Illinois born, he spent his formative years in Paris and later ones in Cuba, but for a decade in between (1931-1939) he called this elegantly colonial Key West mansion home. Hemingway moved here with wife two Pauline Pfeiffer, a friend of his first wife, and left to run off with his third: suffice it to say this chapter of Papa's life was far from dull, and gets brilliantly told on guided tours here crammed with interesting stories. Work-wise, *Green Hills of Africa* and *The Short Happy Life of Francis Macomber* were produced here, as were many cats, descendants of which still run amok in the gorgeous grounds.

SEE IT ! *The Hemingway House is at 907 Whitehead St in Key West.*

328

Watch wild horses wallow at Chincoteague Island

VIRGINIA // Every year on the last Wednesday in July, a handful of riders called 'the saltwater cowboys' climb into the saddle and drive a herd of wild horses across a small channel in northeast Virginia. The Chincoteague Island Pony Swim, famously described in Marguerite Henry's Newbery Award-winning *Misty of Chincoteague*, is followed by a pony parade down Main St en route to the Carnival grounds, where an auction is held the next day. The sale of a select group of foals helps control the size of the island's herd, and also raises money for charity.

☛ SEE IT ! *The Island lies just across from Chincoteague National Wildlife Refuge, which has hiking trails, beachfront, and a lighthouse.*

329

Absorb African American history and culture at CAAM

CALIFORNIA // Opened in impressive quarters at LA's Exposition Park in time for the 1984 Olympics, the landmark California African American Museum (CAAM) is one of the US's most important public collection of African American culture and the first such museum to be fully funded by a US state. It primarily focuses on the huge African American contribution to the heritage of the American West, conveyed through 4000-plus objects from landscape painting to mixed-media artworks. Highlights like recordings of Walter Burrell's interviews with Black celebrities evidence how the CAAM's collection goes far beyond visuals.

☛ SEE IT ! *Close by lies Expo/USC Metro station on Line E.*

330

Walk Birmingham's moving Civil Rights Memorial Trail

ALABAMA // Today's pleasantly leafy and vibrant Birmingham belies a fraught past. Once called 'the most segregated city in the country' by Martin Luther King Jr, it became the center of the Birmingham Campaign, aimed at publicizing the plight of African Americans in the city, which in turn was a catalyst to protests nationwide and ultimately 1964's seminal Civil Rights Act. A poignant walk, over seven city blocks where major campaign events took place, commemorates this history with striking statues, plaques, and photography.

☛ TRY IT ! *Start the self-guided trail at Kelly Ingram Park (cnr 16th Ave N and 16th St N).*

331

Paddle or promenade wildlife-rich Manitou Islands

MICHIGAN // Part of the Sleeping Bear Dunes National Lakeshore, Lake Michigan's North and South Manitou Islands give themselves up utterly to hiking, kayaking, and backcountry camping. Stunningly unspoiled shorelines, dunes, and old-growth cedar forests offer eye-popping topographic versatility. Top trek is the 7-miler to South Manitou's Valley of the Giants: 100ft-tall white cedars in one of Michigan's few surviving stands of virgin timber. Countryside has reclaimed former settlements here: both islands are home to abundant birdlife, including bald eagles.

☛ SEE IT ! *Manitou Islands Transit runs ferries from Leland to South Manitou, a 1.5-hour run.*

332

Drive the rural and historic Natchez Trace Parkway

TENNESSEE, ALABAMA & MISSISSIPPI // Native Americans, rural 'Kaintuck' boatmen, settlers, slave traders, and soldiers all walked this 444-mile trail, now a road traversing Tennessee, Alabama, and Mississippi. It's one of the US's truly great drives, through blackland prairie and sun-dappled forest, passing pastures and crumbling barns untouched in a century.

Running alongside the road is the Natchez Trace Scenic Trail, around 60 miles of hiking and horseback riding path broken into five chunks: explore primeval swamps, sun-blasted grasslands, rocky ravines, and ancient forests. The entire Parkway is a designated bike route, which means no trucks and cars must stay under 50mph. With plenty of

pleasant inns and B&Bs just off the road, it's an ideal setup for a long-distance road trip. And keep an eye out for historic sites along the way, including the grave of Meriwether Lewis, of Lewis and Clark Expedition fame.

☞ SEE IT ! *The Parkway runs from south Nashville to Natchez, Mississippi.*

© Jeff Fladen / 500px

© Esteban Martinena Guerrer / Shutterstock

© Karina Bobinski / Courtesy of Mattress Factory

333

See shadows of WWII history at Manzanar National Historic Site

CALIFORNIA // Just north of tiny Lone Pine, only arid desert and the distant Sierra Nevada bore witness to the suffering of 10,000 people during World War II. In 1942, the American government ordered that people of Japanese ancestry be rounded up and transported to 10 different military-style camps, including Manzanar. Their freedoms were stripped and their possessions sold off.

Driving past a lone guard tower into the site, it feels like you're being watched. Exploring by car or on foot, signposts offer clues to how interred people's lives unfolded in this lonely setting. Only the former school auditorium remains intact, and an ornamental garden stands as a forlorn symbol of hope. An obelisk gleams bone-white in the cemetery, though all but a few of the bodies were reinterred after the war. Even in death, Manzanar's residents left as quickly as possible.

📣 SEE IT ! *Manzanar is 60 miles northwest of Death Valley National Park, or around 90 miles south of Mammoth Lakes.*

334

Be mesmerized by contemporary art at Mattress Factory

PENNSYLVANIA // Mention Mattress Factory to anyone in the American arts world and phrases like 'avant-garde' start popping up straightaway. This art space occupies the former Stearns & Foster mattress warehouse in Pittsburgh's Central Northside neighborhood. Purchased by artist Barbara Luderowski in 1975, it morphed from artist co-operative into an internationally renowned contemporary gallery and global pioneer of site-specific installation art. Its famously edgy exhibits now span several buildings. The main site's roof is itself an installation: giant LED light-sticks seeming to pierce the topmost floor and forming an iconic part of the city skyline. Besides permanent works by artists like James Turrell and many changing exhibitions, it supports a residency program, helping it remain at the vanguard of artistic innovation. Expect the unexpected: room-sized works full of mind-bending perspectives through to sensory deprivation spaces.

📣 SEE IT ! *Start exploring the museum's triumvirate of locations at the main building on Sampsonia Way.*

Find purple sands and pounding seas at beautiful Pfeiffer Beach.

335

Behold breathtaking rocks at Pfeiffer Beach

CALIFORNIA // Reserve the word 'awesome' for dazzling displays of nature like this. As with all truly special places, Pfeiffer Beach needs no fanfare to announce itself. To get to this thrilling stretch of shoreline, take the unsigned, serpentine Sycamore Canyon Drive just south of Big Sur and wind your way down to a parking spot from where it's a short walk to the beach. And there it is, a creek emptying onto a crescent of tawny sand that coaxes your gaze to the jaw-dropping geology ahead. A double-act of towering rock formations stands up to the might of the thrashing ocean, one of which has had a natural rock arch pounded into it with the surf surging spectacularly through. When you've recovered your breath, look at the sand beneath your feet: it's purple in places, due to the presence of manganese garnet in the cliffs.

☛ SEE IT ! *Coming south through Big Sur on Hwy 1, the tight-angled turning is half a mile after Big Sur Station: no RVs or trailers are allowed down the beach access road.*

336

Look for Keys wildlife at Crane Point Hammock

FLORIDA // Bohemian craft stores and breezy waterfront bars are classic spots in the Florida Keys, but they don't reveal much about the natural beauty of this vast archipelago. For a look at a near-pristine Keys ecosystem, visit Crane Point Hammock, a 63-acre reserve encompassing dense tropical hammock, solution holes, mangroves, a butterfly meadow, and lovely coastline. A looping 1.5-mile trail with boardwalk detours takes you into the wild side. Afterward, see dugout canoes, pirate exhibitions, and a simulated reef at the onsite museum.

🖝 SEE IT ! *The reserve is near the town of Marathon, mile 55 of the Overseas Hwy (US-1).*

337

Rediscover pinball wizardry at Asheville Pinball Museum

NORTH CAROLINA // If there is one thing to get old-fashioned gamers goggle-eyed, it's this pinball-machine-packed throwback to the days when these vintage games would have dotted bars and malls of downtowns countrywide. Asheville Pinball Museum exhibits machines with themes from Air Aces through to Game of Thrones, so there is surely a specimen to set your inner silver ball spinning. Some tables hark back to the pinball golden age of the 1940s, while brightly-flashing examples from the 1960s onward are available for a flipper flip.

🖝 SEE IT ! *Your arcade-game utopia awaits at 1 Battle Square, downtown Asheville.*

338

Patrol the perfectly preserved Fort Mackinac

MICHIGAN // Built by the Brits in 1780, this once-embattled garrison saw action in the American War of Independence and two later US–Britain conflicts. Nailbitingly close to the border of then-British colony Canada on an island where lakes Huron and Michigan meet, its location made it a hotbed of action in the late 18th and early 19th centuries. It survived to remain the USA's best-preserved military fort. Costumed characters and cannon firings evoke its storied past and, history aside, million-dollar views tumble back over Mackinac Island and the lake.

🖝 SEE IT ! *Get to Mackinac Island by ferry from Mackinaw City or St Ignace.*

339

Graffiti a car, legally, at Cadillac Ranch

TEXAS // It seems purpose-built for Instagram, but this photogenic and quirky roadside attraction – 10 vintage Cadillacs, buried nose-down in the Texas Panhandle dirt – was dreamed up by an eccentric Texas millionaire in 1974. He considered it a tribute to old Route 66, now I-40 here. Drivers speeding through the cattle town of Amarillo stop to tag the cars with spray paint – there's usually a can or two rattling around on the ground – which means the Ranch has a different look every time you pass. It's the ultimate monument to the Great American Road Trip.

🖝 SEE IT ! *The Ranch is on the south side of I-40 west of town, between exits 60 and 62.*

340

Dig your heels in the sand at Bahia Honda State Park

FLORIDA // The Florida Keys are better known for their mangroves than their beaches. Bahia Honda State Park, however, didn't get the memo, with not one but two sparkling stretches of white-sand shoreline that rank among Florida's loveliest. Mile-long Sandspur Beach makes a magnificent destination for a day of waterside relaxing, though you can also hire kayaks for a leisurely paddle, head off on a snorkeling trip run by the park service, or take in the views from atop the old Bahia Honda Rail Bridge – one of the last vestiges of the railroad that once linked Miami with Key West.

☛ SEE IT ! *The park is off US-1, some 125 miles south of Miami.*

341

Geek out at the Museum of Science and Industry

ILLINOIS // You could spend days in the America's largest science museum and never see it all. So you'll have to prioritize. Clear highlights include the WWII U-boat, the replica coal mine, the Apollo 8 command module, and a 3500-sq-ft model railroad. If you have transportation-obsessed kids in tow, you'll never get out of here. Oh, and there's a 40ft water-vapor tornado, a toy assembly line, and a walk-through human heart. Come to think of it, why would you even want to leave?

☛ SEE IT ! *The museum is in Chicago's Hyde Park neighborhood. Take the Metra Electric Line to 55th/56th/57th St station.*

342

Step back into settler-era America on Tangier Island

VIRGINIA // Quite the island time forgot, this marshy protuberance is marooned in the middle of the US's biggest estuary, Chesapeake Bay. Some 90 miles northwest is Washington, DC, yet Tangier Island feels epochs away. Only ever linked to the outside world by sporadic boat service, it has preserved cultural traits dating back to the early settlers. In an enchanting excerpt from 18th-century Virginia life, locals live in pretty clapboard houses and work on the water, crabbing and oystering just like their ancestors (yes, there are places to try their catch).

☛ SEE IT ! *Tangier Ferries connect the island with Onancock; Tangier Cruise with Reedville. Routes run May-Oct.*

343

View vivid *Seven Magic Mountains* in the Las Vegas desert

NEVADA // Resembling giant many-hued marshmallows upended on skewers, *Seven Magic Mountains* is not what you expect to see driving I-15 south from Las Vegas. Yet the septet of gaudily-painted boulder stacks forming this art installation have been a huge crowd-pleaser since their 2016 public unveiling. Artist Ugo Rondinone's oversized rocks balance atop one another in towers up to 35ft above the desert scrub and in a rainbow-spanning color spectrum – the brightest things around for many miles. By popular demand, they have already stayed standing well beyond the two years they were originally scheduled to exhibit.

☛ SEE IT ! *The artwork is 26 miles south of Las Vegas on I-15.*

Taking a leaf from his father's prestigious book, Lloyd Wright's iconic design for Wayfarers Chapel lets in the outside.

344

Seek sanctuary at picturesque Wayfarers Chapel

CALIFORNIA // The most arresting work of architect Lloyd Wright (son of Frank) towers high above the ocean, in an Edenic clifftop enclave beyond the LA suburban sprawl. Constructed in 1951 almost completely of glass, the striking chapel lets in its natural surroundings to awe worshippers beneath. From the pews, views are of resplendent redwoods encasing the building in a bower that lattices the blue sky and sea beyond.

Small wonder, then, that this is also a popular place to get hitched: Jayne Mansfield famously married Mickey Hargitay here. Wright junior was a landscape gardener too, and the flora making up the 3.5 acres of gardens was a cruicial part of his design; the grounds feature arboreal walkways, a reflection pool, a rose garden, and a hillside stream. Whilst design inspiration for the chapel came from Wright's walks in Northern California's redwood

forests, the idea for its construction began with Elizabeth Schellenberg who, back in the 1920s when this area was mainly farmland, envisaged a little chapel where passers-by could rest and give thanks to God for nature's beauty. Today, it's one of the USA's key examples of organic architecture.

☞ SEE IT ! *The chapel is near Rancho Palos Verdes, 30 miles southwest of downtown LA.*

© ShengYing Lin / Shutterstock

© kavram / Shutterstock

345

346

Relive JFK's tragic assassination at the Sixth Floor Museum

Stumble into a surrealist painting at Mono Lake

TEXAS // Nearly all Americans of a certain age can remember where they were on the fateful afternoon of November 22, 1963. As John F. Kennedy traveled in the back of a convertible through the streets of Dallas, a gunman hidden in a building overlooking Dealey Plaza fired three shots, killing the president and seriously wounding Texas Governor John Connally. The assassination was seen by thousands of spectators who had come to cheer the presidential motorcade, and the shocking news reverberated around the globe. In 1989, the Dallas County Historical Foundation opened a museum dedicated to the infamous event, in the same building where Lee Harvey Oswald pulled the trigger. Fascinating multimedia exhibits tell the story and provide excellent historical context of JFK's time, as well as his life and legacy — and the museum doesn't shy away from the myriad conspiracy theories too.

CALIFORNIA // Let the crowds go to Yosemite National Park. You've discovered somewhere far more curious 22 miles east: Mono Lake, glowing an eerie blue and ringed by toothy towers of limestone.

Sculpted by an Ice Age volcanic explosion, Mono is one of North America's oldest lakes. It's also one of the strangest, as you'll discover along footpaths where limestone structures, known as tufa, squat like goblins by the shore. These calcite towers emerged as the water receded, a slow-grow phenomenon that now lines the shores with rock formations. From Mono Lake Park on the western shore, follow a wooden boardwalk that skirts the lake's glassy surface. Stay a while to watch avocets and sandpipers strutting through the shallows. Wilder walks thread from South Tufa, where you can see a bigger sculpture garden of craggy limestone.

☞ SEE IT ! *The Sixth Floor Museum is a short walk west of downtown Dallas, near the West End light rail stop.*

☞ SEE IT ! *South Tufa is 30 miles north of ski and bike hub Mammoth Lakes, along Hwy 395.*

347

Delve deep at Lanaʻi Culture & Heritage Center

HAWAIʻI // Lanaʻi is the joker in the pack of the Hawaiʻian archipelago: the smallest of the publicly accessible islands and the most culturally un-pin-down-able. This has a lot to do with the legacy of pineapple plantations here, which meant immigrant workers from all around the world settled and gave Lanaʻi its multifaceted heritage. This excellent visitor center and museum is an essential first step in discovering more, covering everything from the island's mysterious place in Hawaiʻian legend through ancient history to the harrowing hardships of pineapple plantation life.

☛ SEE IT ! *The center is located at 730 Lanaʻi Avenue, Lanaʻi City.*

348

Revel in relaxation at Riverbend Hot Springs

NEW MEXICO // Not only have you checked in to New Mexico's most eccentrically named city, Truth or Consequences, but you've arrived at one of the state's finest wellness destinations. Considered to have healing powers by Apache and Mimbres tribespeople, the mineral-abundant waters of the Rio Grande hereabouts can be enjoyed by all at this fetching octet of public thermal riverside pools boasting toasty temperatures of 95–108°F. Shady decking and a barrel sauna wrap up a special pocket of decadent desert downtime.

☛ SEE IT ! *Truth or Consequences is 149 miles south of Albuquerque on I-25.*

349

Roam rugged wilds around Split Rock Lighthouse Park

MINNESOTA // Of all the gargantuan folds of shoreline on the Great Lakes, this state park's 4-mile flurry of craggy, spruce-stippled Lake Superior coast is perhaps the most photographed. There is one standout reason why, and despite a wildlife roll-call of moose, Canadian lynx and black bears, it's a manmade one: the pretty-as-a-peach lighthouse crowning the cliffs. When it was built, following the wild Mataafa Storm of 1905, no roads served this shore, so all construction materials were shipped in then hauled up the rockface. Pretty – and pretty impressive.

☛ TRY IT ! *The nearest significant settlement is Beaver Bay, 5.5 miles northeast; from there head southwest along the lake on Hwy 61.*

350

Watch the sun set over Grayton Beach State Park

FLORIDA // With nearly 2000 acres of marble-colored dunes rolling down to the water's edge, this state park's beauty is genuinely mind-blowing. It's nestled against the wealthy but down-to-earth community of Grayton Beach, home to the famed Red Bar (recently rebuilt after a fire) and to the quirky Dog Wall – a mural on which residents paint portraits of their dogs. Locals flock here for nightly sunsets and to wakeboard on the unique coastal dune lakes that shimmer across the sand from the gulf.

☛ SEE IT ! *The South Walton beaches stretch in a thin line along the 30A coast road, starting about 15 miles east of Destin.*

© Sean Pavone / Shutterstock

© NG-Spacetime / Shutterstock

351

Sample a taste of Philadelphia at Reading Terminal Market

PENNSYLVANIA // Keeping a balance between food market and dining destination, Reading Terminal Market dates back to 1893 and is a city institution. The 75 local stalls provide a strong flavor of Philly's cultural melting pot, embracing everything from Pennsylvania Dutch to Thai cuisine, and attracting everyone from billionaires to blue-collar workers.

Originally accommodated in Reading Railroad Company train shed, the market has had its ups and downs, most notably when the demise of the railway cut passing foot traffic in the 1970s. A welcome rebirth began in the 1990s with the building of an onsite convention center coupled with a growing public interest in artisanal food. Among the many highlights are Bassetts ice cream, DiNic's roast pork sandwiches and Amish meals at Dutch Eating Place.

☛ SEE IT ! *Join the Taste of Philly Food Tour for an in-depth look around the market, including tastings.*

352

Glide through powder snow at the resorts of Alta and Snowbird

UTAH // As you slalom through spruce trees, your skis kicking up great puffs of snow, there can be no doubt: Utah has the best powder on earth, and the fluffiest snow is right here in the Wasatch Mountains.

Almost 45ft of the white stuff cloaks Utah each year; sub-zero temperatures and dry desert air transform it into cloud-like drifts, irresistible to skiers and boarders who flock to the twin resorts of Alta and Snowbird. Alta is reserved exclusively for skiers; the most daring jump aboard helicopters to reach untouched, waist-deep snow. Snowbird, with 2500 acres of mostly advanced-level terrain, brings snowboarders to join the party. It also has the longest winter sports season anywhere in Utah, so you can feel May sunshine warm your skin as you cruise downhill in shorts and a T-shirt.

☛ TRY IT ! *Both resorts have accommodation close to the lifts, but it's cheaper to stay in southeast Salt Lake City and take the ski bus.*

Courtesy of Sevier Distilling Company

© Stephen Moehle/Bartfett / 500px

Imbibe Appalachian moonshine at Sevier Distilling Company

TENNESSEE // The Smoky Mountains have deep ties to moonshine, an un-aged whiskey often made from corn. It's a uniquely American spirit, conjuring visions of hidden copper stills, bearded mountain men, and wild car chases with revenuers in hot pursuit of Depression-era bootleggers. For decades, strict alcohol laws prevented the legal production of distilled spirits across much of southern Appalachia, but a recent loosening of these laws has spurred the opening of numerous new distilleries, and sales of 'legal' moonshine have skyrocketed. Hey presto Sevier, a small-batch distillery offering tours and tastings. They source all ingredients locally and knock out an artisanal moonshine; a tequila spin-off called Tennekeela; and an intriguing Yenoh, an all-honey mead that goes well with Bailey's.

☞ SEE IT ! *The distillery is in Sevierville, 26 miles east of Knoxville, where there's a Greyhound terminal, as well as McGhee Tyson Airport.*

See all creatures great and small at San Diego Zoo

CALIFORNIA // One of SoCal's biggest lures, San Diego's zoo is no standard wildlife park, with an estimated 4000 animals representing more than 650 species. Moreover, the setting is beautifully landscaped, cage-free enclosures typically replicate a species' natural habitat, and some of the plants in the zoo gardens are used for the specialized food requirements of the animals. The park is divided into geographical zones and bioclimatic environments including the 'Elephant Odyssey', home to African and Indian elephants; 'Africa Rocks' replete with lemurs, dwarf crocodiles, leopards, gelada baboons, and meerkats; and the 'Outback enclosure' with the largest colony of koalas outside Australia. Get close-up views of polar bears swimming underwater at the Northern Frontier, and hippos grazing in the water on the Hippo Trail.

☞ SEE IT ! *The zoo is located in the northern part of Balboa Park. Bus 7 will get you there from downtown – it stops at Zoo Place.*

Be wowed by the kaleidoscope of colors at Wailua Falls, but be warned – this is a look-don't-touch experience, to be enjoyed from above.

355

Soak up the tropical beauty of Wailua Falls

HAWAI'I // Made famous by its appearance in the opening credits of 1970s TV series *Fantasy Island*, this two-plumed waterfall is spectacular when in full flow – mist forms in the surrounding tropical foliage and the play of sunlight on water produces mini rainbows. Located on the Upper Fork of the Wailua River, on the eastern side of Kaua'i island, the falls are easily accessible from Lihu'e town and viewable from a parking lot close to the rim.

While officially listed as 80ft, the falls have been repeatedly measured to have a far greater drop. Legend has it that Hawai'ian men in times of old would test their endurance (and sanity) by jumping into the 30ft pool below. Don't try it.

There are two unofficial trails leading down to the falls, although the county advises against using either of them. Heed the sign at the top that warns: 'Slippery rocks at top

of falls. People have been killed.' Many have fallen while trying to scramble down the steep, muddy path beyond.

☛ SEE IT ! *From Lihu'e, follow Kuhio Hwy (Hwy 56) north. Turn left onto Ma'alo Rd (Hwy 583), which ends at the falls after 4 miles. Expect crowds and difficult parking. The alternative of seeing the falls from a helicopter is definitely a superior experience.*

©littleny / Shutterstock

© Elizabeth Felicella / Courtesy of Rothko Chapel

356

Stroll in style along fabulous Fifth Avenue

NEW YORK // Even if you've never visited New York City, chances are you'll know of Fifth Avenue. Considered the main artery of Manhattan, this fabled boulevard stretches for over six miles from Washington Square Park in Greenwich Village to the Harlem River. When visitors 'do' Fifth Avenue, they're often referring to the luxury department-store-studded shopping strips. But make sure you visit the blocks that run alongside Central Park too. These have an eye-boggling array of stunning mansions (this section was once called Millionaire's Row), plus the Museum Mile, so named for its wonderful collection of museums.

👉 SEE IT ! *To see (nearly) the entire length, take the local bus (routes M1 to M4) that head both north and south.*

357

Feel the spiritual power of art inside the Rothko Chapel

TEXAS // Upon visiting the non-denominational Rothko Chapel in a middle-class Houston neighborhood, some people might look around and wonder where the paintings are stored. Others, however, find abstract expressionist Mark Rothko's 14 murals imbued with a power that borders on the transcendent. At first glance they seem an almost uniform black. The longer one spends in this supremely meditative space, the more subtleties appear, and just as Rothko intended, many visitors experience a profoundly emotional reaction. The artist spent the last six years of his life working on the chapel, but sadly he did not live to see its completion in 1971.

👉 SEE IT ! *The Rothko Chapel is 3 miles southwest of downtown Houston, and a short stroll from the Menil Collection.*

Giving thrillseekers a seaside ride since 1927, Cyclone 2 is a Coney Island institution.

358

Soak up the nostalgic, kitschy charm of Coney Island

NEW YORK // The Wonder Wheel! Nathan's Famous hotdogs! Muscle-bound bodybuilders posing on the boardwalk! Coney Island, the beachfront pleasure district in far southern Brooklyn, is a nostalgic blast from the days when a ride on a roller coaster, a bag of saltwater taffy, and a souvenir photo were the highlight of the year for immigrant families, rowdy teens, and tourists alike. A seaside resort since the mid-1800s, Coney Island came into its own around the turn of the 20th century with the opening of amusement parks, aquariums, and sideshows. After a lull later in the century, Coney Island now sparkles again with the same kitschy, slightly seedy charm. Take a teeth-juddering ride on the Cyclone, a wooden roller coaster in operation since 1927, then chow down on kosher hotdogs at Nathan's, host to the beloved annual July 4 hotdog eating contest. If it's warm enough, join the throngs in splashing and sandcastle-building on the wide beach. The New York Aquarium is a must if you've got kids in tow. Most attractions are open from Memorial Day through Labor Day.

☛ SEE IT ! *To get to Coney Island from Manhattan, take the D, Q, N, or F train to Stillwell Avenue.*

359

Enjoy spacious skiing at Big Sky Resort

MONTANA // Big Sky. Big snow. Big skiing. Welcome to the second-largest ski resort in the US: four mountains covering 5850 acres of skiable terrain that get more than 400in of powder a year. Marry all that space with the fact that you're in lightly populated Montana and unimpeded uncrowded skiing is practically guaranteed. When the snow melts, Big Sky offers more than 40 miles of lift-served mountain-bike and hiking trails, making it a worthy summer destination as well.

☞ SEE IT ! *The resort is on Hwy 191 halfway between Bozeman and Yellowstone. Car rental and shuttle service is available at Bozeman International Airport.*

360

Cancel casino crowds at Carson's springs

NEVADA // While Reno and Vegas are the main attention-grabbers in Nevada with their glut of casinos and promises of excitement, Carson City offers a quieter, mellower alternative. Eschewing the roulette wheel, the city is known for its unique, unfussy complex of hot-spring pools, first established in 1849 by settlers on their way to the California Gold Rush (although Washoe Native Americans had been bathing in them for centuries). The savvy opt for a private spa room where you can soak alone, or with a friend, as nature intended – nude.

Put your clothes back on if you want to enjoy the communal outdoor pools and fine onsite restaurant afterwards.

☞ SEE IT ! *Carson City is a zippy 35-minute drive from Reno along Hwy I-580/395, and 40 minutes from South Lake Tahoe.*

361

Immerse yourself in folk-art fun at Tinkertown

NEW MEXICO // Step into the imagination of outsider artist Ross Ward, who built this miniature Wild West village from bric-a-brac: walls of empty bottles; saloons of wagon wheels and scraps of wood; cowboys carved from tree stumps. Entire dioramas come to life with a quarter: ask Esmerelda the Fortune Teller to divine your future. Ross was a carnival backdrop painter who traveled with the circus – many of his displays are circus-themed. He also collected everything from wedding cake toppers to vintage tin toys, all on display.

☞ SEE IT ! *Tinkertown is 25 miles east of Albuquerque on the Turquoise Trail National Scenic Byway.*

362

Wallow in nostalgia at Main Street, USA

FLORIDA // Pass through the hallowed Magic Kingdom entrance gates and find yourself in this copy of a Midwestern town circa 1900. Main Street is modeled after Walt Disney's hometown of Marceline, Missouri (if Marceline had had Cinderella's castle looming in the background). Fans of *Lady and the Tramp* will notice some similarities – the 1955 film was also set in an imaginary Marceline. Main Street's all about nostalgia (and shopping), not adrenaline. Buy a pair of Mickey ears, listen to a barbershop quartet, catch the black-and-white movie reels of old Disney cartoons, sit on the curb to watch the daily parades, and hop on the park-circling railroad to another land.

☞ SEE IT ! *Main Street, USA is a good spot to spend your first hour at Disney before moving on to the livelier parts of the park.*

© IM_photo / Shutterstock

Completed in 1933, Art Deco Coit Tower surveys the San Fran skyline from the top of Telegraph Hill.

363

Marvel at murals and bay views from graceful Coit Tower

CALIFORNIA // From a distance, this fluted tower above San Francisco's Embarcadero looks like a mirage. Named for Lillie Hitchcock Coit, who bequeathed her enormous fortune to the city's firefighters, Coit Tower is somewhere between Art Deco apparition and phallic landmark, and has been a beacon to visitors ever since its completion in 1933. Hike up Telegraph Hill to reach it, listening out for the chattering resident parrots: this colony of cherry-headed conures grew from a single escaped pair in the 1990s. Next, step into the elevator, which whooshes you 210ft above the city for a peerless aerial view of the Golden Gate Bridge. But the view is only a momentary distraction from the tower's centerpiece: the Works Progress Administration (WPA) murals. These wraparound paintings vividly portray harried commuters, busy store interiors, farm workers, and factory laborers. It's a true snapshot of the Depression era, depicting San Fran's industrious nature and indomitable spirit. Initially denounced as communist, the murals were once covered up and kept under lock and key. Now these luminous works of art are a treasured national landmark.

☛ SEE IT ! *Book a tour online. It's a short (but steep) walk from the Embarcadero & Greenwich St light rail stop.*

© Nadya Kubik / Shutterstock

365

Become a music pilgrim at the Rock & Roll Hall of Fame

OHIO // While religious pilgrims flock to Rome or Mecca, the rock & roll faithful head to the slightly less spiritual option of Cleveland, Ohio. In the absence of holy relics, they line up to see Jimi Hendrix's Stratocaster, Keith Moon's platform shoes, John Lennon's Sgt Pepper suit, and a 1966 piece of hate mail to The Rolling Stones from a cursive-writing Fijian. Beyond the quirky memorabilia, this striking museum's clever multimedia exhibits trace the history and social context of rock music and the legendary performers who created it.

☛ SEE IT ! *The museum is in downtown Cleveland on the shores of Lake Erie. Book tickets in advance online.*

364

Take a blossom shower in Brooklyn Botanic Garden

NEW YORK // This 52-acre botanic garden is a flowery refuge from Brooklyn's bustle. Its walking trails wind through woodlands and manicured flower beds, while a Shinto shrine and turtle pond contribute to the feeling of being light-years away from NYC's most populous borough. You'll breathe in the scent of rose gardens, admire delicately twisted bonsai trees, and lead your kids through the touch-friendly gardens. The highlight? Blossom season (from late March/early April to mid-May), when cherry trees shower the ground with rosy petals.

☛ SEE IT ! *Franklin Avenue/Botanic Garden subway station (lines 2, 3, 4, 5) is a few minutes from the visitor center.*

366

Rush in to Klondike Gold Rush National Historical Park

ALASKA // Despite being invaded each summer by hordes of day-tripping cruise ship passengers, the Alaskan town of Skagway retains a palpable gold rush feel. In 1897 this was the famously debauched launch-site for thousands of prospectors heading north to the Klondike gold fields. The US National Park Service has done a fabulous job reimagining the feverish antics of the former 'stampeders' in a museum and visitor center based in the original 1898 White Pass & Yukon Route train depot.

☛ SEE IT ! *Skagway is connected by ferry to other Alaskan panhandle towns and by rail and road to British Columbia and the Yukon.*

367

Get high-altitude lake views on the Tahoe Rim Trail

CALIFORNIA // Completed in 2001, the 165-mile Tahoe Rim Trail follows the lofty ridges of the Lake Tahoe Basin, filled by the blue-green water of the USA's second-deepest lake. Undulating between 6240ft and a head-spinning 10,338ft, day-hikers, equestrians and – in some sections – mountain bikers are rewarded by high-altitude views of the lake and Sierra Nevada peaks while tracing the footsteps of early pioneers, Basque shepherds, and Washoe tribespeople.

There are numerous trailheads, meaning you can break the route into 14 separate day-hikes.

☛ TRY IT ! *Greyhound buses from Reno and San Francisco run to Truckee. From Truckee, take Tahoe Area Rapid Transit buses to the north, west, and east shores of the lake.*

368

Join the party people on dynamic Duval Street

FLORIDA // No-one really remembers William Pope Duval, first civilian governor of the Florida Territory, but the street branded in his honor is where everything seems to happen in Key West. The mile-long strip is a mishmash of raucous music-filled clubs, candlelit wine bars, kitsch cabaret parlors, and palm-fringed patio restaurants well placed for watching the nightly people parade. Booze-fueled revelry aside, there's also browsing boutiques and galleries, plays at the Red Barn Theatre, or fluttering beauties at the Key West Butterfly Conservatory.

SEE IT ! *You can fly into Key West or roadtrip down from Miami (160 miles).*

369

Travel through US history on the Colonial Parkway

VIRGINIA // Connecting Jamestown, Williamsburg, and Yorktown, this 23-mile scenic road was designed to merge with the surrounding leafy landscape, free of commercial distractions. Drive it slowly (speed limit is 45mph) and enjoy the three historic sites that make up America's birthplace. The nation's roots were planted in Jamestown, first permanent English settlement in the New World; the flames of the American Revolution were fanned at colonial capital Williamsburg; and the US won its independence from Britain at Yorktown.

SEE IT ! *You can access the east end of the Parkway in Yorkville from US 17, 40 miles north of Norfolk.*

370

Feel the magic of the movies at Universal Studios

FLORIDA // While Disney is aimed squarely at the kids, the action-packed rides at this entertainment-themed resort appeal to a slightly older crew. It's got eight areas centered around a lagoon, with themes from Harry Potter to New York City. Ride the Hogwarts Express at Diagon Alley; feel your brain bounce around in your skull on the Hollywood Rip Ride Rockit; visit the Simpsons in Springfield; or splash with the kiddos at Curious George's waterplay area. It's hot and crowded and overpriced and thrilling and unforgettable.

SEE IT ! *The closest airport is Orlando, about 10 miles away; some hotels offer free transportation.*

371

Stroll a segment of the Iditarod National Historic Trail

ALASKA // This legendary trail stretches for over one thousand miles from Seward to Nome on the frigid Bering Sea. It's named for a now-abandoned gold rush town and gained international fame thanks to an annual dog mushing race that still follows part of the route every March.

With swampy terrain making much of the trail impassable in summer, few people complete it in its entirety. Instead, most stick to bite-sized sections in the south, including Crow Pass near Girdwood, and the start-point along Seward's waterfront.

SEE IT ! *You can easily access the trail at Mile 0 from the foot of Ballaine Blvd in downtown Seward.*

372

See painting in a new light at the LA County Museum of Art

CALIFORNIA // Los Angeles loves all things artistic, so it should come as no surprise that the city harbors the largest art museum in the western US, pulling in well over one million annual visitors. LACMA's collection is rich and deep and holds all the major players. There's Rembrandt, Cézanne, Kandinsky, 20 Picassos (yes, 20), Mary Cassatt, and Ansel Adams, plus millennia's worth of Chinese, Japanese, pre-Columbian, ancient Greek, Roman, and Egyptian sculpture. And that's before you've even got to the outdoor installations: Chris Burden's *Urban Light*, a surreal forest of vintage LA streetlamps; and Michael Heizer's *Levitated Mass*, a surprisingly inspirational 340-ton boulder perched over a walkway.

In 2020, the museum began a $650-million four-year makeover conceived by Swiss architect Peter Zumthor featuring airy, cantilevered galleries straddling Wilshire Blvd.

☛ SEE IT ! *LACMA is on 'Museum Row' on the Miracle Mile section of Wilshire Blvd, 7 miles northwest of downtown LA via bus 20.*

373

Mix art and rockets at Roswell Museum & Art Center

NEW MEXICO // Modernist painter Georgia O'Keeffe and rocket inventor Robert H. Goddard make strange bedfellows in Roswell, New Mexico. In a city whose name is forever linked with debunked UFO claims, this excellent museum brings a bit of reality back and well rewards a visit. A mix of art, science, outer space, and tales from the Old West (with no UFOs in sight) embellish its 12 galleries. Call by to witness colorful Southwestern artists including O'Keeffe, Peter Hurd, and Henriette Wyeth, along with an eclectic mix of Native American, Hispanic, and Anglo artifacts that illustrate the domestic and spiritual lives of the region's inhabitants. There's also a fascinating display on local rocket pioneer Robert H. Goddard, who launched the first successful liquid fuel rocket in 1926. The museum was founded in 1935 and, in 1968, a planetarium capable of depicting the night sky from any given point on earth was added.

☞ SEE IT ! *Situated on Hwy 285, Roswell is 75 miles north of Carlsbad and about 200 miles southeast of Albuquerque and Santa Fe.*

374

Appreciate classy organic wines at Frog's Leap

CALIFORNIA // Wine lovers have come to the right place. The Napa Valley is one of the world's primary wine regions; the 6650-acre appellation of Rutherford is one of its most unique viticultural areas; and Frog's Leap makes some of its best wines.

Established in 1981, the Frog became Napa's first organic wine producer when it rethought its farming methods in 1988. Since then, the winery has further upgraded its green credentials, now operating with solar power and using water-conserving dry-farming techniques. Cab Sav is the king of grapes in Napa – the American equivalent of French Bordeaux – and Frog's Leap offers some fine renditions, but the place is also rightfully famous for its minerally Sauvignon Blanc and robust Zinfandel. Visitors can follow the vineyard cats through enchanting gardens and drink in the views from the loft of an 1884 barn while sipping delicious, good-time wines.

☞ SEE IT ! *The winery is in Rutherford, 16 miles north of the town of Napa by car. Daily tastings can be organized by appointment.*

© Shawn Levin / Courtesty of AVAM

© Joe Daniel Price / Getty Images

375

See jaw-dropping works by self-taught artists at AVAM

MARYLAND // In 1984, while working at Baltimore's Sinai Hospital, Rebecca Alban Hoffberger was repeatedly impressed by people – patients, family members, staff – who made fascinating artwork but didn't consider themselves artists. Thinking there ought to be a place to showcase these unusual works, she envisioned a museum unlike any other. Fast forward to the present, and Hoffberger's American Visionary Art Museum, which opened in 1994, has become a Baltimore landmark, beloved for its extraordinary collection of artwork created by gifted farmers, factory workers, retirees, homeless people, and other 'outsiders.' You'll find broken-mirror collages, homemade robots and flying apparatuses, elaborate needlepoint sculptures, and gigantic matchstick model ships. The whimsical automatons in the Cabaret Mechanical Theater are worth a closer look. And don't miss the famous Flatulence Post and its, er, 'fart art' in the Basement Gallery.

☛ SEE IT ! *AVAM lies on Baltimore's Inner Harbor. A great time to visit is early May for the museum's human-powered kinetic sculpture race.*

376

Embrace the kitsch on Chicago's Navy Pier

ILLINOIS // Jutting half a mile into Lake Michigan, Navy Pier is one of Chicago's most-visited attractions, sporting a 196ft Ferris wheel, myriad carnival rides, an IMAX theater, a beer garden, and the usual suspects of the franchise restaurant scene. A renovation in the 2010s added public plazas, performance spaces, and free cultural programing. Locals still groan over Navy Pier's commercialization, but it's probably more fun today than in some of its earlier incarnations – which have included a jail for draft dodgers, a training school for the US Navy, and a temporary campus for the University of Illinois.

Polk Bros Park, at the pier's entrance, has a fountain you can splash in and performance lawns for free concerts and movies. Add in lakefront views, cool breezes, and firework displays in summer and you're in for a real treat.

☛ SEE IT ! *The pier is located in Chicago's Streeterville neighborhood, just north of the downtown core.*

© Luther Bailey, Courtesy of the National Park Service

378

Unmask Alaska at Anchorage Museum

ALASKA // The best museum in Alaska explores every facet of the state's history, archeology, science, and art in a modern cubist campus covered with super-reflective glass: a handsome shell that protects equally attractive exhibits. The flagship display is the Smithsonian Arctic Studies Center with more than 600 Alaska Native objects – art, tools, masks, household implements – previously housed in Washington, DC. It's the largest Alaska Native collection in the state and is backed up by the Alaska History Gallery, tracing 10,000 years of human settlement from early subsistence villages to modern oil dependency.

☛ SEE IT ! *The museum is in downtown Anchorage, 15 minutes' walk from the train station.*

377

Pay homage at John Muir's former home

CALIFORNIA // Lovers of the American wilderness owe a huge debt to US–Scottish naturalist John Muir and you can start by paying your respects here, at his former residence on a pastoral patch of farmland in the bustling city of Martinez.

The attractive Victorian Italianate house looks surprisingly refined for a man not known for his love of creature comforts, with a tower cupola, a daintily upholstered parlor, and splashes of white lace. Muir lived here between 1890 and his death in 1914, though he always considered his real 'home' to lie in the Sierra Nevada mountains.

☛ SEE IT ! *The site is just north of Hwy 4. County Connection buses 16 and 98X from nearby Amtrak and BART stations stop here.*

379

Roam alone on Cumberland Island

GEORGIA // Georgia's largest and southernmost barrier island, Cumberland Island National Seashore is an unspoiled paradise, a campers' fantasy, a place for family day trips, and secluded haven for couples – it's no wonder the wealthy Carnegie family used Cumberland as a retreat in the 1800s. The ruins of their former home, the Dungeness Mansion (destroyed by a fire in 1959) have been preserved by the National Park Service. The rest of the island consists of marshes, mudflats, and tidal creeks, plus 17 miles of wide, sandy beach that you'll likely have to yourself.

☛ SEE IT ! *The only public access to the island is by ferry to/from the mainland town of St Marys, located off Exit 1 on I-95.*

© Fernando Garcia Esteban / Shutterstock

© Richard Semik / Shutterstock

380

Romance the storied stones of Gothic Green-Wood Cemetery

NEW YORK // History breathes through the ornate mausoleums and poignant statues of Green-Wood Cemetery in Brooklyn. A massive Gothic gate is the portal to these 478 hilly acres, where more than half a million souls repose. Famous residents include artist Jean-Michel Basquiat, musical legend Leonard Bernstein, and inventors Samuel Morse and Elias Howe, along with numerous writers and abolitionists who made their mark on American history.

Equally deserving of attention are Green-Wood's natural charms, so roam widely from placid lakes to trees where cackling green parakeets roost. As you huff to Green-Wood's loftiest point, Battle Hill, you'll meet a statue of the goddess Minerva, marking the spot where Washington's Continental Army lost a key battle in 1776.

🕮 SEE IT ! *Wear comfy shoes and take the R train towards Bay Ridge, exiting at 25th St; or see the area by trolley-bus tour (book ahead).*

381

Steam up steep slopes on the Mt Washington Cog Railway

NEW HAMPSHIRE // Purists walk and the lazy drive, but the quaintest way to reach Mt Washington's summit is via the cog railway. Since 1869, coal-fired, steam-powered locomotives have climbed a scenic 3.5-mile track up the mountainside. Two of them still run, though these days they're supplemented by faster, cleaner, biodiesel-fueled trains.

Instead of having drive wheels, a cog locomotive applies power to a cogwheel (gear wheel) on its undercarriage. The gears engage pins mounted between the rails to pull the locomotive and a single passenger car up the mountainside, burning a ton of coal and blowing a thousand gallons of water into steam along the way. Boilers are tilted to accommodate the grade. The gradient at the Jacob's Ladder trestle is 37% – the second-steepest railway track in the world.

🕮 SEE IT ! *The base station is 6 miles east of US 302.*

382

Spend an over-the-top night at the Madonna Inn

CALIFORNIA // There are thousands of motels in the US but only one is as wild, weird, unconventional, and fantastically camp as the Madonna Inn. Furnished with a faux-Swiss exterior and an abundance of pink inside, curious international tourists and irony-loving hipsters adore this place for its 110 themed rooms, all of them unashamedly flamboyant. High on the kitsch rating are the 'Love Nest' and the 'Caveman', though the pièce de résistance has to be the waterfall urinal in the men's restroom.

☛ SEE IT ! *The inn is just off Hwy 101 in San Luis Obispo; Amtrak runs daily trains to the city.*

383

Put the 'pop' back into art at the Andy Warhol Museum

PENNSYLVANIA // Before he moved to New York, got a nose job, and became famous for pop art, Andy Warhol lived in Pittsburgh, the son of an East European coal miner, collecting pictures of movie stars. The city has honored him in this dynamic six-story North Shore museum, the largest dedicated to a single artist in the US. Exhibits include early drawings and commercial illustrations, a simulated Velvet Underground 'happening', and scores of his iconic screen prints.

☛ SEE IT ! *Located on the North Shore at Sandusky and East General Robinson streets, the museum is across the Andy Warhol Bridge from downtown Pittsburgh.*

384

Search for the soul of Delta Blues at the BB King Museum

MISSISSIPPI // The former home of string-bending guitar genius BB King, tiny Indianola in the Mississippi Delta is an essential stopover for music aficionados, thanks to this smart modern museum housed in an erstwhile cotton gin building where the 'King of the Blues' once worked. While ostensibly dedicated to King's legacy, it also covers the history of life in the Delta with interactive displays, video exhibits, and an impressive assemblage of artifacts.

You can also visit King's grave; he was laid to rest here in 2015.

☛ SEE IT ! *The nearest major cities to the Delta are Oxford and Memphis. There's a Greyhound station in Indianola.*

© Glynis Jones / Shutterstock

© Anton Foltin / Shutterstock

385

Mark the march of progress at Stonewall National Monument

NEW YORK // Back in the 1960s, being gay was like living in an Orwellian nightmare. You were considered un-American and subversive, surveilled by the FBI and local police. Law enforcement made frequent raids, arresting people in bars and in public places. The Stonewall Inn, which drew a wide cross-section of the gay community, was a frequent target. Yet on June 28, 1969, when the police showed up, patrons revolted. Fed up with the endless harassment, they began bombarding the officers with coins, bottles, bricks, and chants of 'gay power' and 'we shall overcome.' Their collective anger and solidarity was a turning point, giving birth to the modern LGBTIQ+ rights movement in the US. In 2016 President Obama declared tiny Christopher Park, opposite still-vibrant Stonewall Inn, the first national monument dedicated to LGBTIQ+ history. There's little ostentatious memorializing, save a few plaques and the twin *Gay Liberation* statues, a tribute to the normality of gay life.

☞ SEE IT ! *To get there, take the 1 subway line to Christopher St-Sheridan Sq station.*

386

Admire the natural arch of Rainbow Bridge

UTAH // The sandstone Rainbow Bridge National Monument in southern Utah's Glen Canyon National Recreation Area is one of the largest natural bridges in the world, measuring 290ft high and 275ft wide. It has long been held sacred by the Navajo people who christened it Nonnezoshe (Rainbow Turned to Stone). Due to its remoteness, it wasn't properly charted until 1909.

The bridge became more accessible after the damming of the Colorado River in 1963 which led to the formation of Lake Powell. Today, most visitors arrive by boat and make a short 1.2-mile round-trip hike to the monument. Alternatively, experienced backpackers can drive on dirt roads to access two unmaintained trails, each 28 miles round-trip, on the Navajo Reservation. Tribal permits are required.

☞ SEE IT ! *Although the bridge itself is in Utah, the gateway to Lake Powell is Wahweap Marina, 7 miles north of Page in Arizona, where you can arrange eight-hour boat cruises to the monument and back.*

387

Admire music and design at the Walt Disney Concert Hall

CALIFORNIA // A molten blend of steel, music, and psychedelic architecture, this iconic concert venue is the home base of the Los Angeles Philharmonic, but has also hosted contemporary bands such as Phoenix and classic jazz musicians like Sonny Rollins. The 2003 concert hall's visionary architect, Frank Gehry, pulled out all the stops for the building's exterior, a gravity-defying sculpture of heaving and billowing stainless steel. In contrast, the 2265-seat auditorium feels like the inside of a finely crafted cello, clad in walls of smooth Douglas fir.

🖝 SEE IT ! *The hall is in downtown Los Angeles. Free, one-hour audio guides are available from the grand lobby.*

388

Digest Honolulu's Chinatown markets

HAWAI'I // The commercial heart of Honolulu's Chinatown revolves around its markets and food stores. Noodle factories, pastry shops, and produce stalls line the narrow sidewalks, always crowded with cart-pushing grandmothers and errand-running families. An institution since 1904, the O'ahu Market sells everything a Chinese cook needs: ginger root, fresh octopus, quail eggs, jasmine rice, slabs of tuna, long beans, and salted jellyfish. You owe yourself a bubble tea if you spot a pig's head among the stalls.

Nearby, Kekaulike Market displays a full range of whole fish, dry goods, prepared foods, and Hawai'i's plethora of produce.

🖝 SEE IT ! *Honolulu's Chinatown is slap-bang in downtown, just a lei's throw from the harborfront.*

389

Sip Kentucky's favorite spirit at Woodford Reserve

KENTUCKY // Near the town of Versailles (that's Ver-SALES; none of that French pronunciation here), Woodford is the most charming stop on the Kentucky Bourbon Trail. It's the state's smallest and oldest distillery, crafting bourbon the color of an antique penny since 1812. Tour the barrelhouse, where copper-distilled booze gets its color and flavor from oak barrels as it ages, then sit for a tasting in the stone-and-timber visitor center; we recommend the bourbon and chocolate pairing. Bring a bottle home to mix into mint juleps the next Derby Day.

🖝 SEE IT ! *Tours are daily. The distillery is 8 miles northwest of downtown Versailles.*

390

Hike or bike the Golden Gate National Recreation Area

CALIFORNIA // Golden Gate National Recreation Area is a jigsaw puzzle of forests, cliffs, and white-sand beaches. Its 317 sq miles are staggered around the San Francisco Bay area, not only covering the misty Marin Headlands (just north of that bridge) but also diverse preserves like the Presidio, white-sand Stinson Beach, and Muir Woods National Monument. San Franciscans are spoilt for choice, so you'll need to pick your flavor. To cycle past verdant parkland in full view of the Golden Gate Bridge, pedal Crissy Field waterfront. For cliffside rambles, embark on trails from the north end of Ocean Beach past the remains of Sutro Baths. If wild nature appeals, hike the Marin Headlands and visit squabbling seals at the Marine Mammal Center. Billowing fog often obscures the Golden Gate Bridge, but on clear days the views towards it and San Francisco almost shimmer.

🐾 TRY IT ! *It's easiest to take a ride-share to trailheads like Sutro Baths at Lands End or the Tennessee Valley hike in Mill Valley.*

391

Hear the stories behind the science at Biosphere 2

ARIZONA // Built to be completely sealed off from Biosphere 1 (Earth), Biosphere 2 is spread over 3 acres of glass domes and pyramids containing six ecosystems: ocean, mangrove, rainforest, savannah, desert, and city. In 1991 eight biospherians were famously sealed inside for a two-year tour of duty, from which they emerged thinner but in fair shape. Less lengthy modern tours take in the biospherians' apartments, farm area and kitchen, the million-gallon 'tropical ocean', and the 'technosphere' that made it all possible. Though the experiment was ostensibly a prototype for self-sustaining space colonies, the privately funded endeavor was engulfed in controversy, especially after the dome leaked gases and was opened to allow a biospherian to emerge for medical treatment. After several ownership changes, the sci-fi-esque site is now a University of Arizona-run earth-science research institute.

🐾 SEE IT ! *Biosphere 2 is near Oracle, about 30 miles north of Tucson via Hwy 77 (Oracle Rd).*

© Joseph Sohm / Shutterstock

392

Admire the graceful cunning of long-beaked waterbirds at Lake Martin

LOUISIANA // Beginning in January, the skies over Lake Martin fill with the call of birdsong as snowy egrets, great blue herons, and white ibises arrive in their thousands. They nest in the bald cypress trees, tupelos, and buttonwood bushes where they'll stay until June, spending their days stalking through tea-colored waters in silent pursuit of fish and crustaceans. Surrounded by the Cypress Island Preserve, this swamp-like 800-acre lake is one of the most important wading-bird rookeries in North America. Over 200 species nest here throughout the year, including the spectacular roseate spoonbill, sometimes called the Cajun flamingo on account of its bright pink plumage. Birds aside, the fertile swamplands also support turtles, coypu (a hefty, semiaquatic rodent), and 1200 or so alligators, the largest of which can grow to 14ft. The best way to experience the region is to boat across the mirror-like waters with a knowledgeable naturalist guide. You can also spy wildlife on a 2.5-mile walking trail that courses through bottomland hardwood forest and along the water's edge – it closes during alligator mating season though (June to October).

☛ SEE IT ! *Lake Martin is 130 miles west of New Orleans.*

393

Explore Russian and indigenous culture at Sitka

ALASKA // A mystical juxtaposition of tall trees, totems, and Russian architecture in the Alaskan panhandle, small Sitka National Historical Park is riddled with early colonial history and includes the erstwhile battleground where indigenous Tlingits were finally defeated by the Russians in 1804. It's anchored by the Bishop's House, the oldest intact Russian building in Sitka, constructed from local spruce by Finnish carpenters in 1842. Beyond it, a mile-long trail winds past 18 century-old totems set in thick rainforest and often enveloped in mist.

☞ SEE IT ! *On Baranof Island, Sitka is reachable via ferry or airplane. You can walk to the park from the town center.*

© Mark Read / Lonely Planet

394

Go beachcombing on the Gulf Islands National Seashore

MISSISSIPPI // In among the casinos and bling of coastal Mississippi, this maze of wetlands, beaches and offshore barrier islands is the domain of migrating birds, scrubby dunes, and empty white-sand beaches. The islands – Horn, Sand, Petit Bois, and Ship – are the biggest draw, though only Ship has a public ferry. In addition to snorkeling, bodyboarding, swimming, and beachcombing, you can visit Fort Massachusetts on Ship Island, a brick beachside fort built in 1868.

☞ SEE IT ! *Public ferries run to Ship Island in the summer from Biloxi and Gulfport. By car, you can access Davis Bayou, a wet quilt of marsh islands and flat-water horizons on the mainland.*

395

Stand speechless at Yosemite Valley's Tunnel View

CALIFORNIA // If it were possible to freeze-frame a single view to represent the full sweeping majesty of the US National Park Service, this might be it. First glimpsed as you emerge from the dark Wawona Tunnel (which increases the drama), the sight of the Yosemite Valley framed by El Capitan, Half Dome, and Bridalveil Fall is simply jaw-dropping. You won't be the first to be impressed – the scene has been drawn, painted, and photographed to death – nor will you be the only visitor (count on a few coachloads for company), but the memory will remain forever.

☞ SEE IT ! *Tunnel View is 25 miles north of Yosemite National Park's southern entrance via Wawona Rd.*

396

Snake past scenic peaks along the Beartooth Highway

MONTANA // In the competition to name America's finest drive, the Beartooth has a large fan club. Connecting Red Lodge in Montana to Yellowstone National Park's northeast entrance, it snakes and switchbacks for 68 miles cresting the 10,947ft Beartooth Pass, crossing the Montana-Wyoming state-line and motoring alongside 11,000ft peaks and wildflower-sprinkled alpine tundra. It was designated an All-American Road in 2000 for its scenic and recreational properties, one of only 30 in the nation. Heavy snow closes the road between November and May.

🐻 SEE IT ! *It's best to start the drive in Red Lodge, 63 miles southwest of Billings, Montana's largest city.*

Red Sox Go! Taking in a Major League game at Fenway Park is an atmospheric experience.

397

Cheer for the Red Sox at Boston's Fenway Park

MASSACHUSETTS // America's oldest and quirkiest ballpark is such an institution that it has its own lingo. 'Williamsburg' means the bullpens in front of the right-center field bleachers, which benefitted left-handed batters like Ted Williams by reducing the distance from the fence to home plate. 'Pesky's Pole' is the right field foul pole, named for 1940s infielder Johnny Pesky who once won a game with a home run over the right-field wall. The famous 'Green Monster' is the 37ft-high left field wall, an easy target for right-handed hitters.

Learn the legends of Fenway Park on a tour, or join the throngs of rabid Red Sox fans on game night. While the Sox have won four World Series in the past two decades, that followed nearly a century of 'the Curse of the Bambino' – the team's losing streak following the 1918 sale of Babe Ruth to the enemy, the New York Yankees. Though the curse is broken, Bostonians still find it hard to shake their underdog identity. Maybe that's why they seem to cheer harder and boo louder than other MLB fans. Or maybe it's all that beer.

☛ SEE IT ! *Take the T to Kenmore Station; the park's right around the corner. The Sox play from April to October.*

© Maddie Meyer / Getty Images

© Brian Logan Photography / Shutterstock

Courtesy of Sierra Nevada Brewing Company

398

Identify some very famous faces at the Reynolds Center

WASHINGTON, DC // The Reynolds Center is one of DC's finest museums. This Smithsonian venue combines the National Portrait Gallery with the American Art Museum in a whopping collection of American art that's unmatched anywhere in the world. Keep an eye out for famed works by Edward Hopper, Georgia O'Keeffe, Andy Warhol, Winslow Homer, and more. At the Portrait Gallery, test your knowledge of history – one of the most popular sections, unsurprisingly perhaps, it displays the nation's only complete collection of presidential portraits outside the White House. Be sure to hit the Luce Foundation Center on the 3rd and 4th floors too – the open storage area stuffed with more than 3000 paintings, sculptures, miniatures, and folk-art pieces makes for glorious browsing. The glass-roofed inner courtyard on the first floor, dotted with trees and marble benches, is another lovely spot.

☛ SEE IT ! *The Reynolds Center for American Art and Portraiture is one block from the Gallery Place Metro station in downtown DC.*

399

Savor hoppy flavor at Sierra Nevada Brewing Company

CALIFORNIA // In the relatively young world of microbrewing, Sierra Nevada is an ancient relic, founded in Chico, California in 1979, in the early years of the craft beer movement. Unlike many of the other pioneers, it's still going strong – it remains the third largest privately owned brewery in the US. Its flagship brew is the pugnaciously hop-heavy Sierra Nevada Pale Ale, the best-selling pale ale in the country. Backing it up is a long list of seasonals, special releases, and short-run craft beers brewed by beer nerds at invitation-only seminars.

Free brewhouse tours are given regularly and include a rundown of the brewery's cutting-edge sustainable practices – its operations are 99.8% zero waste, its rooftop solar fields are among the largest privately owned solar fields in the US, and the brewery extended a spur of local railroad to increase transportation efficiency.

☛ SEE IT ! *The brewery is in Chico, 90 miles north of Sacramento. Greyhound and Amtrak trains connect to Sacramento and San Fran.*

400—
500

400

Embrace ecological diversity at Denver Botanic Gardens

COLORADO // If you're craving greenery, this 23-acre Rocky Mountains garden is the perfect place to find some. Local flora mixes with relatives from faraway continents such as Australia and Africa to create an incredibly diverse landscape. Exhibits by well-known artists – including Calder and Chihuly – are set among the flowers and fountains to complement the living art. The Mordecai Children's Garden has excellent hands-on exhibits like Pipsqueak Pond water feature. Summer brings outdoor concerts, while winter sees a holiday light show.

☛ SEE IT ! *Run by Regional Transportation District, buses 6, 10 and 24 pass near the park.*

401

Chill out on Kaua'i at Po'ipu Beach Park

HAWAI'I // There are no monster waves or idyllic solitude at Kaua'i's most popular South Shore beach, but it's a go-to spot for pretty much everyone. Patrolled by resident *honu* (sea turtles) in the shallows, the beach is protected by a rocky reef that attracts fish of all kinds. Add lifeguards, picnic tables, toilets, and outdoor showers, and you have one safe, family-friendly beach. A grassy lawn links to Brennecke's Beach just east, where surfers and bodyboarders bob in the water and tourists sit on the roadside stone wall gawping at the action.

☛ SEE IT ! *Most reach the South Shore by rental car. You can also get here with Kaua'i Bus or South Shore Cab.*

402

Sample sweet Kentucky bourbon at Angel's Envy

KENTUCKY // Muhammad Ali isn't the only champion to come out of Louisville, Kentucky. Delivering an equally ferocious knockout punch and amassing several awards are the lovingly crafted spirits of Angel's Envy, a micro-distillery that bucks local tradition by finishing its bourbon in port barrels, giving it a hint of sweetness. Join an intimate tour with tastings at their HQ on Whiskey Row, a mile-long stretch of historic buildings on Main St. Saved from demolition in the early 2000s, the buildings now hold five distilleries, which have breathed new life into the area.

☛ SEE IT ! *Louisville's Muhammad Ali International Airport is 5 miles south of town on I-65.*

403

See speleothems at Carlsbad Caverns

NEW MEXICO // Elaborately carved by the slow hand of time, the magnificent underground rooms and glittering passageways of Carlsbad Caverns National Park feel like a portal into another realm. It's hard to imagine a more dramatic transition than to leave the desert air behind and step through the cool tunnels, with every twist and turn revealing wondrous formations of speleothems (aka stalactites and stalagmites). The cave's creation began about one million years ago, as rainwater, drip by drip, seeped through the layers of the earth.

☛ SEE IT ! *Located 140 miles northeast of El Paso, Texas, the park runs various daily guided tours.*

404

Learn about an all-American religion at Temple Square

UTAH // The Salt Lake Temple, looking more like a fairy tale castle than a church, anchors this 10-acre complex in downtown Salt Lake City, the spiritual center of the Church of Jesus Christ of Latter-day Saints (aka the Mormons). Free walking tours led by young missionaries include the home of early church leader Brigham Young; the 1.4-million-sq-ft conference center; and the Family History Library, where Mormons and non-Mormons alike can do genealogical research. It's a fascinating look into America's biggest home-grown religion.

👈 SEE IT ! *The grounds are open 24/7; buildings are generally open 9am–9pm. The temple is closed to non-church members.*

405

Discover Nola culture at the Backstreet

LOUISIANA // New Orleans' most important traditions are deeply entwined with African American culture, and the Backstreet Cultural Museum is the best place to learn about the city's Black heritage. Amid a small but striking collection of costumes, photographs, and films, check out the dazzling Mardi Gras Indian costumes: elaborate ensembles handmade by local artisans out of thousands of beads, shells, and feathers. Displays also delve into jazz funerals; second-line parades (celebratory street parades still held most Sundays); and Social Aid and Pleasure Clubs (local African American civic associations).

👈 SEE IT ! *Get to the museum via the Rampart-St Claude Streetcar line.*

406

Uncover the roots of counterculture at the Beat Museum

CALIFORNIA // To understand San Francisco's hippie roots, travel back to the 1950s, when Beat Generation writers Kerouac, Ginsberg, Cassady, and Burroughs mingled with the likes of Ferlinghetti, imbuing SF with rebellious, mainstream-rejecting, materialism-shunning, drug-experimenting associations that never left. This homage to key Beat Gen personalities, in the middle of their North Beach hangout spots near Ferlinghetti-founded City Lights bookstore, places their lives in context; exhibits include the banned author-annotated edition of Ginsberg's *Howl* and the 1949 Hudson roadster from 2012's *On The Road* movie.

👈 SEE IT ! *The museum is on Broadway, opposite City Lights bookstore.*

407

Hike or bike the Mount Vernon Trail

VIRGINIA // The Mount Vernon Trail is an 18-mile hiking/biking path that follows the Potomac River south from Rosslyn opposite Washington, DC, past Roosevelt Island, Arlington National Cemetery, and Old Town Alexandria, all the way to George Washington's house at Mount Vernon. There are sights aplenty along the way including Lady Bird Johnson Park, commemorating the First Lady who beautified the capital via greenery-planting campaigns; swaths of tulips and daffodils bloom in spring. The trail is mostly flat, and the scenery is magnificent – DC skyline and all.

👈 SEE IT ! *The multi-use trail can be walked or cycled. There's a parking lot at the north end by the Roosevelt Island pedestrian bridge.*

© MILA PARH / Shutterstock

© Tetra Images / Getty Images

408

Unleash your inner boho in Washington Square Park

NEW YORK // Greenwich Village lets it all hang out in Washington Square Park, a 10-acre hub for jugglers, bongo drummers, speed-chess players, Nietzsche-reading NYU students, anti-capitalism protesters, and the occasional slumming movie star. Once a potter's field, it rests atop the graves of some 20,000 unknown New Yorkers. It's been a bohemian hotspot for more than a century – in 1916 artist Marcel Duchamp famously climbed the park's magnificent marble arch and declared it the 'Free and Independent Republic of Washington Square.'

Come here to sunbathe, listen to guitar-strumming buskers, eat a slice of pizza by the fountain, or challenge one of the resident chess champs to a game. In addition to the arch, look out for statues of George Washington and Italian hero Giuseppe Garibaldi.

SEE IT ! *The park is the southern starting point of Fifth Avenue and is close to an eponymous subway station.*

409

Contemplate the meditative waters of Walden Pond

MASSACHUSETTS // Writer Henry David Thoreau took the naturalist beliefs of transcendentalism out of the realm of theory and into practice when he left the comforts of the town and built himself a rustic cabin on the shores of this New England pond. His famous memoir of his time spent there, *Walden; or, Life in the Woods* (1854), was full of praise for nature and disapproval of the stresses of civilized life – sentiments that have found an eager audience ever since. The glacial pond is now a state park, surrounded by acres of forest preserved by the Walden Woods Project, a non-profit organization.

There's a swimming beach on the southern banks and a footpath encircling the whole pond. The site of Thoreau's cabin is on the northeastern side, marked by a cairn. Visitors are restricted in summer to keep the place appropriately Thoreau-esque.

SEE IT ! *Just off MA 2, Walden Pond is 2 miles south of Concord and 20 miles northwest of downtown Boston.*

© Kathryn Scott Osler / Getty Images

© Stephan Miller

Soak up the suds at New Belgium Brewery

COLORADO // Conceived when its two co-founders went on a bike trip around the European beer heaven of Belgium, this brewery started inauspiciously in a basement in Fort Collins, Colorado in 1991. By 2020, their standard-bearing 'Fat Tire' beer (a pioneering Belgian-style brew) had become the first carbon neutral beer in the US, and their suds were on sale everywhere from Pennsylvania to Peru. A brewery tour brings you face-to-face with the freewheeling essence of Fort Collins' character: a tripartite passion for beer, bicycles, and sustainability. The tour guides are knowledgeable, smart, and playful, and the special selection of beers is among the nation's best. By the time you get to the end, a colorful tasting room with long communal tables, you've probably had enough to consider getting dolled up in one of the flamboyant costumes leftover from their annual bike parade.

🖝 SEE IT ! *Fort Collins is 65 miles north of Denver, just west of the I-25 corridor.*

Follow the path of Paul Revere on the Minuteman Bikeway

MASSACHUSETTS // You're on hallowed ground. Doused in American revolutionary history and punctuated with memorabilia from its second coming as a railway line, this paved bicycle trail is one of Boston's best. Starting near Alewife station, it heads 5 miles northwest to historic Lexington Center, then traverses an additional 4 miles of idyllic scenery to the rural suburb of Bedford. Some of the path coalesces with the route of the famous 'Midnight Ride' made by American hero, Paul Revere, in 1775 to alert the colonial militias of approaching British forces before the battles of Concord and Lexington. It also tracks the path of a now defunct railway line, the Lexington and West Cambridge Railroad, which operated between 1846 and 1980. The wide, straight, paved path also passes meadows, ponds, and a state park replete with herons and ospreys.

🖝 SEE IT ! *The bikeway is accessible from Davis Square in Somerville (Davis T station) via the 2-mile Community Path to Alewife.*

412

Explore a Cold War sub at the USS Albacore Museum

NEW HAMPSHIRE // Like a fish out of water, this 205ft-long non-combative research submarine is now a beached museum on a grassy lawn. Launched from Portsmouth Naval Shipyard in 1953, the *Albacore* was once the world's fastest submarine. It housed a crew of 55 and was piloted around the world for 19 years without firing a shot. A small maritime museum sitting beside the sub explains the background to its story.

☛ SEE IT ! *The sub is located just north of Portsmouth's old town center. Greyhound buses run once or twice daily between Portsmouth and Boston.*

413

See Tlinglit carvings at the Jilkaat Kwaan

ALASKA // Part of a welcome renaissance in Tlingit art and culture in Alaska, this well-curated heritage center guards the ancient Native village of Klukwan on the Haines Hwy. The center includes some of the most prized heirlooms of Alaska Native culture, namely four elaborate house posts and a rain screen – the legendary 'whale house collection' – carved by a Tlingit Michelangelo over 200 years ago and only recently made available for public viewing. The Jilkaat Kwaan includes a museum, clan house, carving studio, salmon-drying room, and shop. There are also regular dance performances and even art classes.

☛ SEE IT ! *The center is located 22 miles north of Haines. You'll need a ride or your own wheels to get there.*

414

Admire art, design, and LA views at the Getty Center

CALIFORNIA // In its multi-million-dollar, in-the-clouds perch, high above LA's grit and glamor, the Getty Center presents triple delights: an engaging art collection (everything from medieval triptychs to Baroque sculpture and Impressionist brushstrokes); Richard Meier's cutting-edge architecture; and the visual splendor of seasonally changing gardens.

On clear days, you can add breathtaking views of the city and ocean to the list. Sunsets create a remarkable alchemy of light and shadow and are especially magical in winter.

☛ SEE IT ! *The center is in the Brentwood neighborhood of LA. Metro bus lines 734 and 234 from West LA Expo station stop at the entrance.*

415

Swim at crystalline Manatee Springs

FLORIDA // In fall and winter it's possible to see bulbous gray manatees swimming with surprising grace through the gin-clear waters of this state park's natural spring. The 72°F temperature makes it an ideal cold-weather shelter for the sea mammals – and a pleasant swimming spot for humans as well.

Stroll the boardwalk through eerie cypress forest hung with Spanish moss, mountain-bike the wooded trails, fish for catfish and largemouth bass in the Suwannee River and – if you're an experienced diver – descend into the underwater cave system.

☛ SEE IT ! *The park is 6 miles west of Chiefland village in northwest Florida. Swimming's forbidden when the manatees are in the springs.*

Courtesy of the Louis Armstrong House Museum

© Action Sports Photography / Shutterstock

416

Walk in the steps of Satchmo at the Louis Armstrong House

NEW YORK // Despite growing up in the musical mecca of New Orleans and touring the world, famed jazz trumpeter and singer Louis Armstrong felt most at home in the modest working-class neighborhood of Corona in Queens. He and his fourth wife, Lucille Wilson, a dancer at the Cotton Club, settled into a modest brick house in 1943, and stayed until Armstrong's death in 1971. Immaculately preserved, the dwelling provides a fascinating window into the Armstrongs' domestic life, with Louis' half-full bottle of Lanvin cologne still sitting on the dresser, and the original living room TV set low to the ground so neighborhood kids could watch. Armstrong's den, of which he was most proud, features a portrait of the great musician painted by singer Tony Bennett. During summer, live concerts are held in the garden.

☛ SEE IT ! *It's a 10-minute walk from the 103rd St Corona Plaza subway station. Guided tours run Wednesday through Sunday.*

417

Watch the Indy 500 at Indianapolis Motor Speedway

INDIANA // Forget the Super Bowl and the World Series. This humongous car-racing circuit, home of the Indianapolis 500 motor race, is the largest sports venue in the world, capable of seating over 250,000 spectators – that's one-third of nearby Indianapolis' population. The big race is held on the Sunday of Memorial Day weekend (late May). Factoring in standing patrons, it's estimated around 300,000 crazed fans pack in to see 33 Indy cars speed for 200 laps around a 2.5-mile circuit. If you can't nail hard-to-come-by tickets, come any time to visit the Speedway Museum, which features some 75 racing cars (including former winners) and a 500lb Tiffany trophy. In summer, take a narrated golf-cart tour of the grounds and track: you're not exactly burning rubber, but it's fun to pretend.

☛ SEE IT ! *The track is 6 miles northwest of downtown Indianapolis. Parking is free on non-race days.*

The Lost Coast Trail is the only way to see this ravishingly remote stretch of Californian coast: shoulder your backpack and go.

418

Find misty magnificence on the Lost Coast Trail

CALIFORNIA // Five hours north of San Francisco, California's coast became 'lost' when the state's highway system deemed the region impassable in the mid-20th century. Today, this is the north coast's ultimate backpacking destination, a magical littoral where narrow dirt trails ascend rugged coastal peaks. Here you'll find volcanic beaches of black sand and ethereal mist hovering above the roaring surf as majestic Roosevelt elk graze the forests. To navigate it, take the Lost Coast Trail, 24.6 miles along rugged shores from Mattole Campground to Black Sands Beach at Shelter Cove. Highlights include an abandoned lighthouse at Punta Gorda, remnants of early shipwrecks, tide pools, and abundant wildlife including sea lions, seals, and some 300 bird species.

The trail is mostly level, passing beaches and crossing over rocky outcrops. However, the prevailing northerly winds make it best to hike from north to south; plan for three or four days. There are campsites with toilets along the way.

SEE IT ! *The closest transport is from Garberville or Fortuna operated by Redwood Transit System. The only reliable shuttle is Lost Coast Adventure Tours' a twice-daily service from Shelter Cove to Mattole.*

© MattManaged / Shutterstock

© Venture Media Group / Getty Images

419

Get the adrenaline pumping at the US National Whitewater Center

NORTH CAROLINA // Half waterpark, half natural wonderland, this outdoor recreation facility is a mecca for adrenaline junkies. Designed to train Olympic-level canoers and kayakers, it's centered around the world's longest artificial whitewater river. Paddle its rapids, scale an artificial rock wall (including the first-ever artificial deep water solo complex, where you climb rope-less and fall into a pool), fly through the forest on a zip line, or traverse a ropes course. Or go old-school with hiking, mountain biking, and flatwater kayaking on the Catawba River. There's a beer garden for winding down after.

☛ TRY IT ! *The center is 15 miles west of Charlotte. Peak season is March through October. Book ahead.*

420

Ski with resplendent lake views at Squaw Valley Alpine Meadows*

CALIFORNIA // As you thunder down the piste, you can't help glancing up to take in views of Lake Tahoe. At Squaw Alpine, connected resorts set among the granite peaks of the High Sierra, the lake's blue expanse is a dazzling distraction from finessing your parallel turns. The resorts form a mighty pair: a total of 6000 skiable acres accessed via 34 lifts. Squaw Valley played host to the 1960 Winter Olympic Games and still attracts pros. Meanwhile Alpine Meadows, its trails stretching across 1800 vertical feet, attracts heavier snowfall – catnip to backcountry addicts. * At the time of writing, the resort was due to change its name.

☛ TRY IT ! *Avoid driving here on the weekends: sluggish traffic and snap highway closures make drive times unpredictable.*

© Leonid Andronov / Shutterstock

© Lebid Volodymyr / Shutterstock

421

Appreciate the arid artistry of nature along Utah's Highway 12

UTAH // The most diverse and splendiferous route in a state not short on eye candy, Hwy 12 winds through rugged canyonland on its 123-mile journey, traversing moonscapes of sculpted rock, crossing narrow ridgebacks, and climbing over an 11,000ft-tall mountain.

Pretty much everything between the bookend towns of Panguitch and Torrey is on or near Hwy 12. Highlights include gourmet cafes in tiny-tot Boulder, a hike in Grand Staircase–Escalante National Monument, and an incredible drive through arches and Technicolor red rock in Red Canyon. Take time to stop at the many viewpoints and pullouts, especially at Mile 70, where the Aquarius Plateau lords over giant mesas, towering domes, deep canyons, and undulating slickrock, all unfurling in an explosion of color.

 SEE IT ! *Most drive Hwy 12 west-east, from Panguitch in southwest Utah. The nearest big airport is Las Vegas, 230 miles southwest.*

422

Stumble upon lost treasure at Point Reyes National Seashore

CALIFORNIA // The windswept Point Reyes peninsula juts defiantly into the Pacific just north of the San Francisco Bay area. It's a rough-hewn beauty that lures marine mammals and migratory birds but has also ensnared scores of shipwrecks. In 1579, Sir Francis Drake landed here to repair his galleon, *Golden Hind*. Sixteen years later, the *San Agustín*, a Spanish treasure ship laden with luxury goods, wasn't so lucky; to this day bits of its cargo still wash up on shore.

Point Reyes National Seashore protects some 100 sq miles of pristine ocean beaches and coastal wilderness hereabouts, and has excellent hiking and camping opportunities. Be sure to bring warm clothing – even the sunniest days can quickly turn cold and foggy.

SEE IT ! *West Marin Stagecoach route 68 from San Rafael stops at the Bear Valley Visitor Center before continuing to the town of Point Reyes Station. It's less than 90 minutes from San Francisco by car.*

423

Trace New England's maritime history at Nantucket's Whaling Museum

MASSACHUSETTS // An early pioneer of whaling in North America, Nantucket island joined the nascent hunting trade in the 1690s and maintained its dominance until around 1850; it was even name-checked in Herman Melville's *Moby Dick*. The evocative museum occupies an 1847 spermaceti (whale oil) candle factory and relives Nantucket's 19th-century heyday as the whaling center of the world. There's a detailed documentary on the island, incredible scrimshaw (engravings and carvings done by sailors on ivory, whalebone, or baleen), and a 46ft sperm-whale skeleton rising above it all. Be sure to head to the rooftop deck for lovely views. The museum itself has something of a history; founded in 1930, it was extensively updated in 2005.

SEE IT ! *Flights arrive at the island's airport, 3 miles southeast of town. Ferries dock at Steamboat Wharf or Straight Wharf.*

424

Snorkel and dive at Makua (Tunnels) Beach

HAWAI'I // One of Kaua'i's numerous too-good-to-be-true beaches, 'Tunnels', on the North Shore, is named for the underwater caverns and lava tubes that pepper the near-shore reef. Not surprisingly, it's one of the island's finest snorkel spots, as well as being the North Shore's most popular dive site (it's even suitable for shore dives). Summer is the best time to head under as in winter the swell picks up and the surf can be heavy. Even those averse to sub-aqua exploration will be quickly smitten by Makua's deluxe crescent of fine sand backed by palm trees, jungle-y foliage and steep-sided pinnacles. Due to its limited accessibility (walk-in only) it's rarely overcrowded. If you're lucky, you may even have turtles and monk seals for company.

🖝 SEE IT ! *Most beachgoers park at Ha'ena State Park, then walk a half-mile along the sandy foreshore. Ha'ena is linked to Hanalei along Kuhio Hwy via several one-lane bridges.*

425

Witness US naval might at the USS Midway Museum

Courtesy of the USS Midway Museum

CALIFORNIA // The hulking aircraft carrier USS *Midway* was the only ship of its type to serve the entirety of the Cold War from 1945 to 1991; it took its last bow during the First Gulf War. Since 2004, it has been a huge museum docked at San Diego's Navy Pier where you can walk right up to two dozen restored aircraft on the flight deck, take an audio tour along the narrow confines of the upper decks to the bridge and the admiral's war room, and duck below to the sick bay, galley, laundry, and engine room.

☞ SEE IT ! *The ship is on San Diego's strollable Embarcadero, an easy walk from downtown.*

426

Climb and create at Chicago Children's Museum

ILLINOIS // Designed to challenge the imaginations of toddlers, 10-year-olds, and adults who haven't fully grown up yet, this interactive museum near the entrance to Navy Pier on Chicago's waterfront gives visitors enough hands-on exhibits to satisfy the shortest of concentration spans. Among the favorites, Dinosaur Expedition explores the world of paleontology and lets kids excavate 'bones'; the ropey schooner imitates a ship's rigging; and Waterways teaches them about hydroelectric power as they get amusingly wet.

☛ SEE IT ! *The pier is in Streeterville, just north of downtown Chicago. Take CTA bus 124 from Ogilvie Transportation Center or Union Station.*

427

Commune with the spirits at Bonaventure Cemetery

GEORGIA // This Savannah boneyard is the very definition of Southern Gothic. On a bluff overlooking the Wilmington River, immense oaks trailing beards of Spanish moss throw shadows over age-worn tombs and angel statues. Established in 1846, it's the final resting place for Confederates, Jewish merchants, Spanish-American War soldiers, and local actors and writers. Look for the eerie statue of Corinne Lawton (said to have killed herself the day before an arranged wedding in 1877) and the sweetly sad statue of Gracie Watson, who died aged six in 1889.

☛ SEE IT ! *The cemetery is 4 miles southeast of downtown Savannah. Visit solo, or take an engaging local tour.*

Courtesy of the Chicago Children's Museum

© Eugenie Robitaille / Shutterstock

An icon of the NYC cityscape, the 1902 Flatiron set the tone for Big Apple 'skyscraper' design.

428

Unleash your inner architect at the Flatiron

NEW YORK // Even if you're not aware of this extraordinary building, chances are it will catch your eye, mainly because of its shape and prominence near Madison Square Park. Designed by Daniel Burnham and built in 1902, the 21-story Flatiron Building has a narrow triangular footprint that resembles the prow of a massive ship, and a traditional Beaux Arts limestone and terracotta facade. This distinctive structure dominated the plaza back in the dawning skyscraper era of the early 1900s. Originally known as the Fuller Building, its construction coincided with the proliferation of mass-produced picture postcards – the partnership was kismet. Even before its completion, there were images of the soon-to-be tallest tower circulating the globe, creating much wonder and excitement. It was later immortalized by short-story writer O. Henry (his publisher Frank Munsey was one of the building's first tenants). The paintings of John Sloan and photographs of Alfred Stieglitz best captured the Flatiron back in the day – along with a famous comment by Katharine Hepburn, who quipped that she'd like to be admired as much as the grand old building.

☞ SEE IT ! *View it from the traffic island north of 23rd St between Broadway and Fifth Ave, where there's seating and a booze kiosk.*

429

Embrace all the colors at Desert Botanical Garden

ARIZONA // Deserts aren't just full of rocks and sand, at least not in Phoenix. Bluebells and Mexican gold poppies are just two of the colorful showstoppers that bloom seasonally at this well-nurtured botanical garden conceived in 1939. It's a lovely place to reconnect with nature while learning about desert plant life like cacti and agave. Trails lead past a profusion of desert denizens, arranged by theme via a Sonoran Desert nature loop and an edible desert garden. It's dazzling year-round, but the flowering spring season is the busiest and most colorful.

☛ SEE IT ! *The garden is 10 miles east of downtown Phoenix, adjacent to the city zoo.*

430

Survey a curtain of cascading water at 'Akaka Falls

HAWAI'I // The Big Island's best 'tourist waterfall' inhabits a lush state park and is easily accessible – hence its fame. A straightforward paved path takes you counterclockwise in a loop traversing cliffs above a river surrounded by orchids, ferns, and bamboo. You'll first pass the modest opening act, Kahuna Falls (100ft), and then behold the grand 'Akaka Falls, which plunge 442ft into a deep emerald pool. Oft-repeated folkloric legends add mystique to the cascading plume of water.

☛ SEE IT ! *To get to the state park turn onto Hwy 220 13 miles north of Hilo, and head 4 miles inland.*

431

Uncover the coastal terroir of Littorai wines

CALIFORNIA // Blending cow pastures, woodland, and companion gardens with neat vineyards, the 30-acre biodynamic Littorai estate is all about the terroir. Here on the fog-shrouded Sonoma coastal mountains (Littorai is derived from littoral, meaning 'coast'), it's all about location, attention to detail and maintaining an integrated ecosystem. Take a tour, or indulge in private single-vineyard tastings to evaluate the difference a year or plot can make to the nuances of taste. The chardonnays and pinot noirs are complex, elegant, and well priced.

☛ SEE IT ! *Located 3 miles west of Sebastopol, the winery is an 80-minute drive north of San Francisco.*

© Leena Robinson / Shutterstock

© Taner Muhlis Karaguzel / Shutterstock

Courtesy of the Georgia Museum of Art

432

433

Play with vintage toys at the quirky Musée Mécanique

CALIFORNIA // Once upon a time, families flocked to seaside penny arcades. More sophisticated pleasures have since replaced these halls lined with coin-operated games, but the Musée Mécanique is a loving homage to these innocent pierside joys – its 300-item collection of vintage games and curios has been a beloved San Fran attraction since 1933. Many exhibits are hands-on: you can play games set in Wild West saloons, squint at belly dancers through a vintage Mutoscope (a 19th-century motion picture gadget), and even learn a cautionary tale about smoking opium. The museum's orchestrions (pipe music boxes), old slot machines, and mechanized figures are charming and occasionally creepy (personally, we give Laughing Sal a wide berth). The entire experience is delightfully weird: this is San Francisco, after all.

☛ SEE IT ! *The collection can be found at Pier 45 on Fisherman's Wharf. You can take the historic MUNI F-Line Streetcar from Embarcadero BART / MUNI metro station.*

Visit the Georgia Museum of Art in innovative Athens

GEORGIA // The word Athens evokes art, sophistication and culture – not just when referring to the ancient Greek city, but also to its smaller American namesake, a creative, laidback college town in Georgia. Closely associated with the University of Georgia, Athens' smart, modern gallery is where brainy, arty types study in the wired lobby, while art hounds gawk at modern sculpture in the courtyard garden. The museum has gone through several incarnations since its inauguration in 1948 and its collection has multiplied concurrently. Strongly represented are late-19th century American Impressionists, American Realists of the 1930s, and masters of tempura canvases from 14th-century Italy. In 2012, the museum was bequeathed 100 works of African-American art dating from the 1890s to the present, providing excellent insight into this important and under-recognized genre.

☛ SEE IT ! *Athens is 70 miles east of Atlanta. Groome Transportation operates 23 shuttles per day year-round between Athens and Hartsfield–Jackson Atlanta International Airport.*

434

Swap Sonoma wine for IPA at Russian River Brewing

CALIFORNIA // Bored of all that pretentious Sonoma viticulture? Come to Santa Rosa, craft-beer capital of Wine Country, where the annual release of this cult brewery's double IPA 'Pliny the Elder' prompts cross-country road trips and campouts at the door. The famous Pliny beers are hoppy, strong, and notoriously bitter – the brain-rattling, triple-IPA 'Pliny the Younger', a wine-barrel-aged sour beer, tops 10% ABV. Both brews pair well with pizza served in the company's large but always busy downtown brewpub. Arrive early and bring a beard.

☛ SEE IT ! *The brewery is in downtown Santa Rosa, an hour's drive north of San Francisco on Hwy 101.*

435

Relive '60s sit-ins at the International Civil Rights Center

NORTH CAROLINA // Poignant, groundbreaking, and still extremely relevant, the downtown Greensboro Woolworth store where four Black students from North Carolina A&T State University sparked a sit-in campaign by ordering coffee at a 'whites only' lunch counter on February 1, 1960, is now a museum honoring the 'birthplace of the Civil Rights Movement.' The museum opened in 2010 on the 50th anniversary of the original sit-in, with three surviving protestors in attendance; exhibits include the historic lunch counter, and a Hall of Shame displaying harrowing photos of atrocities from the era.

☛ SEE IT ! *The museum is in Greensboro, 50 miles west of Raleigh.*

436

Wander between Greek busts and Pop Art at RISD Museum

RHODE ISLAND // Proving that the smallest US state can still deliver a heavy artistic punch, the wonderfully eclectic Rhode Island School of Design's art museum in Providence showcases everything from ancient Greek art to 20th-century American paintings. Track the geniuses of yore from an Egyptian coffin to a 1960s' Lichtenstein etching. Though storied (in operation since 1877), the museum has moved with the times: a 2008 rebuild erected a dynamic new silver cube structure that contrasts delightfully with the surrounding red-brick facades.

☛ SEE IT ! *The museum is just east of the Providence River, close to the city's small, pretty and walkable core.*

437

Delve into the lavish Ringling collections

FLORIDA // The palatial winter estate of railroad, real-estate and circus baron John Ringling and his wife, Mable, is one of the Gulf Coast's premier attractions and incorporates their personal collection of artworks in what is Florida's state art museum. Nearby, Ringling Circus Museum documents theatrical successes, while their lavish Venetian Gothic winter home, Cà d'Zan, reveals the impresario's extravagant tastes.

The Ringlings amassed an impressive collection of 14th- to 18th-century European tapestries and paintings. Housed in a grand Mediterranean-style palazzo, the art museum covers 21 galleries showcasing Spanish and Baroque works, and a world-renowned collection of Rubens canvases. The Circus Museum preserves hand-carved animal wagons, calliopes, artifacts from Ringling Bros' original traveling show, and a truly epic 1:12

scale re-creation of the entire Ringling Bros and Barnum & Bailey Circus in action. The Ringling's Cà d'Zan home displays a theatrical, Venetian-style flair. Ceilings are decorated with painted masterpieces, notably Willy Pogany's *Dancers of Nations* in the ballroom.

🐘 SEE IT ! *The Ringling Museum Complex is in Sarasota, a one-hour drive south of Tampa International Airport on Florida's Gulf Coast.*

438

Watch sunsets over seafood at Menemsha

MASSACHUSETTS // Occupying most of the western side of the island of Martha's Vineyard between Vineyard Sound and the Atlantic, Chilmark is a place of pastoral landscapes and easygoing people. Its pièce de résistance is the ridiculously quaint fishing village of Menemsha, where you'll find shacks selling seafood fresh off the boat. If you start getting strange feelings of déjà-vu, it's because Menemsha was the backdrop to the movie *Jaws* in 1975. Sunsets here are nothing short of spectacular.

☛ SEE IT ! *Martha's Vineyard Regional Transit Authority operates a network of buses from the Vineyard Haven ferry terminal to villages throughout the island. Bus 4 serves Menemsha.*

439

Learn from the past at the Birmingham Civil Rights Institute

ALABAMA // A maze of moving audio, video, and photography exhibits tell the story of racial segregation and the Civil Rights Movement, with a focus on activities in and around Birmingham during the Jim Crow era. Located downtown, the museum has an extensive exhibit on the 16th St Baptist Church (located across the street), which was bombed by white supremacists in 1963, killing four African-American girls. It's also the beginning of the city's seven-block Civil Rights Memorial Trail, depicting 22 scenes with plaques, statues, and photography.

☛ SEE IT ! *Birmingham-Shuttlesworth airport is 5 miles northeast of Birmingham. The city is served by Greyhound buses and Amtrak trains.*

440

Mix beer, food, spirits, and music at Dogfish Head

DELAWARE // Dogfish Head Brewings & Eats is an emporium of good taste in Rehoboth Beach, the closest stretch of sand to Washington, DC. There's a long list of beers available from the iconic brewery, headlined by the colorfully labeled 90-minute IPA. Complementing the beers is a distillery plying vodka, gin, and canned cocktails, regular live music, and food that plays more than a cameo – the wood-fired pizzas are particularly memorable. It's all wrapped up in a large, modern split-level bar-restaurant with high ceilings and warm wood finishes.

☛ SEE IT ! *BestBus offers services from DC and NYC to Rehoboth, running Friday to Sunday in summertime only.*

441

Make time for rhyme at the Amazing World of Dr Seuss

MASSACHUSETTS // Kids can climb on statues of Horton (he who heard a Who), play the Lorax recycling game, enter the railroad tunnel from *Green Eggs and Ham,* and visit Whoville at Christmastime at this museum dedicated to America's best-beloved rhyming children's book author. Born Theodor Geisel here in Springfield in 1904, Seuss wrote more than 60 books, some of which are no doubt imprinted on your own mind from childhood re-readings. See exhibits about Geisel's life, including his collection of 117 bow ties.

☛ SEE IT ! *Springfield is 90 miles west of Boston and 26 miles north of Hartford, Connecticut.*

Inspect bits of Einstein's brain at the Mütter Museum

PENNSYLVANIA // Maintained by the College of Physicians, this macabre museum is dedicated to rare, odd, or disturbing medical conditions. Not for the squeamish, its exhibits include a saponified body, a conjoined female fetus, and incredibly realistic wax models of medical conditions. If that doesn't freak you out, cast your eyes over pieces of Albert Einstein's brain preserved in glass slides, or a collection of 139 skulls. Somewhere in the vaults also lurks a malignant tumor removed from President Grover Cleveland and a fragment of John Wilkes Booth's back.

☞ SEE IT ! *The museum is in downtown Philadelphia. Get off at the 22nd St station.*

Drop into South Walton's manicured beach communities

FLORIDA // Sandwiched between Destin and Panama City along Scenic Hwy 30A are 16 unincorporated communities collectively known as South Walton. Each has its own identity; most are master-planned resort towns with architecture following set themes. If you're wondering what happens when you bake New Urbanism in the Florida sun, here's the answer. If you only make two stops, try delightful Grayton Beach, which feels as though it was settled by old-school hippies who came into money; and the meticulously manicured village of Seaside.

☞ SEE IT ! *The South Walton beaches stretch in a thin line along the 30A coast road in the Florida panhandle.*

Walk in the footsteps of stars at TCL Chinese Theatre

CALIFORNIA // Ever wondered what it's like to be in George Clooney's shoes? Find out by stepping into his foot- and handprints, alongside those of dozens of other stars, forever set in the concrete forecourt of this world-famous LA movie palace. Opened in 1927, it was styled after an Asian-style pagoda complete with temple bells and stone heaven dogs from China. Join the throngs to find out how big Schwarzenegger's feet really are, or search for Betty Grable's legs, Whoopi Goldberg's braids, Daniel Radcliffe's wand, or R2-D2's wheels.

☞ SEE IT ! *The theatre is on Hollywood Blvd. Take Metro B line to Hollywood/Highland station.*

Relish the unique vodka at Hawai'i Sea Spirits

HAWAI'I // There are many ways to make vodka, but this attractive 80-acre organic farm and distillery on Maui island is the only place making it from sugarcane and deep-ocean mineral water. From the sugarcane stalks to the bottling room to the end-of-tour tasting, the 45-minute guided tour at this family-run vodka, gin, and rum distillery tells an interesting story about the company's organic ethos. The flagship spirit, Ocean Vodka, is made with said mineral water sourced off the coast of Hawai'i's Big Island. Tastings happen outdoors, beside the cane fields.

☞ SEE IT ! *The farm is 6 miles southwest of Pukalani, which is 10 miles from Maui's Kahului International Airport. A rental car is your best bet.*

446

Enter the antebellum era at Wormsloe Historic Site

GEORGIA // A short drive from Savannah's downtown area on the beautiful Isle of Hope is the former plantation of one of Georgia's early English-born pioneers, Noble Jones. As soon as you arrive, you feel as if you've been roused from the last snatch of an arboreal dream as you gaze at a verdant corridor of mossy, ancient oaks that runs for 1.5 miles, known as the Avenue of the Oaks.

Beyond, other draws beckon, including an antebellum mansion still lived in by Jones' descendants, some old colonial ruins, and an educational site where you can see modern actors demonstrate blacksmithing and other bygone trades.

© Trisha Ping / Lonely Planet

SEE IT ! *The site is 9 miles south of downtown Savannah. Chatham Area Transit (CAT) buses run here.*

© Serge Skiba / Shutterstock

© Nelson Chenault III. Courtesy of the Clinton Foundation

© LevKPhoto / Getty Images

447

Revisit the '90s at the William J. Clinton Presidential Center

ARKANSAS // A Modernist museum and library in Little Rock lovingly chronicles the impact of native Arkansan (and POTUS 42) Bill Clinton, who was born just 100 miles from this spot. This steel and glass building was designed to maximize river views, and natural light floods the huge atrium. Walk through the main hall to see a detailed timeline of Clinton's presidency (1993–2001) along with painstakingly preserved artifacts, including two million photographs and 80 million pages of documents.

No time to peruse the details of the longest peacetime period of economic expansion in US history? Then pose for pictures in the replica Oval Office, gawp at gifts from foreign dignitaries, and check out Bill's famous saxophone. Snap up an 'I miss Bill' T-shirt before heading outside to stroll the wetland preserve across the road.

☛ SEE IT ! *The center is east of the Arkansas River Bridge on the south side, near Interstate 30.*

448

Spend a whole day immersed in Lincoln Park

ILLINOIS // Chicago's Lincoln Park fills 1200 acres and stretches for 6 miles along the shores of Lake Michigan. On sunny days, locals come out to play in droves, taking advantage of the ponds, paths, and playing fields or enjoying the free-entry zoo and beaches. Guarding the park's southern edge, sculptor Augustus Saint-Gaudens' *Standing Lincoln* shows the 16th US president deep in contemplation. Nearby, take a gander at the Couch Tomb, the sole remainder of the land's pre-1864 use as a municipal cemetery – which included burials of Confederate soldiers who died as prisoners of war at Camp Douglas, a Union stockade on the South Side of town. Further north lie sailboat harbors, golf courses, bird sanctuaries, and rowing clubs out on the lagoons. Walk east from anywhere in the park and you'll come to the Lakefront Trail, an 18.5-mile multi-use path which connects several beaches.

☛ SEE IT ! *Bus 151 from downtown heads along Michigan Ave to the zoo and park sights.*

449

Consider the facts at Dealey Plaza and the Grassy Knoll

TEXAS // Infamous for its location alongside the road where John F. Kennedy's motorcade was ambushed in November 1963, tiny Dealey Plaza park is now a haunting, eerily familiar National Historic Landmark. Lee Harvey Oswald fired the fatal shots from the former Book Depository, immediately north; but witnesses also heard shots coming from the 'grassy knoll' overlooking the plaza. The conclusion of the 1970s' House Select Committee on Assassinations, that a sniper did indeed fire (and miss) from behind the picket fence here, bolstered the belief that Kennedy's assassination was part of a conspiracy.

☛ SEE IT ! *Dealey Plaza is in Dallas' West End Historic District.*

450

Enjoy wine with an Italian bent at Tsillan Cellars

WASHINGTON // On a good day, when the sun is shining, Lake Chelan in Washington State does a good impersonation of Italy's Lake Como, especially if you roll up at the Tsillan Cellars estate with its Tuscan columns, grape arbor-covered terrazzo and belltower overlooking sloping sun-dappled vineyards. The theme continues in the grapes, which include Sangiovese and Barbera, and the onsite restaurant, named Sorrento in a nod to its *cucina italiana*. No small wonder Tsillan was named Washington's 2020 Winery of the Year.

☛ SEE IT ! *Chelan is 170 miles east of Seattle on US 97.*

451

Be a ski renegade at Crested Butte Mountain Resort

COLORADO // Crested Butte is a place where skiing offers something for the renegade spirit. Here, locals occasionally take runs naked, and freedom, irreverence, and the simple joys of fresh powder on a bluebird day still stand true. It's also one of the birthplaces of extreme skiing, and on runs like Rambo, the steepest 'inbounds' run in the US, you can challenge yourself on 55-degree hits. The surrounding forests, peaks, and wilderness areas are as breathtaking as the skiing.

☛ SEE IT ! *Crested Butte is 230 miles southwest of Denver, and 200 miles west of Colorado Springs. In winter, there are regular flights to/from Gunnison Airport.*

With its gondolas, Italianate palazzos, Grande Canal Shoppes, and glitzy casino, the Venetian is Vegas' ultimate destination hotel.

452

Embrace every imaginable excess at the Venetian Resort Las Vegas

NEVADA // Want to gamble hard and wake up with a tiger in your bathroom, *The Hangover*-style? It's hard deciding on a launch-pad into Las Vegas, that infamous oasis of vice in the Nevada desert. But the Venetian Resort is the place to bet it all on red: an Italianate palace of decadence and combined casino space that together make for one of the most impressive, largest complexes in Sin City. There are many reasons why the Venetian

is a quintessential never-leave-the-hotel experience. There are table games and slot machines beckoning beneath ceilings strung with crystal chandeliers. There are the high-rollers who come here purely to explore the upmarket Grand Canal Shoppes. Then there are also the sweet spas ornamented with fountains and marbled statues, and a palm-fringed pool deck (reserve ahead for a cabana). Finally, the resort's nightspots

include a swish Art Deco cocktail bar and three theaters, where you can watch *Chicago* or sing along to ZZ Top. Book accommodation on site and your big, plush room is only a quick elevator ride away – if you sleep at all.

☛ SEE IT ! *The main lobby is next to the Palazzo Casino. Get a ride-share or Deuce public transport to travel up and down The Strip (it's long).*

453

Flex your fingers on Arkadia Retrocade's vintage games

ARKANSAS // Video games were way better back in the day, right? Test the accuracy of your teen memories at Arkadia Retrocade, where $5 gets you hours of fun on old-school arcade games that date right back to the 1970s. Nostalgia is strong among 30- and 40-somethings getting their Donkey Kong on, or playing Pac-Man for the first time in decades. But Arkadia also attracts a younger crowd who play foosball, toy with Atari 2600s and Nintendo 64s, or even go analog with board games.

☛ SEE IT ! *Get gaming at 1478 North College Ave in the Evelyn Hills Shopping Center in Fayetteville.*

454

Gaze from terracotta hills at Corona Heights Park

CALIFORNIA // Offering 360-degree views of San Francisco, Corona Heights Park was formerly the site of a brick factory. Its grassy spaces are still dotted with dusky-orange boulders, but the rock-chiseling production line ground to a halt in the 1920s. Wildlife now flourishes: look out for alligator lizards and red-tailed hawks. Today, the park is also popular with families thanks to tennis courts, barbecue pits, a playground, and the nearby Beaver St climbing wall. Complete the experience at the natural-history-focused Randall Museum.

☛ SEE IT ! *The easiest park access is from Roosevelt Way. From the Castro, hike uphill from Beaver St.*

455

Don't worry, be hoppy at Avery Brewing Company

COLORADO // Like your beers big and your craft breweries bigger? Then two-story Avery Brewing Company (est. 1993) will wet your whistle. The mission of this Boulder-based brewery is to revere traditional production methods while creating category-defying beers. For 30 years they've done just that, collecting the odd gold medal along the way. Order sour ales, crisp lagers, and toasty-vanilla stouts on the patio, or head to the restaurant to pair pork ramen with Imperial IPA. True hop-heads can opt for tasting tours of the barrel-ageing cellar.

☛ SEE IT ! *Find the brewery at 4910 Nautilus Ct, 6 miles northeast of downtown Boulder. Enquire ahead about tours.*

456

Get cultured, Maine-style, at Farnsworth Art Museum

MAINE // On Maine's rocky midcoast, the small-but-mighty Farnsworth punches far above its weight. It's all about American art, with a focus on Maine – see one of the nation's finest collections of works by the Wyeth family: grandfather NC, son Andrew, and grandson Jamie, all realist masters. Other Maine-connected artists represented include Winslow Homer, Marsden Hartley, Alex Katz, and sculptor Louise Nevelson. The pleasant little green campus is an oasis in the heat of a Maine summer.

☛ SEE IT ! *The museum is in Rockland, about 60 miles from Bangor and 80 from Portland, both home to major airports.*

© Z Faulkner. Courtesy of Kingdom Trails

© EE Berger / Courtesy of the Henry Ford Museum

457

Pedal forests and meadows along the Kingdom Trails

VERMONT // This award-winning network of trails offers the best mountain biking in New England, as well as pathways that draw hikers and runners from miles around. Established in 1997, this 100-plus-mile web of single and double tracks and dirt roads weaves through silver birch forests and across rolling centuries-old farmlands. It's especially lovely in fall, when you can fly across the forest floor, kicking up orange and yellow fallen leaves as you pedal through. Come winter, you can swap your steed for a fat bike or clip on some snowshoes to tramp through snow-bogged trails. If you don't feel the need for speed, you can tackle beginner-friendly bike paths like the Village Trails, or embark on easy-going pedestrian paths that meander gently through farmland and meadows.

🖝 TRY IT ! *Buy passes at the Kingdom Trails Welcome Center in East Burke (May-Oct) or Nordic Adventure Center (Dec-Mar). Note that trails close in April and November.*

458

Encounter emblems of US history at the Henry Ford Museum

MICHIGAN // Some moments in history acquire mythic status – and the Henry Ford Museum is remarkable for collecting artifacts from these epoch-defining events and displaying them for more than 1.8 million visitors to see each year. Around this indoor-outdoor museum's 80 acres you can see the presidential limo in which John F. Kennedy was killed; the rocking chair Abraham Lincoln was sitting in when he was assassinated; and the bus on which Rosa Parks defied segregated seating rules. Emblems of innovation are paid homage, too: the Wright Brothers' workshop; a replica of Thomas Edison's lab; and the Ford F-150 factory floor, which explains the history and design of the iconic truck. This colossal collection is like a 300-year timeline of US inventiveness and innovation via railroads, manufacturing, and women's suffrage, with many hands-on experiences along the way.

🖝 SEE IT ! *This museum in Dearborn is big: grab a map at the entrance and save half a day to explore.*

459

Commune with the wilderness at volcanic Mt Shasta

CALIFORNIA // In 1874, naturalist and poet John Muir wrote that his very blood turned to wine at the sight of Mt Shasta. You might feel the same: Shasta is a startling anomaly of the landscape – on clear days you can see this lone, snow-streaked 14,179ft-high peak from 140 miles away. Part of the volcanic Cascade chain, Shasta has been snoozing for more than two centuries. Lace your hiking boots to explore bear-trodden red fir forests on its flanks. In winter, watch purplish sunsets reflect off the snow then go night skiing.

☞ SEE IT ! *Shasta is approximately 220 miles north of Sacramento, a scenic trip along Hwy 5 towards Oregon.*

© Alberto Armas / Shutterstock

460

Browse local bounty at Dane County Farmers Market

WISCONSIN // It began in 1972 with five local farmers peddling their wares; now it's the nation's largest producers-only farmers market. Up to 275 vendors gather twice a week in Madison's Capitol Square to showcase a banquet of Wisconsin goodies. The tradition was originally inspired by European-style open-air markets, but soon took on a life of its own. Browse bright peppers, wipe-the-mud-off potatoes, tempting baked goods, and above all dairy: Wisconsin is the 'Cheese State', so you can't leave without grabbing some of their alpine and Swiss-style

☞ SEE IT ! *Wednesday and Saturday markets run between mid-April and early November. Ask locally for winter hours.*

461

Express your Aloha Spirit on Keawakapu Beach

HAWAI'I // This is it: you've found your step-into-a-postcard moment on Maui. These inviting sands stretch between south Kihei and Wailea's Mokapu Beach. And while many folks come just for the sunsets, Keawakapu Beach is also a magnet for swimmers and boogie boarders; and as its hotels and restaurants are set away from the sand, it's a relatively uncrowded place to sunbathe or paddle. Feel at one with nature by checking out the tide pools at the northern end, or come in winter when you can spot humpback whales from the shore.

☞ SEE IT ! *There are parking lots at all three beach access points.*

462

Photograph serpentine switchbacks along Lombard Street

CALIFORNIA // Nearby signs point the way to the 'Crooked Street,' but the words don't quite do justice to the precipitous, curving folly of San Francisco's Lombard St. The famous 600ft-long stretch has eight hairpin turns, which makes the steep hill's whopping 27% grade (just) drivable. Though plenty of cars queue up for the careful descent, it's even better to enjoy the street on foot. You can take your time strolling down the flower-lined stairway-sidewalks framing the red-brick road, and linger over mesmerizing views across Russian Hill to Coit Tower and the bay beyond.

☛ SEE IT ! *Take Union/Stockton bus 45 to Hyde St.*

463

Dive into Mississippi River Museum & Aquarium

IOWA // Underwater organisms and river-faring humans get shared billing in this fascinating national museum at Dubuque Harbor. As soon as you step inside, tanks show a cross-section of what lies beneath the surface of the Mississippi. Deeper within this huge riverfront development, you'll learn how to crew a steamboat, meet aquatic life-forms like alligators and otters, and get the chance to feed stingrays in the touch pool. There's historical miscellany too, like WWII mess kits and a chair once used by Abe Lincoln.

☛ SEE IT ! *Book ahead to test the boaty lifestyle on the whole family: you can spend an entire night in the 1934 William M. Black dredge boat.*

464

Get lost among millions of books at Strand Book Store

NEW YORK // When the city's best-loved bookstore was struggling during the Covid pandemic, owners asked for help and bibliophiles answered: hundreds of thousands of dollars poured in over a single weekend. It's a sign of how important the Strand is to the city's literary fabric. With its '18 miles of books' (a logo emblazoned on the store's ubiquitous tote bags) spread over three floors, you can easily lose an hour – or a day – browsing its new, used, and antique books. It's occupied the same East Village spot since 1927.

☛ SEE IT ! *The main store is at 828 Broadway, near 14th St-Union Sq subway station; there's a second location on the Upper West Side.*

465

Hear the Gullah perspective at McLeod Plantation

SOUTH CAROLINA // There's no *Gone with the Wind* romanticizing at this James Island plantation, where enslaved Africans and their descendants grew rice, indigo, and cotton in brutal conditions. The historic site tells their story through tours that take in the plantation house, the slave quarters, and the cemetery. The plantation's workers were Gullah people who wove their African heritage into a unique culture and language. Their story is an integral part of America's, and until recently was too often overlooked in favor of glorifying the hoop skirts and white columned porches of the antebellum South.

☛ SEE IT ! *The historic site is 5 miles west of downtown Charleston.*

466

Be inspired at the beguiling McNay Art Museum

TEXAS // The very sight of the McNay Art Museum lifts the spirits. This Spanish-Colonial-Revival-style mansion is flanked by palm trees and surrounded by 25 acres of gardens. It's even more inspiring inside: the 24-room gallery hosts a collection of European and American art, originally the donations of heiress, painter, and art patron Marion Koogler McNay. Today, the works span medieval art right through to the 21st century, with rotating exhibitions cherry-picking the loveliest items – including paintings by the likes of Picasso, Matisse, and Van Gogh.

☛ SEE IT ! *The museum is 5 miles north of downtown San Antonio. Check ahead for intriguing temporary exhibitions in the Stieren Center.*

467

Dream of a lavish country life at Shelburne Farms

VERMONT // This handsome country estate was inspired by the English countryside and a legendary architect. Established in 1886 by William Seward Webb and Lila Vanderbilt Webb, the 1400-acre farm was modelled on the designs of Frederick Law Olmsted, who created New York's Central Park. Stroll along its walking trails to Lake Champlain, then buy farm-made cheese, maple syrup, and mustard. Finding it hard to leave? Stay the night in one of the plush on-site guest rooms.

☞ SEE IT ! *The estate is 8 miles south of Burlington, off US 7.*

© Jay Lyon / Shutterstock

© T photography / Shutterstock

Soar through celestial ski fields in Heavenly

CALIFORNIA // Sunshine is bouncing off the snow as you cruise down to South Lake Tahoe. The sky is California blue, the lake's cobalt expanse shimmers, and at the bottom of the trail, spiked hot chocolate awaits. Heavenly's 4800 skiable acres spread across the California-Nevada border, zig-zagged by tree-lined trails that top out at over 10,000ft. Bit of a ski pro? Somersault through on-snow adventure parks, or test your GoPro in double-diamond canyons. For the rest of us, there's skiing Tahoe's longest run before clinking craft beers in a sun-lounger.

☛ SEE IT ! *Stay in South Lake Tahoe (CA) for snug restaurants and bars or Stateline (NV) for casinos and nightlife.*

© Alisa_Ch / Shutterstock

Dissect aviation history at the Museum of Flight

WASHINGTON // It's no surprise that Seattle, the city that spawned Boeing, has come up with one of the nation's finest aviation museums, chronicling flight history from the Wright Brothers to Concorde. It's a multifarious affair, with a broad sweep of flight-related memorabilia in several hangar-sized galleries. Exhibits include some of the most ingenious human-made objects to have defied gravity, including V2 rockets, Apollo lunar modules, and aerodynamic gliders. It's not all gawping – X-Plane simulators can pitch you into a WWII dogfight.

☛ SEE IT ! *The museum is south of Seattle off I-5. Metro bus 124 runs to the museum from downtown Seattle.*

© Norman Ong / Shutterstock

470

Contemplate a ruined baron's folly at Longwood

MISSISSIPPI // This antebellum mansion traps a historical tipping point in amber. Partly built by enslaved people, it was dubbed Nutt's Folly after its cotton-baron owner Haller Nutt. The mansion was left incomplete when its laborers fled at the start of the Civil War; you can even see their abandoned tools on an upper floor. It remains frozen in time, with lavish, completed lower floors and ghostly, unadorned upper floors.

Longwood has some architectural features common to other mansions in the Deep South, like lacy porch trellising and stately brickwork. But it's a unique design: capped by a Byzantine dome, this octagonal six-story mansion was designed so every room would have a balcony. If it looks vaguely familiar, you might have spotted it in TV vampire series *True Blood*. Contemplating the Nutts' fate as you tour the on-site cemetery, it's hard

to feel much sympathy for the downfall of a family with slave-earned wealth. While many stories of enslaved people here remain untold, Longwood is a rare relic of the transition between slave-holders' prosperity and the post-Civil War South.

☛ SEE IT ! *Longwood is south of downtown Natchez. Drive along Hwy 425, take a right on Lower Woodville Rd, then watch for the sign.*

© Alizada Studios / Shutterstock

© Rolf_52 / Shutterstock

471

Find some fossils at Thomas Condon Paleontology Center

OREGON // Saber-toothed cats once prowled across Oregon, and the proof is right here. Named for the 19th-century scientist who first recognized the significance of local fossil beds, this large interactive center is dedicated to inspiring the next generation of paleontologists.

Start with the 18-minute orientation film, before you contemplate petrified dung-beetle balls and peruse scientifically accurate murals showing plant and animal life throughout 500 million years of history. Watch through a window to see researchers poring over their newest discoveries, or scrutinize finds yourself – it's mind-boggling how the delicate veins of maple leaves are still visible after millions of years. Grab some books from the store to continue playing fossil hunter long after you leave.

☛ SEE IT ! *The center is in real middle-of-nowhere territory, around 230 miles southeast of Portland.*

472

Engage with the past at Plimoth Plantation

MASSACHUSETTS // Learn through immersion at the birthplace of modern America. The interactive Plimoth Plantation allows visitors to experience the early 17th century, exploring the lives of English settlers and showcasing enduring Native cultures. The 'settlers' are in full method-acting mode, as they demonstrate scenes of daily life circa 1627. Ask questions, help them weave and throw pottery, and try age-old furniture-building techniques. Almost half the original pilgrims died of disease or exposure during their first winter, though new arrivals soon added to their numbers, eventually founding the colony of Massachusetts Bay. The fate of Native American people was far bleaker. At the Wampanoag Homesite you can hear their stories, see wattle-and-daub homes and glimpse handicraft traditions.

☛ SEE IT ! *The plantation is around 4 miles southeast of Plymouth, and open from mid-March to the end of November.*

Race to space at the Cosmosphere

KANSAS // Battered rockets and captivating storytelling bring the space race to life at Kansas' only Smithsonian affiliate museum. Inside these walls is the biggest collection of US and Soviet Union space flight artifacts in the cosmos: a whopping 13,000 artifacts, including flown items like the *Liberty Bell* 7 Mercury. The Cold War standoff is explained in gripping detail, with spacecrafts and suits from both sides.

Extra-keen space enthusiasts should opt for the all-attraction pass and experience the planetarium and space simulator – just try not to hit buttons on the command module.

☛ SEE IT ! *It's an easy day trip from Wichita or diversion off US 50.*

Be inspired by words at the Emily Dickinson Museum

MASSACHUSETTS // One of the USA's most important poets, Emily Dickinson spent most of her life (1830-1886) at the green-shuttered custard-yellow-brick home that became known as 'The Homestead.' It was here that she penned most of her 1800 verses, mainly on love, nature, and immortality, though a mere seven were published while she was alive. This insight into Dickinson's world allows explorations around both this residence and 'The Evergreens', the striking Italianate house next door built for Dickinson's brother and his wife. The verdant grounds that so inspired the poet are beautiful for a stroll.

☛ SEE IT ! *The museum sits at 280 Main St in Amherst.*

Surf the waves off Rockaway Beach

NEW YORK // Home to 7 miles of sparkling, sun-kissed shoreline, Rockaway Beach has earned many admirers over the years. In fact, it was a favorite escape for a young Douglas Glenn Colvin – aka Dee Dee Ramone – who immortalized the sandy seaside in the Ramones' 1977 punk-rock hit *Rockaway Beach*. Surfers flock to NYC's best waves, while more casual beachgoers bask on the sands, followed by a stroll along the boardwalk, perhaps getting their fill of lobster rolls, ceviche, and other delicacies. By sundown, open-air drinking and dining spots like Rockaway Surf Club draw the après-sea crowd.

☛ SEE IT ! *Take the A train to Broad Channel and switch to the S train to Rockaway Park.*

Batter up at the Louisville Slugger Museum and Factory

KENTUCKY // When Ted Williams hit .406 in a single season, it was with a Louisville Slugger. Joe DiMaggio's 56-game hitting streak? Louisville Slugger again. When Cal Ripken Jr broke Lou Gehrig's record of playing 2130 consecutive games – you guessed it, he was batting with a Louisville Slugger. Baseball's most iconic bat has been made in downtown Louisville since 1884. Behind an entrance marked by a 120ft Slugger, find famous bats like the one that hit Hank Aaron's 700th home run and an exhibit dedicated to Black ballplayers, or take a factory tour.

☛ SEE IT ! *The museum is on West Main St, a stretch that includes several other museums and cultural sites.*

Drift on up with a Dune Climb

MICHIGAN // Placid Lake Michigan views from atop colossal dunes; water as blue as the Caribbean; enough sand to make you think you've been teleported over to the Sahara. It's all available at Sleeping Bear Dunes Wilderness, a unique pocket of desert-like landscape juxtaposed with forests and a historic rural farm district. The Dune Climb is the area's most popular attraction; a short, sharp trudge up a 200ft-high dune – two steps forward, one step back – before a 90-second run or roll back to where you started. Gluttons for leg-muscle punishment can slog on another hour to Lake Michigan.

☞ SEE IT ! *The Dune climb parking lot is on Hwy 109, 5 miles north of Empire. Bus 11 links to Traverse City (Jun-Oct).*

Frolic in deCordova's art-filled fields

MASSACHUSETTS // Some 60 sculptures are scattered among 30 acres of rolling lawns and woodlands at the magical indoor-outdoor deCordova Sculpure Park, including work by Andy Goldsworthy, Antony Gormley, and Jaume Plensa. You can also explore the airy indoor gallery which displays rotating exhibits of sculptures, paintings, photography, and mixed media art. The gallery has operated since 1950, but it's only in recent decades that sculpture has become its raison d'être. All the better: displaying sculptures outdoors encourages deeper engagement with each piece – as well as garden activities from yoga to nature tours.

☞ SEE IT ! *Find the park 19 miles west of Boston. From Concord, drive east on Rte 2 and turn right on Bedford Rd.*

Try delectable dairy at Cowgirl Creamery

CALIFORNIA // Inside San Francisco's iconic Ferry Building, you file past purveyors of tempting coffee, ice cream, and empanadas. But you're here with one goal in mind: filling your belly (and organic tote bag) at Cowgirl Creamery. Stepping inside, your nostrils flare at the tangy odor, which leads you straight to Cowgirl's signature cheeses: pungent washed-rind Red Hawk and triple-cream Mt Tam. They're certified organic, made from the milk of two dairy farms in nearby Sonoma and West Marin. Shopping complete, order a melty cheese sandwich to munch while overlooking big blue views of the bay.

☞ EAT IT ! *Cowgirl has a small outpost in the Ferry Building or you can visit cheese HQ in Point Reyes Station, an hour's drive north.*

Witness Civil Rights history in Mississippi

MISSISSIPPI // The Mississippi Civil Rights Museum immerses you in the movement's struggles through displays, videos and occasional auditory assaults. It focuses on the fight for equal rights in a state that became notorious for violent opposition to racial equality. The collection is upsetting to explore: aggressive voices bark from overhead speakers while you read about the enslavement of African people during the 17th century, and it's impossible not to be shaken by courtroom footage, photos of lynchings, and hooded Ku Klux Klan robes. The museum's eight exhibition halls provide an unflinching, but essential, education.

☞ SEE IT ! *The museum is at 222 North St in downtown Jackson. Plan to spend at least half a day.*

© GROGL / Shutterstock

© Brenda Kean / Shutterstock

481

Cycle epic desert landscapes along the Kokopelli Trail

COLORADO & UTAH // This mountain biking route is one heck of a ride. Extending from Fruita in Colorado to Moab in Utah, the Kokopelli Trail traverses across rocky plateaus, gurgling creeks, and sandy paths lined by flowering cacti, and rises to quad-burning heights of 8400ft. The dry, mild high-desert climate is great for cycling, and the scenery is glorious: you'll marvel at views of the La Sal Mountains and fly through stony canyons where pinnacles blush pink in the sun.

But make no mistake, this is a hard, 142-mile slog along almost entirely unpaved trails (mostly single track and 4WD roads). Campsites break up the journey but we hope your cycling shorts are well padded – especially for the final descent along Porcupine Rim.

 TRY IT ! *There's an annual race, or you can cycle independently; allow five or six days at a leisurely pace. Riding season extends roughly from March through October, but ask locally.*

482

Hear the twang at the Country Music Hall of Fame

TENNESSEE // Nashville's cathedral to the music that put it on the map, this museum and cultural center takes up a whopping 350,000 sq ft of downtown real estate. It's home to some 2.5 million country music relics: Patsy Cline's cocktail dress; Johnny Cash's black suit; Elvis' 'solid gold' Cadillac; Taylor Swift's rhinestone-encrusted guitar. The central exhibit is *Sing Me Back Home: A Journey Through Country Music*, with objects, sound booths, videos, and touch screens creating an immersive sight-and-sound journey through country's roots. The museum's also home to Hatch Show Print, the country's oldest letterpress print shop, responsible for creating iconic posters for just about everyone in the biz – you'll recognize the style as soon as you see it. Their prints and merch make fantastic souvenirs.

SEE IT ! *The museum is on Demonbreun St. Visit the collections then take a guided tour of Hatch Show Print and/or RCA Studio B, birthplace of the 'Nashville sound.'*

San Fran's Fillmore is best-known for its psychedelic 1960s years, but it's still a vibrant venue today.

483

Commune with rock history at The Fillmore

CALIFORNIA // Rock legends were created within these walls. The former Majestic Hall, built in 1912, began by hosting masquerades, but during the swinging 1960s it became a lightning rod for groundbreaking artists. Santana and The Grateful Dead launched their careers here; The Who, Cream, Jimi Hendrix, and Otis Redding rocked the stage too; and The Fillmore's upstairs bar is still lined with psychedelic vintage posters to prove it. Some traditions endure, like free posters and a 'greeter' who welcomes each guest with: 'Welcome to The Fillmore!'

☛ SEE IT ! *The hallowed venue is on the corner of Fillmore & Geary in San Francisco's Western Addition.*

484

Gaze across the Mississippi from the Gateway Arch

MISSOURI // Soaring 630ft above the Mississippi River, the Gateway Arch is one of America's greatest public works of art. Built in 1965, the shimmering icon – 43,226 tons of concrete wrapped in stainless steel – was a remarkable engineering achievement for its time, built to withstand earthquakes, high winds, and lightning strikes. An eight-car tram, equal parts elevator and Ferris wheel, takes visitors to the top, where views extend 30 miles on clear days. Down below, a museum gives the lowdown on the Arch, St Louis history, and US colonial expansion.

☛ SEE IT ! *The Gateway Arch is in downtown St Louis, reachable by MetroLink light rail (Laclede's Landing station).*

© Lightvision / Getty Images

Strike an iconic pose at the American Gothic House

IOWA // With its striking cathedral window, the Dibble House is instantly recognizable: this is the background of Grant Wood's iconic *American Gothic* (1930). Greatly admired and often parodied, the painting shows a stony-faced woman and man with a pitchfork standing in front of a Carpenter Gothic-style house. Wood noticed the house on a tour around Eldon, hurriedly sketching and later incorporating it into his most famous painting, displayed in the Art Institute of Chicago. Visit the Dibble for a documentary screening and history displays, then recreate your own American Gothic by posing outside – you can even rent props.

☞ SEE IT ! *Eldon is just off Hwy 16; follow the brown signs.*

Bite into legendary cookies at NYC's Levain Bakery

NEW YORK // NYC's icons are often architectural, but just sometimes they take cookie form. Levain Bakery was founded in 1995 by Pam Weekes and Connie McDonald, who turned it into an all-cookie emporium after devising an irresistible recipe. There are four flavors: chocolate chip walnut; dark chocolate chip; dark chocolate peanut butter chip; and oatmeal raisin. They're thick and filling at six ounces each, but don't worry, they last a week. Pro tip: heat them for a few minutes to make them all gooey and delicious-er.

☞ SEE IT ! *Find Levain on the Upper East Side (Third Ave); there are outposts in the Upper West Side, Harlem, and Wainscott too.*

Sing a song of hope at the Woody Guthrie Center

OKLAHOMA // The ballads of Woody Guthrie (1912–1967) touched Americans with their themes of equality, democracy, and overcoming hardship. This uplifting museum honors the Oklahoma-born musician's legacy of grit and positivity, explores the meaning of his music, and hosts live performances. Guthrie's guitar famously sported the slogan: 'This machine kills fascists'. That upbeat defiance laces his folk songs and the center gives context to the lyrics, which evoke the Dust Bowl period and Great Depression. Emerge humming *This Land Is Your Land*.

☞ SEE IT ! *The center is at the southeast corner of Reconciliation Way & Boston Ave in Tulsa Arts District.*

Taste the harvest at United Farmers Market of Maine

MAINE // Saturday mornings in the sweet little seaport of Belfast mean one thing: farmers market. Neighbors chatter as they peruse loaves of sourdough and handmade lavender soaps; friends greet each other as they select wild mushrooms and pyramids of goat's cheese; kids pop fresh blueberries into their mouths and gesture hopefully at the cupcake display. It's year-round, so being Maine this means indoor and heavy on the prepared foods. Maple syrup, artisan jams, pottery, and herbal teas make perfect gifts and souvenirs, and musicians and entertainers lend a community-carnival vibe.

☞ SEE IT ! *Belfast is about 35 miles south of Bangor.*

Tompkins Square Park, the revamped green lung of NYC's East Village.

489

Relish summer in the city in Tompkins Square Park

NEW YORK // A genuine neighborhood gathering place, this East Village park is all about sunbathing students, picnicking families, skateboarding teens, dog walkers, guitar strummers, and chess players. On a sunny summer's day, it's the height of urban bliss – but it wasn't always this way. In the 1980s, the park became one of the most visible sites of New York's drug and poverty problems. The eviction of squatters caused fury and rioting; the park was eventually closed for restoration in 1991. Today, the gentrified green space features a kids' playground, dog runs, ping-pong tables, basketball courts, and free summer movies. On the last weekend of August, the Charlie Parker Jazz Festival brings two days of bebop to the leafy surroundings. And the park's name? It comes from Daniel Tompkins, vice president under James Monroe.

☛ **SEE IT !** *The park is in the East Village, bounded by East 7th and East 10th streets and avenues A & B.*

490

Embrace solitude at Gates of the Arctic National Park

ALASKA // Nature plays by its own rules in this vast and untamed national park. Granite peaks rise to 8200ft, scoured over millennia by intense winds and winter deep-freezes. Muskoxen and moose tread the vast taiga (thinly-spread spruce forests) and birds of prey wheel high above perilous cliffs.

If it sounds like the ends of the earth, that's because it is: these millions of acres of wilderness have no permanent human population. Within the park's boundaries there are no roads, trails, campsites, visitor services, or even cell phone signal. Outdoor survival skills are a must – unless you have the budget for flightseeing or a personal guide. The reward is pristine nature: fishing by mirror-still alpine lakes, hiking along wild rivers, and watching caribou roam wild and free.

☛ SEE IT ! *Visit between June and October. The park is impassable in winter, when temperatures can plummet as low as -40°F.*

© Patrick J. Endres / Getty Images

491

Motor on at Newport Car Museum

RHODE ISLAND // If you appreciate shiny chrome and know your Mopars from your Fin Cars, this sleek exhibition will appeal. Established in 2017 in a former missile manufacturing plant, Newport Car Museum displays more than 75 classic rides. Sigh over swish Corvettes, picture yourself in a 1960s muscle car, and feel inexplicably compelled to buy automotive-themed souvenirs in the gift store. The museum is unashamedly nostalgic for the mid-century golden era of car design, and the displays are lit like treasured items in a sculpture gallery. It's an obsessive homage to vintage vehicles, but beautifully designed for broad appeal.

🖝 SEE IT ! *Find the cars at 1947 West Main Rd in Portsmouth, 7 miles north of downtown Newport.*

493

Visit Mark Twain's Boyhood Home

MISSOURI // Inspiration struck early for Samuel Langhorne Clemens (aka Mark Twain; 1835–1910). The father of American literature grew up in Hannibal and was inspired to base the settings of *The Adventures of Tom Sawyer* and its sequel *Huckleberry Finn* on his boyhood hometown. See Tom Sawyer's whitewashed fence; a replica Huck Finn house; and Twain relics galore including his Oxford gown, first editions of his books, and the death mask of his son. The wider seven-building complex includes two former homes of Twain and also that of Laura Hawkins, the real-life inspiration for the character of Becky Thatcher.

🖝 SEE IT ! *Plan a visit in summer, when an actor gives readings from Twain's works.*

492

Explore a Cold War oddity at Greenbrier

WEST VIRGINIA // It's one of the strangest relics of a strange era in American history: a nuclear bunker the size of two football fields stacked on top of each other, buried in plain sight beneath one of the country's ritziest resorts in the Allegheny Mountains.

Begun in 1959, the Greenbrier Bunker was designed as a bolthole for Congress, complete with cafeteria, hospital, and more than 1000 bunk beds, but was, fortunately, never used. Its cover was blown by *The Washington Post* in 1992; today the Greenbrier Resort runs fascinating public tours of the declassified facility.

🖝 SEE IT ! *The Greenbrier is in White Sulphur Springs, a stop on Amtrak's Cardinal route.*

494

Swirl a glass of pinot at exceptional ROCO

OREGON // 'Pinot noir' and 'Oregon' are almost synonymous for discerning drinkers, and this standout vineyard in the Dundee Hills offers a great introduction to this complex varietal. 'ROCO' is a portmanteau of the owners Rollin Soles and Corby Stonebraker-Soles, pioneers of Oregon sparkling wine who approach their craft with scientific precision. Their grapes are plucked from three different vineyards, and they aren't all destined for smooth, berry-rich reds: well-rounded chardonnays, fruity rosé and sparkling wines provide something for every oenophile. You'll leave laden with bottles.

🖝 SEE IT ! *Reserve ahead for the tasting room. The winery is 30 miles southwest of Portland.*

495

Dig into the ancient and modern at Brooklyn Museum

NEW YORK // Set in a lavish Beaux-Arts building, the Brooklyn Museum is a five-story colossus of culture stuffed with 1.5 million objects. Established in the 1890s, it has a lower profile than other NYC museums, but step inside and you'll wonder how you could have missed it from your New York must-see list. Between delicate 19th-century period rooms and Roman artifacts, don't miss the permanent installation *The Dinner Party*, Judy Chicago's homage to paradigm-shifting women throughout history.

🐦 SEE IT ! *The museum is next to Eastern Parkway/Brooklyn Museum subway station, lines 2 and 3.*

496

Lose hours getting merry at Lagunitas Brewing Company

ILLINOIS // The largest brewery in Chicago, Lagunitas is designed to appeal to almost every style of drinker, with a book exchange for solitary sippers and big wooden tables for beer-clinking groups. Specialty IPAs and pale ales ensure a lingering visit, and there are free tours showing how brews get from barrel to brimming glass. Be wary of having 'just one more' – many beers have a high alcohol content that catches you unawares. It's a good idea to mop them up with pretzels or nachos, or wind down with zero-alcohol IPAs.

🐦 SEE IT ! *The suds are served in Douglas Park, west of downtown Chicago. The nearest L station is California.*

497

Find American icons at Washington National Cathedral

WASHINGTON, DC // With its flying buttresses, carved gargoyles, and soaring vaulted ceiling, Washington National Cathedral was inspired by Western Europe's grand Gothic churches. But American accents remind visitors that they're very far from Chartres or Cologne. A lunar rock is embedded in the 'Scientists and Technicians' stained-glass window, Darth Vader's head numbers among the 112 gargoyles, and carvings depict Rosa Parks, Eleanor Roosevelt, and Helen Keller. And Martin Luther King Jr gave his last Sunday sermon at the Canterbury Pulpit here.

🐦 SEE IT ! *It's a 20-minute walk to the nearest metro station (Cleveland Park); the N6 bus from Dupont Circle gets you closer.*

498

Get artistic overload at the Philadelphia Museum of Art

PENNSYLVANIA // Step inside the PMoA's imposing Great Stair Hall, its gilded statue of Diana framed by towering columns, and it's clear that this is a titan of the arts scene. Take your pick from 200-plus gallery spaces: perhaps Renaissance and Romantic masterpieces; weapons and armor of bygone days; European Impressionism; or photography. Works by Cézanne, Degas, and Monet dazzle, but don't miss the galleries dressed in period splendor – play time-traveler in a French medieval cloister, admire a Japanese teahouse, and stroll the sculpture garden.

☛ SEE IT ! *The museum is at the northwestern end of Benjamin Franklin Pkwy. Your ticket covers two days of entry.*

499

Rove from sea caves to clifftops on Santa Cruz Island

CALIFORNIA // Santa Cruz combines the best of California's nature in its 97 sq miles. It's the largest isle in Channel Islands National Park and a playground for water- and land-based pursuits. You can hike along rugged cliffs, wander windswept beaches, peer into tide pools, and paddle into grottoes, like the lovely and lichen-splashed Painted Cave. Canoeing and kayaking are popular, while hikers can traipse to sublime views at Cavern Point, or try the challenging trail to Smugglers Cove.

☛ SEE IT ! *Boats travel here year-round, arriving at Prisoners Harbor or Scorpion Anchorage. The island's eastern section is managed by the National Park Service; you'll need a permit to see the rest.*

500

Face off with the monstrous *Mothman* statue

WEST VIRGINIA // Ruby eyes glare from his metallic skull. Veiny wings stretch from his bulging torso. His fanged mouth contorts into a snarl. Luckily, this steampunk vision of horror is only a sculpture – artist Bob Roach's 12ft-high tribute to a local legend, the Mothman of West Virginia. Numerous sightings of a 'man-sized bird creature' in the Point Pleasant area were reported in newspapers in the 1960s. The legend was cemented with the publication of John Keel's 1975 *The Mothman Prophecies*, packed with strange sightings and conspiracies.

☛ SEE IT ! *The statue is on 4th St, Point Pleasant; each September, you can don wings and join revelers at the Mothman Festival.*

Index

First Edition
Published in August 2021
by Lonely Planet Global Limited
CRN 554153
www.lonelyplanet.com
ISBN 978 1838 69458 6
© Lonely Planet 2021
Printed in China
10 9 8 7 6 5 4 3 2 1

General Manager, Publishing Piers Pickard
Commissioning Editor, Publisher Robin Barton
Designer Kristina Juodenas
Editor Cliff Wilkinson
Indexer, Proofer Polly Thomas
Image Research Ceri James
Print Production Nigel Longuet

Written by: Brendan Sainsbury, Anita Isalska, Emily Matchar, Kate Armstrong,
Regis St Louis, Luke Waterson

Lonely Planet Global Limited office

IRELAND
Digital Depot, Roe Lane (off Thomas St), Digital Hub, Dublin 8, D08 TCV4

STAY IN TOUCH
lonelyplanet.com/contact

Paper in this book is certified against the
Forest Stewardship Council™ standards.
FSC™ promotes environmentally responsible,
socially beneficial and economically viable
management of the world's forests.